A Harvest for God

Christian Initiation in the
Rural and Small-Town Parish

Michael Clay

LTP

LITURGY
TRAINING
PUBLICATIONS

A HARVEST FOR GOD: CHRISTIAN INITIATION IN THE RURAL AND SMALL-TOWN
PARISH © 2003 Archdiocese of Chicago: Liturgy Training Publications, 1800 North
Hermitage Avenue, Chicago IL 60622-1101; 1-800-933-1800, fax 1-800-933-7094,
e-mail orders@ltp.org. All rights reserved. See our website at www.ltp.org.

This book was edited by Victoria M. Tufano. Kris Fankhouser was the production
editor. The design is by Larry Cope, and the typesetting was done by Kari Nicholls
in Papyrus, New Baskerville, and Professor. The cover photo is by Wilmar
Zehr/Painetworks © 2003.

Printed in the United States of America.

Library of Congress Control Number: 2003106650

ISBN 1-56854-367-0

Font and Table Series

The Font and Table Series offers pastoral perspectives on Christian baptism, confirmation and eucharist.

OTHER TITLES IN THE SERIES:

Baptism Is a Beginning

The Catechumenate and the Law

Celebrating the Rites of Adult Initiation: Pastoral Reflections

The Church Speaks about Sacraments with Children: Baptism, Confirmation, Eucharist, Penance

Confirmation: A Parish Celebration

Confirmed as Children, Affirmed as Teens

Finding and Forming Sponsors and Godparents

Guide for Sponsors

How Does a Person Become a Catholic?

Infant Baptism: A Parish Celebration

La iniciación cristiana: un recurso básico

One at the Table: The Reception of Baptized Christians

Readings in the Christian Initiation of Children

Welcoming the New Catholic

Year-Round Catechumenate

RELATED MATERIAL AVAILABLE THOUGH LITURGY TRAINING PUBLICATIONS:

The Rite of Christian Initiation of Adults (ritual and study editions)

Rito de la Iniciación Cristiana de Adultos (ritual and study editions)

Catechumenate: A Journal of Christian Initiation

Baptism Sourcebook

Forum Essays series:

 The Role of the Assembly in Christian Initiation

 Eucharist as Sacrament of Initiation

 On the Rite of Election

 Preaching the Rites of Christian Initiation

 Liturgical Spirituality and the Rite of Christian Initiation of Adults

 Images of Baptism

 The Reception of Baptized Christians: A History and Evaluation

In memory of

JOANNA NINTEMAN CASE

1938–2001

Pioneer of the Rural Catechumenate

Contents

Introduction

In a culture where "bigger is better" is a way of life, the notion of "small is beautiful" may appear quaint, especially to those who have never lived or ministered in the rural and small-town parishes of the United States. The estimated 20 million U.S. Catholics (not to mention all of the non-Catholics) who live in this setting would beg to differ. If the choice is between a world where someone asks how you feel and actually takes the time to listen to what you say because he or she cares and one that generally does not, there's no doubt what a rural person would choose. Despite this and many other wonderful qualities and characteristics, rural and small-town communities frequently remain underappreciated and undervalued both in society and religious denominations.

During the first generation of pastoral implementation of the *Rite of Christian Initiation of Adults* (RCIA) in parishes throughout the United States and Canada, significant strides were made through the efforts of pastoral leaders and scholars. Not surprisingly, urban and suburban parishes have been the primary beneficiaries of these initial efforts since these are the places where resources, both human and material, are available and where the theologically educated generally reside.

Rural and small-town ministers have also attempted to implement the rite in their parishes. Their instincts and experiences tell them that the models developed for urban and suburban parishes frequently don't "translate" in their setting. This is due to the fact that the culture and social dynamics are different.

This book is a first-generation attempt to assist initiation ministers in their efforts to help rural adults and children of catechetical age as they discern their way through the process of Christian initiation. It is practical in its structure and explanations. In the first chapter, an overview of rural society and culture is provided, primarily to assist leaders who are not indigenous rural people to understand this world and to give a language to those who are so that they may engage their non-rural colleagues in the conversation that is necessary to implement the rite in a culturally sensitive manner.

The remaining chapters take the reader through the four periods and three steps of the initiation process. You will follow the faith journey of a rural unbaptized, uncatechized adult; a rural baptized, uncatechized adult; and two elementary-age rural children in the process. You will learn how to assist a baptized, catechized adult who desires full communion with the Catholic church; how to prepare and conduct inquiry, catechumenate and mystagogy sessions; and how to prepare, celebrate and reflect on the rites associated with the process in a rural-friendly manner. Appendixes appear in the back of the book, some of which may be photocopied for the purposes of preparing catechetical sessions of initiation.

Many people have been instrumental in bringing this book to life. At the risk of overlooking someone, I nevertheless wish to acknowledge them. I am deeply appreciative of my bishop, the Most Reverend F. Joseph Gossman, for granting me a sabbatical to write this book. I am honored to serve a bishop who sees beyond his own diocese to the larger church, who is generous in sharing his priests with that church, and who desires to serve the *entire* people of his diocese. I am grateful to the bishops, diocesan initiation leaders, pastors, pastoral leaders and parishioners of the dioceses of Alexandria-in-Louisiana, Belleville, Bismarck, Portland-in-Maine, Raleigh, Saginaw, Sioux City and Springfield-in-Illinois, where many of the ideas presented here were field-tested in workshops geared specifically for rural and small-town parishes.

The financial commitment and moral support of the North American Forum on the Catechumenate also needs to be noted. They have been instrumental in making rural and small-town parishes a priority in the allocation of funds for workshops in the above-named dioceses and others. Their commitment to this important segment of church life in North America is appreciated.

My thanks go to Sister Gael Gensler, Mrs. Mary Sellars-Malloy and Sister Mary Ellen Theriot for reading and critiquing this book throughout the process. John and Patti Byrne provided a place for me to stay during the writing process. Thanks for opening such a quiet and beautiful place to me. To Vicky Tufano and Liturgy Training Publications go my gratitude for making this book a reality.

Lastly, I cannot conclude without acknowledging the enormous contributions of my dear friend Joanna Case. Her love of God, people and the church, her rural heart, and her catechetical wisdom have irrevocably influenced my ministry and this book. It is in her memory that this book is dedicated.

A Harvest for God: Christian Initiation in the Rural and Small-Town Parish

Chapter 1

Initiation Ministry in the World of Rural and Small-Town People

A few years ago, a woman religious from the urban Northeast responded to an invitation to minister with Native Americans in the Southwest. She had spent many years as a religious educator, and one of her responsibilities in her new community was the preparation of children and their parents for first sacraments. About a dozen mothers arrived for the first parent session for first reconciliation with "Sister Ann." From some casual comments by the mothers during the session she learned that there were many more children eligible for first sacraments. When she heard this, she passed a piece of paper around and asked the mothers to write down the names of eligible children not represented at the meeting so she could invite their parents to the next session. As she was closing up the room at the end of the meeting, Sister Ann found the sheet of paper she had passed to the mothers sitting on a chair. It was blank.

The next day Sister Ann went to the parish secretary, a Native American woman wise in the ways of both Natives and non-Natives, to describe the events of the previous evening. The secretary listened to her story, smiled inwardly and proceeded to explain some things about the new world this sister had entered. She said, "Sister, I'm not surprised there were no names on your sheet of paper. Let me tell you why. First, the absent parents are their relatives, and they would never want to embarrass members of their family. Second, if you got a name from them and then went to visit, the first question an absent mother or father would ask is, 'How did you get my name?' If you told them, the parent would become very angry at the person who provided the name because it's none of that person's business to share that information with a stranger.

"Sister, you're new here, and we're happy to have you among us. Let me offer a suggestion to you. For the first year, spend your time getting to know us and our ways. If you do this and learn who we are, we'll learn to trust you and slowly you'll be able to reach some of those absent parents and children."

Sister Ann has just been given some of the most valuable advice she'll ever want as a non-rural person coming to serve a community of rural people.

She has entered a relation-based society where relationships are everything and belonging (being an "insider") is very important. It is a world quite different from the urban and suburban "mega-parishes" she has served most of her life. If she can enter, accept and honor this new world, she will become a beloved member of the community and an effective minister of God's kingdom.

WHAT IS RURAL?

Sister Ann has entered the rural world. While this particular setting is Native American and Southwestern, many of her experiences will look and feel like rural and small-town settings in other parts of North America. The U.S. government recognizes over 40 varieties of "rural." Consequently, a universal description of a Catholic rural and small-town parish is impossible. Consider the following examples. Catholics number less than one percent of the population in rural Appalachia, while in rural North Dakota the baptized are mostly Catholic or Lutheran. In small towns 30 miles from St. Louis, more and more people are relocating from the city to the countryside, changing the face of local church and civic communities to one that is more blended, called "rurban" by some sociologists. In contrast, people are leaving rural areas in some parts of Saskatchewan due to lack of work, creating yet a different experience of rural life. Along the coast of rural Maine, summer tourism changes the entire rhythm of life for locals, many of whom earn nearly all of their annual income in three months.

Despite these and other variables, there are many commonalities among rural and small town communities and parishes. This chapter will examine some of these commonalities, illustrating them with examples whenever possible. Awareness of and familiarity with these dynamics is critical for effective implementation of initiation in rural North America. For those whose life experience is rural or small-town, what follows will constitute a review but may also provide a language to help them assist and educate urban/suburban people, especially those who may serve as leaders in their parishes or dioceses. For those whose background is urban/suburban, this overview will provide critical information that is absolutely essential if one is to minister effectively in this setting.

LIVING IN A RELATION-BASED SOCIETY

What follows are some of the qualities and characteristics of people who live in rural society. To the extent that there is intermingling with urban/suburban people (for example, through marriage or immigration from the city or suburbs) or to the extent that a rural person has been "urbanized" (for example, by attending college in an urban area or having lived in an urban/suburban setting), these dynamics may not apply 100 percent to every rural person or community. What will be described is generally true of indigenous rural people and is presented as a profile of them.

The Importance of Relationships

The importance of relationships is one of the central dimensions of rural life. Being together and sharing life are primary goals. As such, relationships tend to be ends unto themselves and generally do not exist for utilitarian purposes. Because relationships are more important than tasks for rural people, a meeting will typically begin with those present spending time visiting with one another, catching up on news and life. The agenda of the meeting tends to be secondary to the value of finding out what is going on in the lives of those present. In other words, the utilitarian purpose for gathering this group of people together is less important than simply being together. This is not to say that the group omits business as part of its gathering; it is simply to note that before the agenda can begin the visiting has to have occurred. This means that less will be accomplished in a given period of time in a rural setting than might be in an urban setting. For the urbanite or suburbanite who is more likely to manage the meeting time to complete the agenda first or is driven to accomplish a lot, this can be frustrating.

In the preparation of a formation session in the catechumenate, it will be important that time be set aside at the beginning of every gathering for people to visit with one another. It means that the catechist will need to consider carefully what can realistically be covered during any given formation session. An ambitious agenda may prove frustrating for both catechist and participants when sensitivity to the value of relationship in the rural setting is overlooked.

Why is this so? A number of factors present in the rural community contribute to this dynamic. Populations in rural communities are small. Consequently, rural people tend to have fewer relationships than people living in cities, and their relationships tend to be lifelong ones because rural people are less mobile than their urban counterparts. Because people do not frequently see each other on a regular basis in the rural setting, spending time chatting with friends is highly valued.

Belonging to the Group

In rural society, being an insider is very important. If someone is perceived as belonging to the group, opportunities exist that are not available to an outsider. Being an insider gives a person a sense of identity and well-being. People who move into a rural community generally remain social outsiders for some time. Notable exceptions are teachers, bankers, doctors and pastoral leaders. If, however, one of these newcomers is insensitive to the ways of rural people, he or she can lose the status of insider. This is a lesson Sister Ann will need to learn.

This is one reason why there aren't many inquirers in a rural catechumenate. In addition to the scarcity of people, becoming an insider with one group is usually at the expense of becoming an outsider with another group. There is a lot of pressure to maintain the status quo of groups in rural life. If the husband of a Catholic woman has been raised in the Methodist church but is worshiping with his wife and children in the local Catholic parish, it may be many years before the husband expresses interest in joining the denomination where he and his family worship regularly. The network of relationships that the Protestant spouse has with his own relatives, who are probably Methodist, and with the local church where he may still be on the roll, are very difficult to sever. To do this gives the appearance of being disloyal and is perceived as a diminution of the group, and should therefore be avoided. If he does express interest in switching denominations, he may receive not-so-subtle pressure from relatives to reconsider. So the Protestant spouse may remain in the pew of a rural Catholic parish for his entire life and never come into full communion. He would rather live with the limitations that come with being a Methodist in a Catholic parish than to rock the boat with his parents and other blood relatives.

Resistance to Change and Conflict

One of the most fascinating dimensions of rural life is the way rural people make sense of their world. Among traditional rural people, the present makes sense to the extent that it is consistent with the past. As a result, life is viewed as habitual and constant rather than new and innovative. Urban people are frequently more comfortable in a present that is oriented to the future. Innovation and improvement are characteristic of this thinking. Rural people are more comfortable leaving things as they are because "we've always done it this way." Urban people are generally at ease with reflecting on the present with a view to change when the result will an be improvement.

Rural people can do the same, but it will require much more time and effort because they are less willing to take the result of moving into an unknown future until they are fairly convinced that the result will be an improvement and have considered all the ramifications of the change, especially in terms of relationships. Someone has suggested that rural people move and change like a glacier. They move and change, but very slowly.

The resistance to change is tied to the perception by the community that change will upset the delicate equilibrium they have achieved (whether real or imagined). Leaving things as they are is more highly valued by indigenous rural people than making progress. Consequently, change is resisted.

Conflict is also resisted. In a social setting where keeping everyone in his or her place and keeping up appearances is highly valued, conflict is avoided. If conflict is necessary, it is frequently addressed in an indirect manner, such as storytelling or the use of parables, proverbs or witty one-liners. Direct criticism, if used, is meant to keep people in their place. A grandparent, parent, aunt or uncle may criticize, but it is usually done to startle someone younger back into conformity regarding behavior that is considered unacceptable or to challenge a new idea they may have. And it is usually kept within the family. Peers are unlikely to criticize each other directly.

Those on the faith journey of the catechumenate are called to conversion. Dying to self and rising with Christ is a dimension of this journey. In some cases, the conversion to which the individual is being called can be significant. Racist and sexist attitudes will be challenged. Abusive relationships and addictions will be confronted by the gospel and the Lord of life.

These are difficult issues to address in any social setting, but they are especially difficult in a setting where resisting change and avoiding conflict is considered normal. Addressing these issues will require much time and patience, and the individual will have a better chance of making progress if the one who challenges is held in high regard. The temptation will be to avoid these issues due to the tension they create. This temptation has to be gently but persistently resisted if initiation ministers are to be faithful to their role. In these situations, the status of the pastor or a catechist with significant standing in the community will frequently be of great importance in guiding the one on the faith journey toward conversion.

Image of God

Those who study rural people tell us that God is usually very important to them. This probably has something to do with their connections to the land and to nature. Worship has a more prominent role in their lives than in the lives of urban people. At the same time, God tends to be seen in a stricter and more judgmental role than is the case among urban people. Experts suggest that God is relied upon as an ultimate corrector of the wrongs that are frequently left unresolved in rural communities. If conflict is generally avoided and keeping things in their place is highly esteemed, the need to right wrongs has to be resolved by someone. God becomes the one to do this, whether in this life or the next. Consequently, God is perceived in a more legalistic and moralistic manner.

Expanding the images one has of God is important in the process of Christian initiation in order that the inquirer, catechumen or candidate come to a fuller understanding of the truth of God. Beginning with the period of inquiry, or precatechumenate, it will be important that biblical images describing God as more than a divine judge be included in formation sessions and reinforced later on as the inquirer moves into the later periods of the process.

Discipleship and Social Justice

There is nothing people will not do for you when you are in need in the rural community, unless you are an outsider. This generosity is in the bones of rural people. They grow up helping each other. This makes the invitation to discipleship as a component of Christian initiation fairly easy. The stretch may lie in the call to expand the list of those who might qualify for help to include the outsider and to resist the inclination to refuse help from others. Social justice issues are extremely difficult to address in the rural world, where people feel completely overwhelmed to do anything about them. Experts in this area suggest keeping social justice issues local and connecting the issue with a face that people know.

If the conditions of migrant farmers is an issue, helping the parish and those in the process of initiation meet and know migrant farmers on a personal level might be a significant way to get them to consider one concrete step they can take to improve the situation. Having rural mothers meet migrant mothers or rural children interact with migrant children may also help. Compassion motivates people more than knowledge in the rural world. The problems of migrant farmers will continue to exist for a long time, and knowing how to fix these problems is probably beyond the scope of rural people. But helping them develop a compassion based on personal relationship may move everyone in the right direction.

LIVING IN AN ORAL CULTURE

Having addressed some of the sociological dimensions of rural and small-town life, we now turn to some cultural realities found in this setting. As in the previous section, it should be noted that to the extent that rural people have intermingled with urban/suburban people and/or been "urbanized," the following issues might not apply to them completely. What follows is considered generally true of most indigenous rural people and provides a fascinating snapshot of them.

Preferred Manner of Communication

Anthropologists refer to the culture in which rural people live as "oral." This expression may need some explaining. To say that someone lives out of an oral culture means that his or her preferred way of communicating is through the spoken rather than written word. This is not to say that rural people are illiterate, although some are, or that the written word is unimportant. It simply means people in this culture tend to process reality and daily life through the spoken word more than the written word. Enduring wisdom and guidance is gleaned more from proverbs, stories and relationships than from books. Life is understood through experience rather than intellectual discourse. This preference has significant implications for those who are responsible for the formation of inquirers, catechumens and candidates in rural and small-town parishes. It also constitutes perhaps the biggest challenge for ministers whose training in initiation catechesis is based on methods found in literate culture, where the printed word and critical reflection are commonplace.

It is believed that nearly half of the people in the United States engage life through this cultural lens.[1] If this is true, the implications for initiation ministry could be vast and might explain the number one frustration expressed by rural and small-town people over the years about catechesis, homilies, liturgy and pastoral care in their parishes: They are not as effective as they could be because they are frequently done or led by people operating out of a literate rather than an oral culture.

Faith Is More Experiential Than Theoretical

Asking rural people to read a chapter in a book or some paragraphs from the *Catechism of the Catholic Church* as part of a formation session may be disturbing to them. In oral culture, you *know* what you can recall more than what you can find in a book. Recalling information provided in an instructional book on the faith will be less appealing than recalling a story, parable, proverb or relationship that communicates the same information. The wise rural catechist understands this and builds the catechetical session around stories from the scriptures, the lives of the saints, traditional practices of the faith, faithful folk theology, folk stories and legends, and the experiences of the local community.

Rural people remember stories, folk wisdom and clever sayings because they live in a culture where these things are part of daily life. They get repeated with some frequency and become part of the repertory of the local community. Words they might read in a book once will not have the same staying power. However, selected words they might read or hear repeatedly from a book (for example, the Bible) or liturgical rituals they encounter over and over again will become an ingrained part of their lives.

I recall being present in a small-town funeral home for the wake of an elderly African American gentleman several years ago. People from many denominations were present as well as some who had never darkened the doors of a church. As the service progressed, I invited the people to recite the antiphon to the responsorial psalm, Psalm 23. When I prayed the first line of the psalm, I was astounded as everyone, including the Catholics, began to recite the King James version in unison. So much for a responsorial psalm! Afterward, I noted my amazement to one of the mourners, and she simply noted that everyone grew up learning this passage from the Bible.

Initiation catechesis is not simply storytelling, however. The astute catechist knows that the stories he or she uses must illuminate some point of church teaching and that inquirers, catechumens and candidates must get a good dose of both. Catechists teach the faith by connecting church teaching to people's lives through examples and images they can easily relate to without necessarily presenting it explicitly as "theology." Turning a catechetical session or a homily into a theology lesson can be deadly in an oral culture. When a certain rural parishioner was told that his new pastor was a doctor of theology, he wryly said, "Theology? What disease is that?"

To illustrate initiation catechesis in oral culture, it might be helpful to describe a catechetical session based on the liturgical feast of the Baptism of the Lord. The obvious church teaching for the catechetical session is baptism. The rural catechist wants her catechumen and uncatechized candidate to know something about the Catholic approach to this sacrament. She is not going to give them a chapter to read out of a book or primer on Catholicism. She is going to read these materials herself, perhaps discuss them with her pastor, and then devise a session that describes the truth about baptism in language and images that are rural-friendly.

After reviewing the many issues associated with a Catholic understanding of baptism, she decides to approach church teaching more from a relational than academic perspective. Again, this is not done because rural people are unintelligent. They are as intelligent as any other segment of society. They simply engage life more affectively and relationally than cognitively.

This catechist knows her audience and prepares accordingly so that what they learn will remain with them for more than 24 hours.

She chooses to emphasize baptism as the establishment of two types of relationship: 1) between God and the one being baptized and 2) between the one being baptized and the community of faith into which the child or adult is baptized. She uses stories of newborns to prime the pumps of her catechumen and uncatechized candidate. She gets them to talk about newborns in their own families and the significance of the newborn to the parents, siblings and members of the extended family. Because the catechist knows that rural people view their livestock almost like family, she will not be surprised if someone tells a story about a newborn piglet instead of a story about a newborn child.

Having listened to the candidates' stories of newborns, the catechist then tells them the story of one who is a spiritual newborn in the waters of baptism. She tells them about the two types of relationships established in baptism and explains the importance of these relationships. Afterward, she invites them to see the connection between spiritual rebirth and human birth. The human connection will help them to remember that baptism establishes two types of relationships: divine and ecclesial.

She does not present a historical development of the theology of baptism in her session. While important, rural people will find this too abstract and irrelevant to their daily life unless it provides answers to practical questions, such as infant baptism versus adult baptism. If these issues emerge, the rural catechist knows how to explain them in practical ways without getting too caught up in theological and historical detail.

Oral people live their faith experientially and seek assurance and trust in their faith more than discourse and explanation about it. History and theology may be very appropriate in a college setting where discourse is esteemed. For oral people they are largely irrelevant. Life and faith are lived on simpler terms and are more in the heart than in the head. The rural-friendly catechist knows this and shapes her session to connect the faith more to the hearts of her catechumen and uncatechized candidate than to their heads.

Again, this is not to say that information about the faith is irrelevant. It is as relevant to rural people as it is to urban/suburban people. They simply do not need as much of it because their priorities are elsewhere. If something arises and they need more information, they will go to their pastor or catechist, especially if they have shown themselves to be sensitive to rural people.

Introspection and Critical Reflection

Rural people live life intuitively. They generally rely on their instincts more than their intellect to make sense of their world. Analysis and critical reflection are not particularly important to rural people. Critical thinking is a skill developed in a literate world, where attention to nuances and subtleties are necessary for discourse and new insights. While this is very important in the study of theology, it is not important for the daily life of a farmer. Because the rural catechist knows this, he avoids a lot of fancy words and is careful how often he uses "why questions" during his conversations with those in the initiation process. "Why questions" are introspective and invite rural people to enter a realm many of them find unnecessary in order to make sense of the world in which they live.

Understanding occurs more tacitly than explicitly among rural people. Because life is simpler, with fewer contexts to incorporate into the thinking process, rural people tend to understand each other and the events of life without the need for a lot of critical thinking. People in this setting have much more in common with each other than is the case in the literate world. Consequently, they are more likely to know the context in which a question is asked or a discussion is taking place. The catechist who is not attuned to the local context may frustrate her rural inquirers, catechumens and candidates if she keeps asking them to be more explicit in their answers or in explaining what they mean. They think it's as plain as the nose on your face.

Initiation catechists may turn to resources to help them prepare a catechetical session. They should be sensitive to the literate culture out of which most of these resources operate.[2] These resources frequently ask people to ponder the meaning of some theological point or invite people to wonder why something is the way it is. Indigenous oral people will often be unable to respond to these types of questions because they frequently haven't developed these types of reflection skills. Their wisdom comes from a different place, from the experiences of life and the bonds they have with others in their community.

Also to be avoided are "feeling questions" such as "How did you feel about that?" These questions are similarly introspective, and rural people often don't know what to do with them, so they tend not to answer them.

This type of introspection is thought to be the fruit of the social and behavioral sciences that have increasingly found their way into church ministry. Rural people will be more responsive if they are invited to ponder life through the stories they know and have experienced. Consequently, questions or statements that keep the *story* flowing will be more helpful in getting oral people to new insights and affirmations than why or feeling questions. As rural people reflect on their lives through their stories, asking questions like "What did you do?", "What happened next?" or "How did you get through that?" will be more effective.[3]

Witnessing to the Faith

"Oral people approach faith in terms of survival and coping far more than they do in terms of systematic understanding and coherence."[4] This is due to many things, principal among them the difficulties of rural life brought about by economic hardship and the difficulties associated with addressing family and community problems. Consequently, faith is strengthened more by trust, assurance and a sense of belonging than by intellectual discourse.

It is very important that rural initiation ministers be people who are strong in their own faith and know firsthand what it means to lean on God for assurance during the difficult moments of life. It has been said that the most effective evangelists are those whose lives are a personal witness of God's fidelity to them. The catechist who has personal experience that God is trustworthy and never abandons those whom God has created is a very powerful evangelizer and is highly desirable as an initiation minister.

The catechist who has survived the death of her husband and the economic hardship it has brought her and still believes that God is faithful is a true treasure in a rural or small-town parish. Likewise, the catechist who is willing to talk more about his relationship with God than his (or someone else's) view of God will be appreciated by initiates who live in an oral culture.

Showing Rather Than Telling

Rural people prefer informal structures to formal ones. They also appreciate a catechetical approach that is more relational than theoretical. A classroom, a book and an instructional methodology are perceived by oral people as formal and may be uninviting for many of them. Meeting in someone's home and taking an approach where the catechist is perceived to be a peer who has traveled down the path of faith a little longer, as opposed to a superior who knows it all, is enormously important for rural people. It's all about relationship, and the preference is that of friend to friend or, in the case of the spiritual leader of the community, shepherd to sheep.

Rural people view life more through the lens of apprenticeship than study. Consequently, formation for life as a Catholic Christian will be more effective if it looks more like an apprenticeship for living in the faith than like a class. Someone who apprentices others has described the process of apprenticeship among oral people:

What I hear, I forget.
What I see, I remember.
What I do, I understand.

A catechesis that is practical and experiential is more helpful to rural people than one that is full of fancy words and theology. Singing "Amazing Grace" will probably be more helpful in an understanding of grace than a long lecture on it. Visiting someone who is homebound will be more effective than any presentation on discipleship. Going to Mass will probably be more helpful than a series of classes discussing it. Again, this is not to say that presentations of the faith of the church are unnecessary or beyond the capabilities of rural people. It simply means that the more successful approach to formation in the rural or small-town setting will incorporate substantial hands-on opportunities and will engage the body and senses in very practical ways so that faith becomes an experience felt in one's bones.

Notes

[1]This contention is made by Tex Sample in *Ministry in an Oral Culture: Living with Will Rogers, Uncle Remus, and Minnie Pearl* (Louisville: Westminster/John Knox Press, 1994), p. 6. Several of the ideas contained in this portion of the chapter are based on Dr. Sample's insights.

[2]While I find them personally very insightful, intellectually stimulating, and useful in parishes operating out of literate culture, resources such as *Word and Worship Workbook* by Mary Birmingham (Paulist Press) and *Foundations in Faith* by Resources for Christian Living will not be very useful for people living in oral culture without major revisions.

[3]These insights come from Tex Sample in *Ministry in an Oral Culture,* p . 20 ff.

[4]Ibid., p. 77.

Chapter 2

The Period of Evangelization and Precatechumenate

This chapter will examine:

- ways of integrating people from rural society/oral culture into the precatechumenate

- the differences between the catechetical method of the period of evangelization and precatechumenate and the catechetical method of the catechumenate period

- the problems with using a predetermined topical outline for the sessions with inquirers

- determining when someone may skip the precatechumenate altogether

- knowing when sufficient evangelization has occurred

- welcoming new inquirers at any time of the year

- the difference between those who are baptized and/or catechized and those who are not, and their participation in this period

- incorporating scripture and prayer into each inquiry session.

Joe works at the local farm-goods store in Oakville. He was restocking the shelves one day when a young woman named Maria approached him and asked for assistance in locating some gardening supplies. As most rural men would, he immediately stopped what he was doing and took her to the gardening section of the store. He asked what she was looking for, and she told

Boy meets girl/ First dates	Commitment to go steady	Building the relationship Meeting the family Learning the traditions	Engagement	Pre-Cana/ Marriage prep	Wedding	Honeymoon/ First year of marriage
Precatechumenate	Rite of Acceptance into Order of Catechumens	Catechumenate	Rite of Election	Purification and enlightenment	Sacraments of initiation	Mystagogy

him that she was having problems growing healthy vegetables in her garden. Insects and other pests kept attacking them. She wanted to try a different pesticide this year, and she needed some help deciding what to use.

Joe asked her what kind of vegetables she had grown in the past, what she intended to grow this year, what kind of pests she had, and what kind of pest control she had been using. He also told Maria about his own interest in gardening and even shared a story about the prizewinning pumpkin he had grown in his garden the previous fall. Maria had heard about that. Everyone in the county had!

Joe suggested a pesticide that he had found to be both effective and environmentally friendly. Maria thanked him, bought the suggested pesticide and left, but not before Joe told her to come back if she had any further questions or problems.

With both of them being from the Oakville area, Joe and Maria had known each other for many years but had never really spoken personally; she was four years younger than he and lived quite far from town. As they spoke in the store, something seemed to click with them. There was chemistry! He liked her smile and she liked his kindness.

A few weeks later, Maria came to the store looking for more garden supplies. Not surprisingly, Joe was there to help her. About a week later, she was in town doing some banking and dropped by to chat with Joe at the store. A few days later, she was at the drugstore and stopped by to see Joe again. Each time they chatted a little longer.

One day Joe asked her if she might be interested in hanging out with him and a few of his friends. They were going into Springfield, the county seat, for dinner and a movie. She accepted. Joe and Maria, along with his friends Bob, Martha, Gladys and Peter, went to Springfield the next Saturday. They had a great time. Maria and Joe sat next to each other in the car and at the restaurant, where they talked about everything under the sun. The movie was awful, but it gave them something to laugh about as they returned to Oakville. Both said they had enjoyed the evening.

After a few more outings with Joe and his friends, Maria invited Joe to join her for a picnic with some of her friends. Joe accepted and enjoyed getting to know Maria more and meeting some of her friends the following Saturday, even though she drank a little too much that day.

Joe and Maria began seeing each other more and more, at first with other couples but soon by themselves. After a few months, Maria expressed her growing affection for Joe and suggested that they date each other exclusively. Joe had been thinking the same thing, so it was easy for him to agree with her suggestion.

EVANGELIZATION: ATTRACTING OTHERS TO CHRIST AND THE CHURCH

The period of evangelization and precatechumenate, commonly called the precatechumenate or inquiry period, is to the process of initiation what the meeting and getting acquainted phase is to a relationship in a rural or small-town community. Like Maria and Joe, who knew each other before that fateful pesticide conversation in the store, potential inquirers in the small-town setting will, for the most part, already be acquainted with Catholic Christians. They may know a neighbor or someone who works in town is a Catholic Christian. What they know about the Catholic faith through that person may be minimal, but they will have an opinion of Catholicism based on the lifestyle of the Catholics they know. This lifestyle is a form of evangelization. As Joe went out of his way to assist Maria with her pesticide inquiry, it may also be that an inquirer is evangelized to consider the Catholic Christian faith as a result of some outreach by a member of the local Catholic parish.

A story is told of a farmer who had a heart attack and needed help harvesting his fields during his recuperation from surgery. Four Catholic families who lived nearby decided to help this man and his family. They brought his crops in, putting in long hours after working their own farms all day. He was so impressed with their generosity that upon recovery he began to worship at the local Catholic church, bringing his entire family with him.

In rural and small-town communities, those who may become future inquirers frequently are connected to the local parish in some way already. Because relationship is so important in rural society, most inquirers are not newcomers to the parish or strangers to its parishioners. For example, in one countryside parish there is a man who has been married to a Roman Catholic for over 20 years. He worships weekly with his family in the local Catholic parish and assists with taking up the collection. While the decision to become a member of the church must be that of the individual in dialogue with the initiation ministers, the influence of family and friends as a catalyst for taking the first step towards initiation cannot be underestimated.

Evangelizing in a Rural Community

Many of those from small towns who eventually become inquirers have already been part of a Christian faith community and formalized their relationship through baptism in that community. Evangelizing a person in this situation must be approached with great sensitivity, especially if they have remained active members of their church of baptism. Churches in the rural and small-town setting are frequently small in size, and their survival depends on a stable membership. They function like a family. Because of the high value placed on family in rural communities, there may be great resistance shown by both church family and birth family (many of whom belong to the same church family) to someone who expresses interest in leaving their baptismal denomination for another. Hence, evangelization efforts might concentrate on (and be more successful with) the unchurched.

This raises a question about evangelization itself. In the rural and small-town setting, where there are few people to start with and where quantitative growth is not highly valued, efforts to evangelize aggressively will generally be of little interest to most people. In fact, it may backfire on those who are attempting to bring more people to the church. Rural people generally do not make this mistake because they know evangelization of this kind simply does not work, but urban people living and ministering in rural or small-town communities may be tempted to evangelize in this more explicit manner. They should resist this temptation.

The combination of these and other dynamics explains why there are frequently few if any inquirers in a given year in the rural or small-town parish. A "bigger is better" mentality is not a high priority in this setting when it comes to community, both civic and religious, so rural ministers tend to remain unperturbed when no one is in the process of Christian initiation.

Joe and Maria's relationship began informally with a conversation about gardening, something they shared in common. This is similar to what happens before one formally begins inquiry. It is a form of evangelization. It may begin when a parishioner has a conversation with a non-parishioner that is characterized more by listening than talking, and when that parishioner humbly shares a helpful insight from the Catholic tradition with the non-parishioner. Such an encounter may result in an awakening or reawakening to something important in the life of a non-parishioner. For Maria it was primarily an awareness of an effective form of pest control, but also an awareness that Joe possessed something she did not.

Maria returned a couple times over a period of several weeks to chat more about gardening and pest control. But while this was happening, a relationship was taking root. She found that Joe explained things to her in such a way that they made sense and she began to see progress in keeping pests off her plants. In the same way, a non-parishioner may meet someone from the church community who seems to possess some life wisdom that makes sense to the non-parishioner, who gains some personal benefit as a result of hearing this wisdom. This might be called a *pre*-catechumenate. All this is casual and informal, gradual and episodic, but vitally important in the rural setting where relationship, wisdom and trust are highly valued.

INQUIRY

Joe invited Maria to join him with some of his friends for an outing, for a date. This was the first invitation Joe extended to her to enter his world. This is like the invitation to inquiry with the church, the formal invitation to the precatechumenate. Notice what has gone on before Joe extends an invitation to Maria for the first date. They have laid the groundwork for the relationship. Likewise, inquirers in the rural and small-town setting do not generally fall from the trees. They show up because parishioners have slowly but surely cultivated relationships in informal, casual ways, offering wisdom from their own faith journey to those who seek it.

This wisdom need not be sophisticated in language or complex in thought. Rural people have a wisdom that is earthy and straightforward. As one rural man said to a young man who was keeping bad company, "Son, if you sleep with dogs, you'll wake up with fleas." In those few words we will find an excellent summary of moral theology that the father of modern moral theology, Alphonsus Ligouri,[1] would be proud of.

Maria accepted the invitation and went on what would be the first of many dates with Joe. During this dating period, she was introduced to Joe's friends and the world he and his friends have created together. This is how inquiry functions. It is an experience of community, becoming acquainted with the people who make up the parish. And as is true of community, not everyone does the same thing or possesses the same talents. Some will be good at hospitality, making sure the inquirer feels welcome. Others will be good storytellers, sharing the wisdom of faith in a manner that can be understood by a rural person. Others will be good at listening, hearing not only the words spoken by the inquirer but also the silent voice that speaks beneath the spoken words. These are the people who are needed for the precatechumenate. Blessed is the community where a person or two who possesses most of these gifts can be found.

Note that the first date was to a neutral place. Inquiry does not have to occur on church property. It can occur in someone's home or backyard, on a park bench, or over lunch. It also does not have to involve many people. While Joe invited Maria to go on a group date, it may be that in the local rural parish a group of people does not exist to do inquiry. (In large suburban parishes, "teams" may exist for the precatechumenate.) While it is certainly fine if a rural parish can cultivate a few people to handle the inquiry period, it is not required or necessarily preferable. What is needed is for the inquirers to have someone with whom they can develop a relationship, someone who is willing to listen to them and can announce the good news to them in a rural-sensitive manner.

Revealing Brokenness

Maria has had several opportunities to hang out with Joe and his friends. She is growing in her bond with this group of people and trusts Joe enough to invite him more deeply into her world. So she invited Joe to a picnic with her friends where he entered her world. While spending time with Maria and her friends, Joe learned more about her, including the possibility of a problem with alcohol. He does not judge her and break off the relationship because she was slightly inebriated. Rather, he views her as a beautiful person who may be broken in some way and in need of healing. Gradually, they grow in trust, and Joe is able to get Maria to talk about her life. She talks about the premature death of her father and how that has created severe hardship for her family. She talks about how she sometimes uses alcohol when the responsibilities of her life become overwhelming. She finds acceptance in Joe rather than condemnation, and experiences something of a healing that

A Harvest for God: Christian Initiation in the Rural and Small-Town Parish

she attributes to his love for and acceptance of her. Over time, she finds that she does not resort to alcohol as much as before to deal with stress. Rather, she turns to Joe and his friends, and the positive values they exemplify.

This is what evangelization does. It invites people into the love of God, Christ and the church so they can receive the courage and strength they need to "give up, abandon, and renounce other [things] that have shaped their lives in false and distorting ways."[2]

Rural people bring much brokenness with them. Those who study and work in rural settings report a disproportionate share of the nation's poverty; sixty percent of the nation's substandard housing; decreased services for the rural poor; decreased health care, especially for infants, children and the elderly; a disproportionately high level of unemployment; poor working conditions; divorce; depression; suicide; teen pregnancy; and alcohol and drug abuse. Getting rural people to discuss these issues, however, is a very delicate matter. There is fear in admitting that something is wrong in a culture where keeping up appearances no matter what is a way of life. This is why relationships and trust are so important at this phase of the initiation process. With a trusting relationship well established, it might be possible to crack the tough veneer that keeps the brokenness from being brought into the light with at least one other person and healed. The astute person from the parish who is listening to the story of the inquirer's life may find that she/he can pierce the veneer with a story or song that both resonates with the struggle of the inquirer and proclaims the good news of healing and reconciliation that God's love has unleashed in the world through the passion, death and resurrection of Jesus Christ.

Asking Deeper Questions

Joe and Maria continue to date each other, sometimes including others and sometimes not. During this time together, they grow in their trust and affection for each other. As that trust and affection grow, Maria asks Joe more personal questions. She wants to know about his family, friends, beliefs, values and work. She wants to know about his world. As he unfolds his life before her, she too begins to unfold her life before him.

In the same way, the inquiry period is a time when the inquirer asks questions of the initiation ministers and others who represent the local parish, whether it's in a group setting or one on one. Some of their questions will be peculiarly Catholic and frequently asked through a relationship lens: the exclusion of non-Catholics from holy communion, the relationship between Catholics and the pope, confessing sins to a priest, and praying to Mary and the saints, for example. Other questions are more generically Christian: reading the Bible, loving one's neighbor, going to church on Sunday. Some questions are profound: Why does God allow suffering? Others are more trivial: Why is the Catholic version of the Lord's Prayer different from the Protestant version?

Listening

Joe believes in the saying that God gave us two ears and one mouth and that they should be used in that proportion. So Joe listens more than he speaks. He receives more than he gives. He lets Maria go first in the initial exploration of their relationship, rather than control it by only talking about the things that are important to him. This is because he knows listening and letting her go first will strengthen their bond better than anything else. Sometimes when there is a lull in the conversation, Joe will ask a question of Maria or bring an issue forward for consideration, but he always allows her to go first.

Conversations during the precatechumenate will be more faithful to the vision of the rite and fruitful in an oral culture if the facilitator listens more than speaks and allows the inquirer to set the agenda for the conversation. By allowing the rural inquirer to set the agenda during this period, the facilitator is saying that he or she values the inquirer. This facilitates the relationship because it respects their dignity, something very important to rural people. Without relationship, rural people will be more likely to drop out of the process.

Building Relationships

Rural people believe a relationship with God (spirituality) is more important than ideas explaining God (theology). This first period of the initiation process should reflect this preference in order to be most effective. This period is evangelical in nature; its purpose is to awaken inquirers to the fact that God loves them, desires an eternal relationship with them, and sent Jesus to die and rise so that nothing would separate them from that relationship. It awakens them to the fact that this relationship is deepened and lived out in the midst of other believers. Once this relationship has been established, then theology can make a lasting impression on the believer. Consequently, the issues of this period are primarily of an evangelical nature: Who is God? Who is Jesus and what difference does his death and resurrection make in my life? What difference does belief in God and Jesus make in my life? What good news does Jesus have for me? What roles do community and prayer play in my relationship with God?

Having 30 predetermined topics is not the vision of this period, nor is it sensitive to the rural world. A predetermined topic approach says that establishing a relationship (with God, Christ, his church and the world) is secondary to knowing what the church teaches. The importance of helping inquirers know what the church teaches is beyond dispute. The issue is one of priority and method. Relationship is the first priority in this period; theology is second. The witness of initiation ministers and other parishioners concerning their relationships with God, Christ, the church and the world is valued more by rural people than studying proofs for the existence of God or other theological explanations in this phase of formation.

Witness bespeaks relationship that is personal; study is frequently more impersonal. People from an oral culture prefer relationships to study because they prefer the spoken word to the printed word. Perhaps the following example expresses it best: One Sunday a parishioner came out of small-town church and said to a her new pastor, a recent graduate from the seminary, "Father, I know you put a lot of work into that homily and I appreciate your effort. But may I offer you a suggestion? Next time don't tell me so much about what somebody else said about Jesus. Tell me more about what Jesus said to you."[3]

Inquiry ministers do ask questions, but they are secondary to the questions raised by the inquirers. They present theology, but in a way that responds to the needs of the inquirers and is rural-friendly, using storytelling, parables and proverbs rather than abstract concepts, for example. Life is discussed in this period more than concepts. For rural people life is experiential rather than theoretical; it is lived more in the heart than in the head. And it is relational. In the precatechumenate, keep relationships with God, Christ, the church and the world in the forefront of any conversation with inquirers.

Sponsors

Should the inquirer decide to continue into the period of the catechumenate, someone will be needed to accompany him or her through the rest of the process. It is important that this person establishes a relationship with the inquirer some time before the first rite is celebrated. Because those who live in rural communities are few in number, inquirers will frequently know many people from the church community. The *Rite of Christian Initiation of Adults* allows an inquirer to have a sponsor for the initial phases of formation (through the end of the catechumenate period) and then to choose another person to serve as godparent in the later phases of formation (beginning with the rites of sending and election). With the exception of parents,[4] most fully initiated members of the parish may serve as godparents. It is the general experience of rural communities that the person selected as sponsor is the person who becomes the godparent. Changing the relationship toward the end of the process seems unusual in a culture where relationships are characterized as long-term and stable.

DISCERNMENT FOR ENTRY
INTO THE CATECHUMENATE PERIOD

After several months, Joe and Maria are ready to deepen their commitment to each other by forgoing other romantic relationships. From their first months together, they have discovered feelings of love for each other and have established a trusting relationship. It is just a beginning, but they believe they are off to a good start. They know a lot about each other but, at the same time, they realize there is much more to know. As they discuss the idea of seeing each other exclusively, they realize they are not making a commitment to marriage, only to an exclusive dating relationship with each other. After reflecting on how their relationship has grown and how much they enjoy being with each other, they decide to go steady.

The precatechumenate comes to an end when inquirers are ready to declare that they want to enter into a formal relationship with God in Christ.[5] They reach this conclusion because they have experienced both divine and human love during their experiences of the precatechumenate. The inquirers have a clear sense that God loves them, have accepted from God the gift of faith in Christ,[6] and believe the church community values them. They are ready to move to the next phase of formation because they have had their questions answered.

In the same way that Joe and Maria talk to each other about their readiness to go deeper in the relationship, the unbaptized inquirers enter into dialogue with the initiation ministers of the parish about being admitted to the order of catechumens through the celebration of the rite of acceptance into the order of catechumens.[7] If they are baptized but uncatechized inquirers (including Catholics baptized in infancy who received little or no catechesis), they discern their readiness to celebrate the rite of welcoming the candidates.[8]

These inquirers meet with those charged by the parish to discern their readiness for one of these celebrations.[9] This discernment is not a test. Rather, it is a conversation in which the inquirer and one or more delegates from the parish reflect on the growth that has occurred in the inquirer's relationship with God, Christ and the church. It is a conversation in which the parish delegates affirm what the inquirer has come to discover: that they are loved by God, Christ and the church; that they have accepted Christ as the savior of the world; and that they are ready to begin to reciprocate that love.[10]

It will be important for rural people that this conversation be casual and informal. If inquiry sessions have occurred in someone's home, it may be beneficial that this discernment conversation occur in the same setting. Because of the importance of relationship, it will also be critical that the people with whom the inquirer discerns be people with whom the inquirer has had a relationship. For example, if the pastor has not participated in the inquiry period with the inquirers, it may seem strange in the eyes of the inquirers for him to be inserted into the process at this moment, unless they have cultivated a relationship with him in some other setting. Or if a sponsor is being introduced into the process with the rite of acceptance, it might seem strange to the inquirer that this individual is included in a discernment conversation along with people the inquirer has come to know and trust over the course of the inquiry period.

Focusing the Conversation for Discernment

How might the discernment conversation be focused? Be careful that the questions and/or statements used as prompts for the inquirer are not ones that require introspection or are designed to elicit feelings. These are more characteristic of a literate culture. Let the prompts be concrete and experiential. Invite the inquirers to use stories, parables, proverbs and similes to

A Harvest for God: Christian Initiation in the Rural and Small-Town Parish

describe the journey on which they have been. Doing this is a kind of introspection, and feelings will be expressed but in an oblique rather than direct way. Some sample prompts might look like this:

- When you think about your relationship with God now, as compared to what it was like a year ago, what would it be similar to?

- Tell us a story about God or Jesus that has been helpful to you.

- Tell us about someone you have gotten to know at our church since you started coming to our inquiry sessions.

- How would you describe your relationship with Jesus today?

THE BAPTIZED CANDIDATE

In the United States, it is estimated that 75 percent of those seeking admission into the Catholic church are already baptized. The reality in rural and small-town parishes is that most of those seeking initiation are already baptized and some are already catechized: They are grounded in the teachings of the Christian faith, they understand the importance of community and worship, and they realize that discipleship is not an optional way of life.[11] The process for the baptized will look a little different from the one used with the unbaptized. Perhaps a few scenarios typical of rural parishes might help us figure out where they fit in.

Richard

Richard Schmidt, a baptized Lutheran, is married to Ruth, a baptized Catholic. They have been married for 25 years and have five children between the ages of 16 and 24. Richard has worshiped with his family at St. Aloysius for nearly 20 years. He is a member of the parish Men's Club and helps with the annual pig roast fundraiser. He was raised in the Lutheran church, going to church every Sunday and attending Sunday school until he graduated from high school. He started going to the Catholic church when his first child was old enough to go to church. He thought it was important that his family worship together and that he set a good example for his son. He has a job in town, but does some farming as well. He has a neighbor who is a widow and who lives on social security. He always makes sure that she has food and fuel in her home and does not hesitate to provide these things for her out of his own resources when she is in need. Richard tells the pastor one day that he would like to "take communion" with his family and wants to know what he needs to do to become a member of the parish. Does he need to go through the entire initiation process?

The answer is no. According to National Statute 30,[12] the preparation period for those who are already baptized and catechized should be modified to reflect their status as baptized, catechized Christians. In Richard's case, he would not participate in a precatechumenate, and probably would not participate in much, if any, of the other parts of the initiation process. He would probably meet with someone one on one who could help him complete whatever doctrinal and/or spiritual preparation he might need in order to come into full communion with the Catholic church. He would celebrate the sacrament of reconciliation, according to his conscience, prior to his reception.[13] Consequently, his formation period might consist of a handful of conversations with someone from the parish (perhaps the pastor or catechist) who could assist Richard in whatever areas he needs to explore more thoroughly. He would not participate in any of the preliminary rites recommended for baptized but uncatechized Christians. After this brief period of preparation, he would be received into full communion, be confirmed, and receive the eucharist at the Sunday Mass he normally attends with his family.

Joan

Joan, a baptized Methodist, is married to John Burnett, a baptized Catholic. They have been married for 12 years and have two school-age children. Joan regularly attended the Methodist church until she was approximately 10, but stopped going when a new minister arrived whom her parents did not like. John gradually stopped going to church after he was confirmed in the seventh grade, despite the disapproval of his parents. They were married at St. Aloysius at the insistence of John's mother, but they have not been back to the church except for the baptism of their children, which was also at the insistence of John's mother.

Joan works on the School Auction Committee of the local Parent Teacher Association of the public school her children attend. On the committee are two Catholic women, Phyllis and Pauline, who work hard to ensure the success of the major fundraiser event of the school and who have a very friendly, inclusive manner about them. Joan grows in her admiration of these two women and gradually spends more and more time with them over the course of the months leading up to the auction.

During their time together, these two women occasionally talk about what their pastor said in his homily, a quilting project that their parish Women's Sodality is doing, and about a neighbor they visit who has cancer. Joan likes these women and is happy to be included in their lives.

One day Pauline asks Joan if she goes to a church and Joan tells Pauline her story. Pauline listens carefully to her story and when she is finished asks her if she has ever thought about returning to church. Joan tells her she has on occasion but is afraid to go alone since her husband is not a Methodist and her parents still do not attend. Pauline asks her if she would like to come with her to the Catholic church some Sunday. Joan says yes because she likes Pauline and they arrange to go to St. Al's the following Sunday. Joan feels a little out of place at first, but after a few weeks she begins to feel at home with the order of worship and the people she meets, especially those whose children attend the same school as hers.

After a few months of worshiping with Pauline and her family, Joan tells Pauline she is interested in learning more about the Catholic church. Pauline puts her in touch with the couple in charge of the parish's initiation process and Joan begins her journey of exploration with the Catholic church. Does Joan need to go through the entire process?

The answer is probably most of it, but not all of it. According to National Statute #31, baptized individuals who have lived some portion of their lives as Christians should not be asked to undergo the full process of Christian initiation. In Joan's case, some discernment might be needed over the course of a few initial conversations to determine if she has been evangelized about God, Christ and the church. Does she believe Jesus is the savior of the world? If she has been evangelized, she may need a period of time to ask some preliminary questions about the Catholic church.

The initiation coordinators decide, after consulting with Pauline and Phyllis, that Joan might benefit from some kitchen-table conversations with these two women to get many of her questions answered. After all, Phyllis and Pauline are her friends. This is Joan's precatechumenate. What she will do later will be covered in subsequent chapters.

Ned

Finally, there is Ned, a baptized Roman Catholic. He is a widower with four grown children. His wife died two years ago in an automobile accident. Apart from his baptism and a friend's wedding, he has never been inside a church. His wife's death devastated him, and he began to drink so heavily that he was in danger of losing his job at the mill.

One day his foreman, Frank, who had concluded that Ned had a problem with alcohol, told him the story about a woman who had become addicted to pain killers and how she had found sobriety. Ned listened to the story and continued working. On another occasion, Frank told Ned a story about a man who gambled so much that he had to sell his farm. Ned listened and commented how tragic it was to lose something as important as a farm. Eventually, Frank told a story about a man who had become addicted to alcohol but who eventually found sobriety. Actually, it was Frank's story. When Frank told Ned the story was autobiographical, he asked Ned if he ever experienced the same thing. Ned said he did and Frank invited him to consider going to a meeting where people gather to help each other stop drinking. Ned went with Frank later in the week to his first Alcoholics Anonymous meeting. It was difficult at first, but eventually Ned was able to achieve sobriety with the help of Frank and his friends.

One day Ned asked Frank about his "higher power" and Frank told him about Jesus and about receiving him in holy communion. Ned was intrigued by this and asked how he could learn more about Jesus and the church. Frank invited Ned to his church, where he found a friendly community, two others he recognized from his A. A. group, and a service that gave him a sense of the holy. Frank brought Ned to church every Sunday and after several months Ned asked how he could become a member. Frank introduced him to Bill and Alice Smith, who coordinated the initiation process at St. Aloysius, and he began a faith journey that, when completed, will culminate in the celebration of confirmation and holy eucharist. Does Ned need to go through the entire process?

Probably. RCIA, 400–472, and National Statutes, 25–29, provide guidelines for the formation of a baptized uncatechized Catholic. RCIA, 401–402, indicate that the timeframe for Ned will probably be the same as it would for someone who is not baptized while recognizing and honoring the privileged status Ned enjoys as a baptized Christian. The Smiths will want Ned to experience the precatechumenate in its fullness and will ask Frank to be his sponsor. Ned will need to be evangelized while he asks the kinds of questions that might occur for someone coming to the Catholic church for the first time.

Different Needs, Different Paths

Richard, Joan and Ned are all baptized. Each has a different level of formation in the Christian life and so the experience of initiation formation will be different. Richard needs very little while Ned needs a lot. Notice how Bill and Alice utilize the people in the community who have reached out to Joan and Ned. They become a part of the early formation. Phyllis, Pauline and Frank were evangelists who became mentors for Joan and Ned (but please don't tell them they were evangelists; they think they were just being friends). Notice that it was through relationship, storytelling and discipleship that Joan and Ned were attracted to Phyllis, Pauline and Frank. It wasn't through an ad in the newspaper or a bulletin announcement; it was through the everyday events of life where people spend time with each other. This is how evangelization and inquiry might be utilized with the baptized in the rural world.

BEGINNING INQUIRY AT ANY TIME

Parishes in cities and suburbs frequently have many people in the process of Christian initiation. Being generally larger than most parishes in rural and small towns, many have an initiation team, a group of parishioners who share the responsibilities of initiation ministry. The reality in rural and small-town parishes is quite different. Between small membership in a parish, a small general population, and a comfort with smallness in general, the notion of an initiation team may be wishful thinking and certainly is not necessary. It is commonly noted that a rural or small-town parish may not have anyone in the initiation process in any given year. Accounts from several rural dioceses indicate that generally there may be one or two people in the process in a rural or small-town parish at any given time with some dry spells in which no one is in the process. Given the circumstances of rural and small-town communities, this should be considered normal and not an indication that the parish is failing to evangelize.

The circumstances that bring someone to the attention of the parish regarding Christian initiation are varied. Regardless of the circumstances, potential inquirers do not all arrive in late August with the hope of beginning right after Labor Day and finishing by Memorial Day. Theoretically, an unbaptized, uncatechized inquirer (whom we shall call Teresa), Richard, Joan or Ned could show up at any time. How are they incorporated into an inquiry process when they show up in November, February or May? From the description of our four searchers, it should be clear that it is possible to incorporate them into some kind of inquiry experience no matter when they show up. In the rural context, an informal approach is preferable to a formal one. A classroom model is not a good way to begin with rural people who prefer relationship, experiential-based learning and informality.

Bill and Alice Smith are the coordinators of Christian initiation at St. Aloysius. They do not run everything. Rather, they act as mentors for other adults in the parish who might be able to facilitate conversations during the precatechumenate phase of the process, and they provide resources to help these other parishioners respond to the issues that might arise in these informal conversations. With this model, it is possible for our four searchers to begin whenever they show up. Bill or Alice may join Phyllis, Pauline and Frank—the friends who became evangelizers and then sponsors—from time to time when specific questions arise that need a more in-depth response. Richard, the baptized, catechized Lutheran, may be paired with Father Dan or the Smiths to help him in his short-term preparation for full communion. People with little or no catechesis, like Teresa, Ned and possibly Joan, may be paired initially with Bill and Alice or with a parishioner who is comfortable talking about the importance of God, Christ and the church in his or her life, is a good listener, and is willing to spend time with them.

The rural or small-town parish does not need to follow the precatechumenate model frequently found in the urban or suburban setting. Frequently, it is geared to large numbers, may follow a school-year timeline (which creates a graduation and class mentality), and often places a higher priority on tasks (teaching the information) than relationships.

Occasionally, a rural or small-town parish is blessed to have a few people who want to serve in initiation ministry. In such a blessed parish, it may be helpful to have someone responsible for the precatechumenate portion of the process. In the rural world, it will be important that this individual be rural-friendly. Such a person believes in the value of relationship; is at home with experiential-based learning that utilizes storytelling, parables and proverbs; takes time to be with people and is not in a hurry to get to the task of teaching; is a good listener; and believes that apprenticeship ("Come sit here beside me and let me show you how" rather than "Sit there and let me tell you what I know") is a good way to be formed in the Christian life. Doing so tells the inquirers that they are valued for who they are.

PUTTING A PRECATECHUMENATE CONVERSATION TOGETHER

One of the most frequent requests of rural initiation catechists is for advice on preparing and facilitating a precatechumenate conversation or session. Let us now turn our attention to the components and process of such a conversation/session.

Evangelization Sessions

When the time comes for the unbaptized to celebrate the rite of acceptance into the order of catechumens or the baptized to celebrate the rite of welcoming the candidates, a number of issues are presumed to be in order. First and foremost is this concern: Has the inquirer experienced an awakening about God, Christ and the church? For the inquirer, this means they have discovered God and that God's love is perpetually available to them; that Jesus Christ incarnates—makes visible—this love and that through his life, passion, death and resurrection declares to those who accept him and his good news that nothing will ever separate them from the love of God; and that Christ makes this love visible in the life of a faith community, the word of God and the sacraments. Someone, perhaps the pastor or one of the Smiths, should chat with Richard and Joan to see if these fundamentals are in place. If they are, the facilitator concentrates on other issues. Teresa and Ned, however, will need someone to apprentice them in these areas.

Those who are willing to apprentice Teresa and Ned will be most effective if they keep in mind how essential relationship is in the rural precatechumenate. It is crucial, therefore, that the facilitator of these evangelization conversations develop a relationship with the inquirer and already has a living, breathing relationship with God, Christ and the church, and can witness to those relationships credibly and personally. What rural people look for in these relationships is assurance and trust. Life is sometimes hard for rural people and will continue to be hard after they are initiated. They want to be assured by church people that life on the other side of initiation is better with God, Christ and the church than it is without them.

Explanations about the faith need to be done in plain, everyday language. Inquirers from an oral culture will probably be mystified by a term like "paschal mystery." Tell them the story of Jesus' *passion, death* and *resurrection* from one of the accounts in the Bible and describe it using these terms. Read it together. Then tell them how Jesus' passion, death and resurrection have made a difference in your life. Tell them your story. Follow that up by some stories of how others' lives became better because of Jesus' passion, death and resurrection. Tell them a story of one of the saints. Keep it relational and informal, like two friends getting together to swap stories on the front porch in the summer with a cold drink in hand. Conclude with a short prayer from the tradition of the church; perhaps the acclamation of faith from the eucharistic liturgy could be used: "Lord by your cross and resurrection you have set us free. You are the savior of the world." This could be printed on an index card and given to Teresa or Ned for future reference.

As can be seen from this brief example, it is not imperative that the facilitator of this conversation be an expert in christology. It is imperative, however, that the facilitator be a true believer in Jesus' passion, death and resurrection, and comfortable telling how it has made a difference in his or her life. If theological questions arise, the facilitator can jot them down and ask the parish priest or the initiation coordinator(s) to provide an answer that the facilitator can then pass on to the inquirer the next time they see each other.

Other Types of Inquiry Sessions

There are two levels of conversations during this period. The first level might be called foundational evangelization, and focuses on God, Christ and the church. The catechists of the inquiry period take the lead in discussing these issues with uncatechized inquirers. The second level focuses on issues to which the inquirers seek answers. These issues are surfaced by the inquirers and come in the form of questions they have about God, Christ, the church and life, such as the following: What's so important about Mary? Is there really a hell? Does God know everything we do? Does God really forgive all of our sins? How can I love my enemies when they've hurt me so badly? What is purgatory? It's very important that time be allowed for these kinds of questions. Answering them says the inquirers are valued and the catechist is there to serve their needs. It will be very important during these first conversations to focus on their issues and questions so that when the church asks them to focus on the issues and questions of the church during the catechumenate period, they will be open to them.

Having described how to have a conversation concerning the primary issues of evangelization, let us direct our attention to structuring a conversation about an issue raised by an inquirer. For this structure I am especially grateful to the late Joanna Case, who gave me permission to use her model in this book. The template for this model is found in Appendix 1 in the back of the book and may be reproduced.

In a conversation with Teresa and Ned about Jesus' death and resurrection, the topic of heaven and hell came up. As Bill and Alice Smith discussed heaven and hell, Teresa asks if people who die with sin on their souls go to heaven or hell. Bill and Alice tell her they go to either purgatory or hell. Teresa has never heard of purgatory and asks about it. Because it will divert them from what they want to finish saying about Jesus' death and resurrection, they ask Teresa and Ned if they could discuss purgatory the next time they get together. Teresa and Ned agree and Bill and Mary continue their conversation about the paschal mystery. Joan, who has been meeting with Phyllis and Pauline on Saturday mornings, is invited to join Teresa and Ned, as she has done on other occasions when an issue has arisen that the Smiths think might be of interest to her.

In preparation for their next conversation, Alice reads up on purgatory by consulting the *Catechism of the Catholic Church*, a high school level religious education book that contains an explanation of purgatory, and a *Catholic Update* on the topic. (For a list of resources, see Appendix 2). Using her

Inquiry Session Preparation Form (Appendix 1), Alice begins to sketch out how the conversation on purgatory might unfold. She starts by filling in "Box 3: Question(s) from the Inquirer" (see page 37), which identifies the question from Teresa. Alice is aware that rural people view life more experientially than theoretically, so she must be able to relate purgatory to the inquirers' everyday life. She decides to use an analogy from everyday life to approach the topic: What happens when we don't resolve the hurts we inflict on or receive from others. With that in mind, Alice fills in "Box 4D: Summary of Church Teaching" and "Box 4A: Key Stories/Issues Linked to Human Experience" on the form. Alice wants to connect the topic of purgatory to the scriptures but cannot think of a connection, so she calls her pastor and asks him if there is a one. Father Dan tells her the story from the second book of Maccabees about the dead Jewish soldiers who are discovered with amulets used to worship pagan gods on their bodies and how the ruler of Israel interceded on behalf of these Jewish soldiers because they had violated the first commandment. After telling her the story, he gives her the citation. She is now ready to fill in "Box 4B: Key Stories from Scripture." (See Appendix 3 for some popular Bible stories). Next she wants to connect purgatory to a tradition of the church and thinks of All Saints Day and All Souls Day and the burning of vigil candles in the church as a symbol of intercessory prayer for the dead. She writes these down in "Box 4C: Key Stories from the Tradition." She now has the heart of what she needs for her conversation with the inquirers.

Alice wants the inquirers to see the effect of believing in purgatory in their daily lives, so she asks herself how her belief in purgatory challenges her. As Alice thinks about an argument in her own life that was left unresolved, she remembers a deceased aunt who betrayed a confidence of hers and how she never spoke to that aunt again after the incident. As she recalls what she has read about purgatory, it occurs to Alice that she should pray for and forgive her aunt. So she fills in "Box 5: So What? The Challenge to Living Faith Daily" with her own responses. She wants to conclude with a prayer as they do every time they gather, so Alice goes to her *Handbook for Today's Catholics* and finds the prayer used at the end of funerals ("Eternal rest grant unto . . .") and writes it in "Box 6: Prayer from the Treasury of the Church." She also writes it on index cards so she can give the prayer to the inquirers. Thinking they might like to pray for some of their deceased relatives and friends, Alice decides to bring a small vigil candle from the church, so that when they conclude their conversation they can light the candle, remember some of their (and Alice's) deceased relatives and friends, and conclude with the "Eternal rest grant unto . . ." prayer. She notes the candle in "Box 2: Appropriate Prayer/Music/Symbols, Etc." She also wants to put the Bible out with the passage from the second book of Maccabees marked, so she notes it in Box 2 so she won't forget. Finally, it is always important to extend hospitality to those who come into one's home, so Alice notes that she will need to make some coffee and have something to eat while they visit and catch up on each other's lives and writes this down in "Box 1: Building Relationships/Community/Hospitality." (Alice would probably not need to fill in Box 1 because theses things come naturally to rural

INQUIRY SESSION PREPARATION FORM

Date of Session: *June 14*

1. Building relationship/community/hospitality:

    Coffee, cake, catching up on each other's lives

2. Appropriateprayer/music/symbols, etc.:

    Vigil candle from vigil rack at church, bible

3. Question(s) from the inquirers:

    Purgatory: What happens when you die with sin on soul but don't deserve hell?

4. Responses to the question(s):

    A. Key stories/issues linked to human experience:

    Story about what's left over after an argument when there's no apology/forgiveness

    B. Key stories from scripture:

    2 Maccabees 12

    C. Key stories from tradition:

    All Saints' Day/All Souls' Day: lighting vigil candles as symbol of prayer for dead

    D. Summary of church teaching:

    We are made in God's image and likeness. When we return to God we stand in the presence of pure love. Whatever is left from our earthly life that is "unlovely" because of our sins (with the exception of mortal sin) is purged so that we can live in the fullness of God's love forever.

5. So what? The challenge to living faith daily:

    I need to forgive N., a deceased relative who betrayed me. Pray for her.

6. Prayer from the treasury of the church:

    Eternal rest grant unto them, O Lord. And let perpetual light shine upon them. May they rest in peace. Amen. May their souls and the souls of all the faithful departed, through the mercy of God, rest in peace. Amen.

people, but it is included for non-rural people serving as initiation ministers in rural and small-town parishes for whom this might not naturally occur in the course of preparing for a session.)

Doing a Precatechumenate Conversation/Session

Teresa, Ned and Joan come over to the Smiths' home on Thursday evening at 7:30 in the evening. As always, Alice and Bill have a pot of coffee made and a little something sweet to eat. On the kitchen table are a Bible and an unlit vigil candle. They sit down in the kitchen and visit for a little while, catching up on the news of each other's lives since they last met.

When they seem caught up, Alice asks Teresa and Ned if they have any thoughts or questions that occurred to them after their last visit. Ned indicates he has no specific questions or comments and Teresa says that nothing in particular came up, but that she has had a growing sense of peace as she has prayed each day the short prayer given to her last week (Acclamation of Faith D: "Lord by your cross and resurrection . . ."). She has even memorized it (something oral people like to do) and found herself praying it a few times over the weekend when things got stressful at home. Alice tells her that it is a prayer used sometimes at Sunday Mass. With that, she asks Bill to bring in their missal and Alice shows the inquirers where the acclamation is located in the eucharistic prayer. Bill then volunteers to return the missal and asks if he can be excused to do some work in the cellar.

After Bill leaves, Alice tells the inquirers a story: One day a young woman came to tell her father, John, that she had fallen in love and wanted his blessing to marry. The father would not give his blessing because the man his daughter wanted to marry was Hispanic. The daughter was very upset and pleaded with her father to give his blessing. Her father refused. After several months of pleading, the young woman eloped with her beloved and moved to the next county.

For the next 30 years the two had no contact with each other. Both lived good lives. John was an excellent husband and a good father to his other children. He went to church regularly and worked hard. His estranged daughter was a wonderful wife and mother. She too went to church regularly and was a productive member of the community.

One day the daughter received a telephone call from her mother telling her that her father had died of a heart attack. Although 30 years had passed since she last spoke to him, she wept like a little child over the death of her father. That night as she was sleeping her father appeared to her in a dream. At first she was startled but noticed how sad her father looked. Then he spoke. "Margaret, I have come to you to ask for your forgiveness. When I arrived before God's heavenly throne, God told me he loved me very much. God then said that before he could give me his blessing and allow me completely into his presence I must heal the wound I created between you and me. Standing before God, I could see for the first time how foolish I was about you and Carlos. I was a fool to have forbidden your marriage to Carlos. So I come asking for your forgiveness."

She said to him, "Dad, it has been very difficult these past 30 years without you in my life. You hurt me very badly when you would not bless my marriage to Carlos. There were so many times I wanted to share the events of my life with you, things like the birth of your grandchildren. Despite your rejection, we have had a good life and your grandchildren have grown up to be fine members of the community. I know you did not like Carlos because he wasn't one of us, but he has been a wonderful husband and father." There was a long silence and John's head was down. Finally, Margaret said, "Dad, I forgive you." With that, her father's face broke into a smile and with tears in his eyes he said to her, "Margaret, I'm sorry for being such a fool. I want you to know that I never stopped loving you and that I will always love you, and from heaven I will pray for you, your children and Carlos." With that, he disappeared and Ellen awoke from her dream.

Alice then tells a personal story about her Aunt Bertha. It seems Alice had shared a confidence with Bertha and later discovered that Bertha had broken her confidence by sharing the story with others. Alice was mortified to discover her confidence had been broken and became furious with Bertha and never spoke to her aunt again. Alice goes on to say that that wound is still in her heart and that when Bertha went before the Lord, that wound was still in Bertha's heart as well because they had never been reconciled with each other. Bertha was a good but imperfect woman, and Alice said she thinks Bertha is probably now in heaven. But before she could enter the fullness of God's presence in heaven, she had to be purified of her unresolved sin of betrayal. Alice then concludes by saying this purification is what she understands as purgatory, and this is what occurs when someone dies with sin on their soul but doesn't deserve hell. After being purified, the person experiences the fullness of heaven.

Alice goes on to say that while God is total love, he is also total justice. This means that we do have to make an account of our lives before God at the time of our death, including the sins that were not forgiven before we died. She then says that because of God's great love, he provides an opportunity for a final purification so that Bertha and anyone else who dies with sin on their soul—but who doesn't deserve hell—will be fully in heaven, for this is where God wants us all to be.

Alice then explains that we know virtually nothing about the process and duration of purgatory, but that it has been a teaching of the Catholic church for a very long time. She then opens her Bible to the passage from the second book of Maccabees and reads it to the inquirers. Alice says this text describes a group of soldiers who died with a major sin on their soul: idolatry. Those who discovered their sin offered prayers asking God to be merciful to these deceased soldiers.

Then Alice discusses the place of intercessory prayer on behalf of the dead. She explains that Catholics believe they maintain a relationship with the dead and that prayers are a wonderful way to communicate with them and with God about them. She then explains how two days, the feasts of All

Saints and All Souls, are set aside every year to pray for all of the faithful departed.

She picks up the vigil candle and tells the inquirers about its location in the church and its purpose. Alice lights the candle and invites them to tell her a story about a significant deceased relative or friend. Teresa tells about her grandmother who died a few years ago and her father who died while driving intoxicated when she was 10 years old. Joan tells a story about a high school friend, and Ned talks about his wife. Alice then asks them if they would like to pray for their relatives and friends. They all agree. So they begin to mention aloud their deceased friends and relatives. Alice goes first and mentions her Aunt Bertha and a few others she knows. Joan mentions her friend, and Ned mentions his wife. Teresa mentions her grandmother, a cousin and a former teacher she greatly admired. Alice notices that Teresa does not mention her father's name, but she decides to make no comment.

Alice pulls the index cards from the Bible with the "Eternal rest" prayer. She distributes them and shows the inquirers where they can pray the response portion of the prayer. Then they read the prayer aloud. To conclude, Alice tells the inquirers that that is what she understands about purgatory and that they can learn more about it after they become a Catholic. She gives them the cards and suggests they use them from time to time when they want to pray for their deceased relatives and friends.

Because Alice is a rural person herself, she intuitively catechizes using stories. Because relationships are so central to rural people, Alice uses relationship stories to convey the truth about purgatory (John and Margaret, John and God, Bertha and Alice). She also invites the inquirers to view purgatory in light of their own relationships (Teresa and her relatives, Joan and her friend, Ned and his wife).

Then she asks them if they have any questions. Ned expresses an interest in learning more about prayer. He has never really prayed in his life, and he is intrigued by all of the prayers that Catholics have available to them. Alice tells him that Bill and she would be happy to talk about prayers and praying. Teresa agrees this would be a worthwhile issue to explore and Joan asks if she might join them. They agree to meet in two weeks. They share a little more coffee and then depart.

Before they leave, Alice privately mentions to Teresa that she noticed that Teresa did not mention her father when they were praying. Teresa admits that she omitted her father's name, saying that she is not ready to pray for her father just yet because of her anger about the way he died and the difficulty it brought to the family. Alice simply takes Teresa's hand and says that it is all right to feel that way and that if she would ever like to talk about it she was willing to listen. Alice gives her a big hug as she leaves their home and later tells Bill to pray that a healing may take place between Teresa and an important person in her life. Alice goes to bed that night and dreams of Aunt Bertha, who has a big smile on her face.

DISCERNMENT

The Smiths will meet with Teresa and Ned over the course of several months while Joan will continue to sit down at Pauline's kitchen table on Saturday morning for coffee and conversation, joining Teresa and Ned on Thursday evenings from time to time. Gradually, Joan's children, Keith and Sue, accompany their mother, especially on those Saturdays when their father must be away from the home. They too will begin to experience evangelization and express some interest in joining the church.

Eventually, Bill and Alice discern that Teresa has a foundation in faith and believe she is ready for the next phase of the initiation process. Alice speaks with Phyllis and Pauline about Joan's progress. They tell her that Joan is ready to make a deeper commitment as well. Alice then speaks to Teresa and Joan about this and they confirm their readiness. After a conversation with Frank, Ned's friend, Bill and Alice ask Ned about his disposition about moving on to the catechumenate period. Ned says he is not yet ready. Because of his infrequent attendance and some behaviors Frank has noted, Bill and Alice affirm this decision and tell Ned they will continue to meet with him as long as he wants to.

The Smiths arrange for a meal in their home one Sunday afternoon, to which Father Dan, Phyllis, Pauline, Teresa and Joan are invited. Teresa and Joan have met Father Dan a few times and have listened to his homilies when they have come to Mass. During the meal, Alice broaches the topic of the inquirers' progress and in a very casual way invites Teresa and Joan to talk about their experiences over the past few months. The Smiths, Phyllis and Pauline also speak favorably about the progress each has made.

This informal conversation about the growth of their relationship with God, Christ, the church and themselves is their discernment for the catechumenate period. It is very casual and occurs among people whom both Teresa and Joan trust.

Father Dan is happy to hear of their progress and asks if they think they are ready to make a deeper commitment to God, Christ and the church. They say they are, so he suggests they set a date to celebrate the combined rite of acceptance into the order of catechumens and the rite of welcoming the candidates.[14] They set a tentative date, and Father Dan asks Teresa and Joan if they know anyone in the parish they would like to have as their sponsors. Teresa knows some parishioners, but none closely enough to make this kind of request. She asks Alice if she would help her find someone. Alice agrees. Joan immediately thinks of Pauline but is uncomfortable asking her on the spot. Joan says she will think about it and asks Pauline if she will help her with this decision. Pauline says she is glad to help her make this decision and then volunteers to sponsor Joan if Joan will accept her, because her role as catechist will end once Joan celebrates the rite of welcome and begins the next phase of her formation with the Smiths. Joan is happy to hear this.

Joan tells the group that her children also might be interested in moving to the next phase of the process. Pauline affirms this and, because she knows how the initiation process for children works, volunteers her own children to serve as faith companions for Joan's children.[15] Alice and Father Dan ask Pauline to chat with Keith and Sue to determine if they want to do this, and if they are ready to do this. Pauline agrees to speak with them in the coming week.

After dessert, they all pray together and then leave for home. During the week, Alice confers with Father Dan about a sponsor for Teresa. She thinks Phyllis might be a good choice. Father Dan concurs and Alice calls Phyllis to see if she would be willing to sponsor Teresa. Phyllis is honored to be asked, but has several questions about the responsibilities of a sponsor. Alice answers her questions and adds that Pauline has done this before and would probably be glad to help her if she has any practical questions. After further conversation, Phyllis agrees and asks Alice to contact Teresa with the proposal. Teresa gladly accepts and Phyllis arranges for them to get together so they may become more acquainted with one another before the rite is celebrated.

Notes

[1] St. Alphonsus Ligouri (1696–1787) is acknowledged as being the first theologian to have provided an exhaustive synthesis of moral theology in the modern church. His writings became the basis for the moral theology manuals used in seminary education for many centuries.

[2] Walter Brueggemann, *Biblical Perspectives on Evangelism* (Nashville: Abingdon Press, 1993), p. 10.

[3] Adapted from *Ministry in an Oral Culture: Living with Will Rogers, Uncle Remus, and Minnie Pearl* by Tex Sample (Louisville: Westminster/John Knox Press, 1994), p. 73.

[4] Because most sponsors eventually become godparents in the case of the rural unbaptized, parents might be better excluded from serving as sponsors since this would necessitate a change later in the process.

[5] See RCIA, 42.

[6] See RCIA, 42, and the Decree on the Church's Missionary Activity *(Ad gentes)*, 14.

[7] See RCIA, 41–47, for the meaning and discernment associated with this rite and RCIA 48-74 for a description of the rite.

[8] See RCIA, 400, 411–415, for the meaning and discernment associated with this rite and RCIA, 416–433, for a description of the rite.

[9] RCIA, 43, says that it is the responsibility of sponsors, catechists, deacons and parish priests to participate in this discernment.

[10] RCIA, 42, describes the signs one is to look for that indicate readiness for the rite of acceptance into the order of catechumens.

[11] See the *General Directory for Catechesis*, 85–86, for a description of a catechized person.

[12] Found in Appendix III of the U.S. edition of the *Rite of Christian Initiation of Adults*.

[13] See RCIA, 482, and National Statute, 36.

[14] See RCIA, 505–529.

[15] RCIA, 254.1, speaks of th importance of Catholic children from the parish serving as companions to those children seeking initiation.

Chapter 3

The Rite of Acceptance into the Order of Catechumens

This chapter will examine:

- how to celebrate this rite in a rural-friendly manner

- how to conduct a mystagogical catechesis on this rite in a rural-friendly manner

- how to prepare rural inquirers and the rural community for this rite

- the differences in this rite for unbaptized and baptized inquirers

- the structure of the rite of acceptance into the order of catechumens.

Joe and Maria have come to a threshold moment in their relationship. They have been dating on and off for a few months. When they were first getting to know each other, Maria was also occasionally dating Craig, a young man she had known since high school days. It was a casual relationship, more a friendship than a romance. Joe, too, had dated other women, although most of the time he asked them out so that he would not feel like a fifth wheel when he got together with his friends Bob and Martha and Gladys and Peter. As their relationship grew, Joe and Maria increasingly found themselves spending more and more time with each other. Maria eventually stopped accepting Craig's invitations for a date, and Joe was no longer interested in calling just anyone to join him when he was hanging out with his friends. Eventually, they decided that they wanted to date only each other.

Maria and Joe went into Springfield one evening for dinner and a movie. During the meal Maria told Joe that she really enjoyed spending time with him and that she might be falling in love with him. She told him she had no interest in dating anyone else and wanted to know if it would be okay if they dated only each other.

Boy meets girl/ First dates	Commitment to go steady	Building the relationship Meeting the family Learning the traditions	Engagement	Pre-Cana/ Marriage prep	Wedding	Honeymoon/ First year of marriage
Precatechumenate	Rite of Acceptance into Order of Catechumens	Catechumenate	Rite of Election	Purification and enlightenment	Sacraments of initiation	Mystagogy

Joe was happy to hear Maria say this. He too had been growing in his affection for her and told her so. He told her how much he enjoyed it when she stopped by the store to visit, even when it was for just a few moments. He told her that he loved her sense of humor and her fondness for having a good time, and that he might be falling in love also. So Joe said that if she was willing to date only him, he was willing to date only her. She agreed. Then he leaned over and kissed her on the lips.

When Maria arrived home, she told her mother that Joe and she had made a decision to go steady. Her mother could tell how happy she was! Joe too called his family to tell them the news and then told his four friends. Everyone congratulated them and told them what a lovely couple they were.

THE RITE OF ACCEPTANCE INTO THE ORDER OF CATECHUMENS

At the restaurant Joe and Maria crossed a threshold in their relationship. They made an initial commitment to each other by declaring they would date each other exclusively, declining all other dating relationships. In the same way, unbaptized inquirers cross a threshold with this rite. Their status changes. Before the celebration they were inquirers; afterward they are catechumens. As catechumens, they are now members of the household of Christ.[1] Joe and Maria were good friends before that important evening in the restaurant. When they left they were a couple. By celebrating the rite of acceptance into the order of catechumens, unbaptized inquirers publicly proclaim their exclusive relationship with the Catholic church. In much the same way, Joe and Maria announce the exclusivity of their relationship by informing their families and friends of this new dimension of their relationship. There are visible rituals and symbols that the unbaptized inquirers experience in the rite of acceptance, such as the signing of their senses with the sign of the cross and the reception of a Bible. Joe and Maria ritualize the new dimension of their relationship with each other by the giving and accepting of a kiss.

Teresa and Joan, whom we met in chapter two, have been part of St. Al's precatechumenate for several months; they are now ready to deepen their commitment to Christ and the church. After their discernment with the Smiths, Father Dan, Phyllis and Pauline, they are ready to cross the threshold

A Harvest for God: Christian Initiation in the Rural and Small-Town Parish

into the period of the catechumenate. Teresa will cross the threshold through the ritual and symbols of the rite of acceptance. Because Joan is already baptized, her threshold rite is the rite of welcoming the candidates (RCIA, 411–433), which is similar in many ways to the rite of acceptance. If the parish welcomes Teresa and Joan into their new status at the same liturgy, they celebrate what is referred to as the combined rite (see RCIA, 505–529).

Three Rites for Admission into the Catechumenate Period

1. Rite of Acceptance into the Order of Catechumens: unbaptized only

2. Rite of Welcoming the Candidate: uncatechized baptized only

3. Combined rites of acceptance and welcome: unbaptized and uncatechized baptized together

---

Father Dan plans to celebrate the combined rite because there is only one Mass on Sunday at St. Al's at 10:00. A Sunday in August, the Nineteenth Sunday in Ordinary Time, Year A, is selected because the gospel lends itself to the meaning of the rite, it is a date when everyone can be present, and it is a date when the Women's Sodality can prepare a reception. But even the best plans sometimes need to be set aside.

On the Saturday morning before the celebration, Joan's son Keith fell out of a tree and broke his leg. While at the hospital getting his leg set, Joan called her friend and sponsor, Pauline, to tell her the news. Joan said that she doesn't think she and her children would be able to make it for the special liturgy the next morning. Pauline called Father Dan to tell him the news. Father Dan asked if the boy is all right and Pauline assured him that Keith was fine and that it was just one of those life experiences kids have. He sized up the situation for a few moments and asked Pauline to assure Joan that another date in the near future would be arranged to celebrate the rite of welcoming. Then he mentioned that he would stop by to see them on Sunday afternoon.

After hanging up, Father Dan opens the lectionary in his office and looks at the readings for the next few weeks. He notes that the gospel on the Twenty-second Sunday in Ordinary time goes well with the focus of the rite of welcoming and decides to propose that Sunday as the rescheduled time to celebrate the rite. He gives thought to moving the combined rite to that Sunday, but knowing how upset some of those who are preparing food for the reception the next day become over last minute changes, he decides against that idea. He calls the chair of the Women's Sodality to tell her the news about Keith, which she has already heard about, and asks her if it would be possible to do a second reception in three weeks. She thinks it will be all right, given the circumstances and promises to get it organized.

PREPARATION SESSION FOR THE INQUIRERS AND THEIR SPONSORS

On the Thursday evening before the rite is to be celebrated (and before Keith fell out of that tree), Teresa, Joan, Joan's children, Phyllis and Pauline all meet at Bill and Alice Smith's home. Pauline's husband, Jim Schneider, is also present because he will be sponsoring Joan's children. The Schneider children are also present because they will companion the Burnett children during their time of formation. There is a great deal of excitement and just a little anxiety about the upcoming rite and the conversation is very animated. Once they have had a chance to visit with each other and share some refreshments, they all gather in the living room and sit down.

Alice begins by asking them if they are curious about what they'll be doing at the church on Sunday. They all say yes! Alice tells them that they're going to spend the evening talking about some familiar things. She says that after talking about these things, they will have an idea about what they will be celebrating on Sunday.

She begins by telling everyone that she is going to say a sentence that they need to complete. She says, "I believe in God because. . . ." She repeats the statement, pauses and says, "I believe in God because when I look at the night sky and see all the stars, I know they did not get there by themselves." She repeats the statement and looks around to the others in the room.

Joan's third grader, Sue, says, "I believe in God because of the way all the seeds turn into flowers or plants."

Teresa speaks next and says, "I believe in God because of the wonderful people he has sent into my life."

Joan then says, "I believe in God because of the miracle of my two children."

Pauline says, "I believe in God because the Bible tells me so."

Keith says he believes in God because his mother believes in God and if she believes in God, he must exist because his mother doesn't believe in anything stupid.

Teresa says she believes in God because Alice and Bill believe in God and they have shown her that belief in God makes a difference in life. She goes on to say how dedicated they are to open their home every Thursday night and that it must be because of their belief in God. They continue on for a few more minutes, allowing everyone, including the sponsors, an opportunity to complete this sentence.

Next Alice tells them about her family. She tells them briefly about her mother and father and how important they were in her life, especially her mother. After speaking for a few moments, she asks them to describe their family briefly. Everyone tells stories about their family. Sue and Keith embellish the family story that Joan tells, and the Schneider children do the same when Pauline and Jim tell a little about their family.

Then Alice turns the conversation to the subject of Jesus. She asks them to name one thing they know about Jesus. Joan says that she knows he suffered and died on the cross so that everyone, including her, could have the chance to live forever. Keith says he knows that Jesus could walk on water and heal blind people. Sue says that she knows that he loves children. Teresa says that she knows he came to forgive sins. The others also respond to Alice's question.

Next she asks them to tell her something about the Bible. Sue says that it's a big book with a lot of words she doesn't understand, but that they must be good words because they are God's words. Laughing, Joan agrees with her daughter! Teresa says it's a holy book with stories to help us live our lives well, and Keith says it's a book with cool stories in it like David and Goliath and Noah and the Ark. The other children describe stories they know, like Adam and Eve, Jonah and the whale, and the Good Samaritan. Alice reminds Teresa and Joan that they have heard many Bible stories over the past several months and that it sounds like Joan has been sharing some of those stories with her children.

Then she asks them to tell her something about prayer. Teresa mentions that she knew nothing about praying before she started coming to the inquiry sessions and that she has kept all the index cards with Catholic prayers on them that Alice has given her over the past few months. She says that she reads through many of them daily and that they help her get through the day. Joan talks about how her parents taught her to pray as a little child and that she was teaching her children to pray. She expresses appreciation to Alice for helping her find some basic prayers to teach her children. She concludes by saying that prayer is a way for her to talk to God, but that she needs to learn more about how to listen to God. Sue recites a prayer her mother has taught her. Not to be outdone by his sister, Keith recites another prayer his mother has taught him.

Next Alice asks the group if any of them have ever made a promise. Teresa is the first to respond and tells them about a promise to finish high school that she made to her mother when she was thinking about quitting. She tells them that it was difficult keeping the promise at times, but that she managed to keep it with the help of her mother and one of her teachers. The others tell stories of promise making. Keith tells a story about making a promise with his friends and sealing it by pricking their fingers and mixing their blood together. (Joan makes him promise not to do that again!) Sue thinks this is gross. She then recalls a promise she once made to her father about helping her mother prepare the table for supper. Joan thanks her for keeping her promise and tells her how helpful she is by setting the table. Joan talks about the promise she has made to her husband John to be a loving and faithful wife no matter what.

Alice says that, based on what they have just said, they are ready to celebrate the upcoming rite. She tells them that on Sunday they will be making a public promise about God, a church family, Jesus, the Bible and prayer.

She compares it to the public way Joan and her husband made a promise to each other in a wedding ceremony. She tells them that they will commit themselves to grow in their relationship with God, Jesus and a spiritual family called the church, and to deepen their commitment to the Bible and prayer. She asks them if this sounds difficult to do. They all respond that it does not. She repeats that she believes they are ready to celebrate the rite on Sunday.

She then explains that the sponsors will come to the church for a rehearsal on Saturday afternoon to make sure everything goes smoothly on Sunday. She tells the candidates that they will not go to the rehearsal and that they just need to trust that their sponsors will walk them through everything smoothly. She tells Teresa, Joan and her children that they will be asked three questions at the beginning of the ceremony: What do you seek from the Lord as you make this first or renewed promise today? What do you seek from this parish to help you keep your promise? Are you ready to make or renew this promise?[2] She has these three questions printed on index cards and distributes them to the four candidates. She asks Jim Schneider to read the questions to her and, as he does, she answers, "Divine strength," "Support" and "I am." She tells them their answers do not need to be long, but that they should be ready to give their responses aloud to Father Dan when he asks them these questions on Sunday.

She concludes by telling the sponsors that they will be asked by Father Dan to present their candidates to the parishioners at the beginning of the ceremony. She tells them it should be brief, no more than 40 words, and that if they would like to write it out and go over it with Father Dan at the rehearsal they are welcome to do so. Alice asks Phyllis to stand up. Phyllis does so and Alice walks over, puts her arm around Phyllis' shoulder and says, "Good morning. It is my privilege to sponsor our good friend, Phyllis Lerner, in today's ceremony. As you know, she is married to Tom and has three lovely children. She is a baptized Catholic." She tells the sponsors this is an example of what they might say on Sunday.

She asks if they have any questions. Keith wants to know if he has to wear a tie, and Alice wisely tells him that that's a decision between his mother and him. There are no other questions, so they conclude with a prayer and leave for home.

Analysis of the Preparation Session

Alice held this session in order to prepare both the candidates and the sponsors for the upcoming liturgy. She wanted to make the purpose of the liturgy clear to them, because going into an unknown future is very intimidating for people from an oral culture. This is because rural life is habitual and makes sense when the present is repetitious of the past. So she shows them what they already know from the past about God, Jesus, family, the Bible and prayer, and tells them they are publicly committing themselves to it.

She focused on making a promise and then got them to illustrate their familiarity with making a promise by remembering promises they have made in the past. Promise making and promise keeping are important ways of negotiating relationships in the oral culture. Rural people keep their word, and promises are frequently made without any written agreements. Alice knew that framing the liturgy in this light would make it easier for them to understand what they were actually going to do on Sunday and reduce their anxiety about an unknown ritual.

Alice's methodology for the session is quite simple and incorporates three important dynamics useful in oral culture: relationship, storytelling and apprenticeship. She used simple examples to communicate deep truths about the rite. Her format may be summarized as follows:

- Hospitality and informal conversation

- Rite of acceptance as promise making about

    - Belief in God: "I believe in God because . . ."

    - Faith family: stories about their blood families

    - Jesus: "One thing I know about Jesus is . . ."

    - Bible: stories they know from the Bible

    - Prayer: describe prayer

- Rite of acceptance as making a public promise

    - Storytelling: examples of making a promise

- Nuts and bolts

    - Rehearsal: who rehearses and who does not

    - Answering three ritual questions (with role-play)

    - Sponsor introduction of candidate (with role-play)

- Other questions

- Prayer and conclusion.

Alice made sure that there was time for everyone to interact and strengthen the bonds of friendship throughout the session. Storytelling was another way she built relationships. One story led to another, which led to another. The stories bonded the storyteller to all who listened. Alice then took the stories and connected them to the rite. In doing this, the fabric of the stories became interwoven with the fabric of the rite. Alice's role-play of the three answers to be given by the candidates and the introductions to be given by the sponsors apprenticed those for whom those parts had implications and made the prospective of doing something unknown less daunting.

REHEARSING FOR THE CELEBRATION OF THE RITE OF ACCEPTANCE

Phyllis, Teresa's sponsor, comes to the church on Saturday afternoon to walk through the rite with Father Dan. She had already heard of Keith's accident and called Father Dan to find out if there would be a change in plans. He told her they would celebrate with Teresa since she will have some guests present and a big reception was in the works. At the church, Father Dan walks Phyllis through the rite, showing her where she will stand, what she will do and what she will say. Phyllis expresses some anxiety about remembering everything, but her pastor reassures her that he will give her clear directions throughout the ceremony so that she will not get lost. She asks if she may read the brief introduction of Teresa that she has been asked to prepare. Father Dan listens and tells her that it's just fine. He thanks her for coming and reminds her that Teresa, her guests and she should be at the church by 9:45 the next morning in order to get everyone settled before the Mass begins.

THE CELEBRATION OF THE RITE OF ACCEPTANCE INTO THE ORDER OF CATECHUMENS AT ST. AL'S

On the following Sunday morning, Teresa and some members of her family arrive at St. Al's. Phyllis is already there and greets them in front of the church where a few other parishioners have already gathered. When they are ready, Phyllis takes Teresa and her guests into the church and escorts them to the pew where Phyllis and her family always sit. When Father Dan enters the church, he goes immediately to Teresa and welcomes her and her guests to the church. As rehearsed, Teresa and Phyllis sit at the end of the pew so they can move easily into the aisle when it is time. Just before the Mass is to begin, one of the ushers comes and invites Teresa and Phyllis to the doors of the church. As they walk to the doors, the organist invites the assembly to repeat a few simple sung refrains after her that will be used for the rite of acceptance. Finally, Father Dan walks to the front of the church and says a word of welcome to everyone, especially Teresa's guests. The opening hymn is announced and the liturgy begins.

After the hymn concludes, Father Dan invites the assembly to have a seat. He then speaks a few words to the people about the importance of the rite that is about to be celebrated.[3] He mentions that Joan Burnett and her children are unable to join them because Keith has broken his leg. Many heads nod, indicating that they had already heard the news. He goes on to say that they will celebrate the rite of welcoming in three weeks' time for the Burnetts, but that the parish could not let a broken leg keep it from rejoicing with Teresa and having a wonderful reception to honor her first commitment to God and the church, especially since all the food was already made! He reminds them that it has been over two years since they last celebrated this rite and asks if they remember when John Carson was welcomed as a candidate for full communion. He looks over to John, who is seated in the church, and asks him if he remembers it. John nods his head yes. Father Dan concludes his introductory remarks by asking the parishioners to participate as enthusiastically in today's celebration as they did over two years ago for John.

He then walks down the short aisle, accompanied by one of the acolytes with the processional crucifix, to the place near the doors where Teresa and Phyllis are waiting. The church is fairly small, seating about 200 people, so everyone can see Phyllis and Teresa easily. The pastor has elected to have them stand inside the doors of the church rather than outside. Teresa has been sitting in the midst of the assembly for several months. It makes little sense to Father Dan to ask her to go outside, where it is already becoming quite hot, in order that she may ritually cross the threshold as though for the first time.[4]

Turning his attention to Phyllis, who is standing beside Teresa and holding her hand, Father Dan asks her to introduce Teresa to the assembly. Phyllis says, "Good morning. It is my pleasure to present Teresa Marino to you, the people of St. Aloysius, so that God and this community may accept her as a catechumen. I am proud to be her sponsor." She looks at Teresa, smiles and gently squeezes her hand. Father Dan then turns his attention to Teresa and asks her the first of three questions found in the rite.[5] He asks her what she seeks from the Lord as she makes her first promise to God and the church. She responds, "His all-powerful love." He then asks her what she seeks from the people of St. Aloysius to help her keep her promise. She responds, "Your patience and encouragement."

Taking the processional crucifix from the acolyte, he places it in front of Teresa and brings her hands up to touch the feet of the Christ figure. He enfolds her hands with his, looks her in the eyes and says, "Teresa, this is all-powerful love: Christ crucified for the redemption of the world. You have come to know him and his wonderful love for you over the past several months and now you come today asking for his love to possess you completely. Are you ready to begin your journey today under the guidance of Christ crucified, the one who is the visible sign of God's all-powerful love? Are you?"[6] Teresa responds, "I am."

Turning toward the assembly, the pastor asks them, along with Phyllis, "Are you ready to help Teresa by your patience and encouragement so that she may follow Christ crucified? Are you?" The people answer, "We are." He concludes the promise-making portion of the liturgy with a concluding prayer found in the ritual text.[7]

Next he invites Teresa to the front of the church. With the processional crucifix leading the way, Father Dan, Teresa and Phyllis process to the front of the church while the assembly sings the acclamation "Glory and praise to you, Lord Jesus Christ!" a few times. The pastor asks Teresa to step up into the sanctuary and to turn and face the assembly. As she does so, Phyllis stands beside her, and Father Dan moves into the main aisle in front of Teresa. When the acclamation stops, he reaches up and makes the sign of the cross on her forehead saying, "Receive the cross on your forehead. It is Christ himself who now strengthens you with this sign of his love. Learn to know and follow him."[8] The assembly repeats the acclamation they sang during the procession. As they are singing, Father Dan backs away from Teresa into the aisle and nods to Phyllis to move in front of Teresa as they had practiced the day before.

Once Phyllis is in place, the pastor invites her to make the next sign of the cross on Teresa's ears. He proclaims the text found in the ritual book while Phyllis makes the sign of the cross on Teresa's ears, followed by her eyes, lips, heart, shoulders, hands and feet.[9] Father Dan concludes the signing by making the sign of the cross over her and then uses the prayer found at paragraph 57b of the ritual text to conclude this portion of the rite.

Next he goes to the ambo, brings the lectionary to Teresa and opens it in front of her. He asks her to place her hands on the book. As she does, he says, "Teresa, you seek God's all-powerful love. In the word of God you hear proclaimed from this book, you will encounter all-powerful love. Listen to the words proclaimed from this book carefully and faithfully all the days of your life."[10] Teresa and Phyllis are then invited to return to their seats in the assembly for the liturgy of the word.

After the homily, the assembly is invited to rise. Teresa and Phyllis are invited to the foot of the sanctuary and the lector comes forward to lead the intercessions that also include special petitions on behalf of Teresa. Following the intercessions, Father Dan stretches out his hands over Teresa and offers the prayer for the catechumen (RCIA, 66). Since Teresa will not be dismissed at this time as recommended by the rite,[11] she is invited to return to her seat, accompanied by Phyllis, for the remainder of the liturgy. But before she returns to her seat, the pastor invites the assembly to express its support again for Teresa by a round of applause. Following the Mass, all go to the fellowship hall for a reception in Teresa's honor.

ANALYSIS OF THE CELEBRATION FROM THE PERSPECTIVE OF ORAL CULTURE

Much thought went into planning and celebrating this rite so that is would be a positive experience for both Teresa and the parishioners of St. Al's. The rite of acceptance is perhaps the most complex of all the initiation rites. Consequently, it may require the most preparation in order for it to be well celebrated. In order to understand how this rite may be celebrated in a rural setting, six terms will be used as a guide: assembling, making covenant, signing, listening, praying and sending.[12]

Assembling

Liturgy begins long before the people rise for the opening song. Hospitality and preparation of the assembly encourage the full, conscious and active

A Harvest for God: Christian Initiation in the Rural and Small-Town Parish

participation by everyone in the liturgical rites of the church. They "prime the pump" of the liturgical celebration. Phyllis was vigilant about the importance of hospitality by being at the church in time to greet Teresa and her guests and providing an opportunity for them to meet other members of the community.

Phyllis conducted this time of introductions and welcome outside the church building. In many traditional rural parishes, it is common that parishioners inside the church before Mass are quietly praying while others are socializing outside in front of the church. Both activities are acceptable at this time, but they are frequently kept separate. Because the parishioners of St. Al's maintain this kind of separation between worship and fellowship, Phyllis showed respect for those inside the church by keeping the visiting before the liturgy to the front of the church.

As the time to begin the Mass approached, the pastor recognized visitors and prepared the community for the rite. Recognizing visitors is an act of hospitality, and preparing everyone for the rite enables them to participate fully, consciously and actively in the rite as recommended by the church.[13]

The last time the rite of acceptance was celebrated at this parish was over two years ago. Wisely, the organist and pastor spent a little time preparing the assembly for its important role in the rite. The organist reviewed the ritual responses and chose simple, repetitive refrains or acclamations to facilitate participation.

Finally the liturgy begins. The last element of assembling centers on the placement of Teresa and Phyllis at the beginning of the rite. The rite of acceptance invites the candidates, their sponsors and some of the faithful to gather outside the church whenever possible. This is done because the candidates are about to cross a threshold. In many rural churches, "outside the church" is literally outside. Frequently there are no gathering areas adjacent to the church proper that are under the same roof. Weather may be a problem depending on the time of year and time of day the rite is being celebrated. Almost always, the candidate for the rite has already been a part of the community's worship, sometimes for many months. That he or she would be asked to formalize an already established relationship by beginning outside makes little sense to rural people for whom relationships are negotiated informally. So Father Dan asks Teresa to stand inside the door of the church to ritualize the crossing of a threshold in a way that would not strike her as artificial. Since everyone knows Teresa, it is unnecessary to ask her to state her name at the beginning of the rite. As an act of hospitality, however, Phyllis introduces her to the parishioners and clarifies her relationship to Teresa as her sponsor.

Making Covenant

Making covenant is the heart of the rite of acceptance. Promises are made. Teresa makes a promise to follow Christ while Phyllis and the assembly promise to support her on her faith journey. As Father Dan describes to Teresa the promise she is about to make (to become a follower of Christ), he simplifies the words found in the ritual text (RCIA, 52). He has learned over the years that this text is frequently difficult for people to absorb while it is being voiced in the actual ritual. Therefore, he has simplified the language and strengthened it with a tangible symbol: the cross. The presider seals the covenant through a prayer addressed to God (RCIA, 53).

To assist both Teresa and the parishioners in making their promises, he ends his question to them by repeating the words "Are you?" He does this because he knows that this assembly, like most, is made of people of habit. When they are in an unfamiliar place or situation, such as this infrequent rite, they may be confused about what, if any response, they are to give to the questions.

Signing

The rite calls for the signing of the catechumens with the cross (RCIA, 55), at least on their foreheads. The rite provides the option of signing other senses (RCIA, 56). Father Dan has learned over the years in his ministry with rural people that this additional signing is very powerful. He knows they are a people who live life more out of their hearts than their heads. They labor with their hands and feet and bear many burdens in life. They engage a world that is filled with wonderful sights, sounds, smells and tastes. Marking these senses with the cross of Christ tells them that Christ permeates everything in their lives. He had Teresa face the assembly for this signing. Facing an assembly in such a manner causes anxiety for rural people because they are not accustomed to standing in front of a crowd of people, but Father Dan wants the community to witness this marking as a way of keeping them invested in the ritual. The responses they will sing with the signing of each sense will also help. During the signing Phyllis looks Teresa in the eyes as much as possible, as the pastor suggested in the rehearsal. This helps reassure her and keeps her focused on the rite, not on the fact that everyone is looking at her.

Listening

Teresa has been initiated to the table of the word through this rite. It is the place where her promise will be strengthened. Before Teresa returns to her seat, the lectionary is brought from the ambo and Father Dan invites her to place her hands on this book while he explains the importance of the word of God, incorporating the answer she gave in response to his first question at the beginning of the liturgy. Again, he ritually strengthens the meaning of his words by asking Teresa to place her hands on the lectionary, a book she will see weekly for the rest of her life, and by recalling that what Teresa is seeking from the Lord as she makes her first promise will be found in this book and experienced at this table to which she is now initiated.

A Harvest for God: Christian Initiation in the Rural and Small-Town Parish

Praying

The lector announces the regular intercessions for the Nineteenth Sunday in Ordinary Time, and then adds some from the rite of acceptance. Father Dan concludes the intercessions with the prayer over the catechumens (RCIA, 66). Both options for this concluding prayer seem appropriate for Teresa, but he likes the reference in the first prayer to the "God of our forbears and God of all creation," so he selects that one.

Sending

As noted earlier, the rite prefers that those who are not ready to celebrate the liturgy of the eucharist be dismissed at the conclusion of the rite of acceptance. Since there is only one Mass at St. Al's and since the catechists want to participate in the liturgy of the eucharist, Teresa is not dismissed. Teresa knows that she is not eligible to receive holy communion so she remains in her pew with her family when the members of the parish go forward to receive.

MYSTAGOGICAL CATECHESIS ON THE RITE OF ACCEPTANCE

After the reception is concluded and Teresa's family has left, Teresa, Phyllis and Alice adjourn to Father Dan's kitchen to reflect on what they had just experienced. As they settle in at the table, Alice offers congratulations to Teresa and thanks to Phyllis for her help in the ritual. Alice tells them that they are going to spend a few minutes reflecting on what they celebrated in the church so that they might appreciate what happened more deeply.

Alice asks Teresa, "As you think back on the ceremony we celebrated this morning, what memories stand out for you?" After a few moments of silence, Teresa begins by saying how nervous she was before the Mass began but how it disappeared after she answered her questions at the beginning of the ceremony. She looks at Phyllis and tells her how grateful she was to have her beside her through the whole ceremony either holding her hand or placing her own hand on Teresa's shoulder. She tells the two women that she was moved when Father Dan made the sign of the cross on her forehead but even more moved when Phyllis made additional signs of the cross over her whole body, especially her feet. Phyllis comments how powerful it was for her to make the sign of the cross all over Teresa's body and thanked Teresa for helping her up after she signed her feet. Teresa mentions the moment in the liturgy when she was asked to hold the crucifix as she made her promise by saying, "I am." She says that when she said those words, she felt a real oneness with Jesus. She says that she felt reassured when Father Dan placed his hands over hers at that moment.

Alice asks Teresa if she remembers their conversation from a few months ago when they talked about having a relationship with Jesus. Teresa says she does, and Alice reminds her that she said she really wanted to know Jesus and be one with him, and that Jesus had answered her prayer.

Teresa is invited to continue her recollection. She remembers the moment in the liturgy when she was invited to touch the lectionary and how her comment about seeking God's all-powerful love at the beginning of the rite was repeated in relation to the scriptures.

Alice reminds Teresa of their preparation session last Thursday evening during which they discussed making promises. Referring to Teresa's recollection of the cross and the lectionary in the rite of acceptance, Alice asks her what kind of promise she made at those two points in the ceremony. Teresa is quiet for some time and then responds that when she touched the cross she made a promise to follow the Lord, and when she touched the lectionary she made a commitment to listen to his words. Alice agrees.

Teresa looks at Alice and asks why Father Dan made her touch the feet of the body of Jesus. Alice explains that following Jesus sometimes involves suffering as he did and that this is part of the promise. Alice then goes on to say that because suffering is sometimes part of discipleship, Father Dan enfolded her hands with his to reassure her that there are others to help her when this happens. Then she tells Teresa that this is why Phyllis was with her during the ceremony and why the people made a promise to encourage her. After explaining this, Alice gives Teresa a simple crucifix and asks her to place it somewhere in her house where she will see it often and asks her to remember the importance of Christ's death for the salvation of all, including her, every time she looks upon it.[14]

To refocus Teresa, Alice asks again about the promise connected to the lectionary. Teresa answers that she made a commitment to listen to the word of God. She says that touching the lectionary somehow connected her to the scriptures in a way she never experienced before. Alice explains that as a catechumen, Teresa has made a commitment to become a devoted disciple of the word of God and that this word is kept in a special book from which it is read when the community gathers to worship. After this brief explanation, Alice gives Teresa a copy of the lectionary readings for Year A[15] and asks her to bring it with her when she comes for her weekly sessions.[16] She suggests that Teresa read the scriptures before coming to Mass so that she may be more familiar with the passages when they are proclaimed by the lector and get more out of them when they are proclaimed.

Alice ends her reflection with Teresa by telling her that the parishioners of St. Al's have made a promise to support her and that they are happy that she has become part of the parish. Teresa comments on the feeling of welcome she has experienced from the community and how impressed her family was by both the hospitality extended to them before the service and at the reception. Alice then says that God has also made a promise to Teresa in this liturgy and that God has promised to remain with her and to protect her as she continues on her journey of faith. Teresa smiles at this comment and says how lucky she is to have God and people like Phyllis, Father Dan, Alice and the people of St. Al's on her side.

Alice ends the session by reminding Teresa that her sessions will now follow the Mass every Sunday and that Alice's husband Bill will be her primary catechist. Alice asks them to join hands, and Alice repeats the prayer Father Dan prayed at the end of the general intercessions. They embrace, clean up the kitchen and return to their homes.

Analyzing the Mystagogical Session

Alice has used a simple format to reflect with Teresa on the Rite of Acceptance. This session is referred to as a mystagogical catechesis. This is a reflection on the rite in order to discover the meaning of the rite, especially for those who celebrated it. Her format might be summarized as follows:

- Welcome and brief explanation of session

- Remembering the rite:

  - Prompt: "What memories stand out for you from this morning's liturgy?"

  - Responses by catechumen (and others present)

- Connecting the rite and its meaning:

  - Promise of catechumen to follow Christ as disciple and its implications

    - Presentation of a cross/crucifix

  - Promise of catechumen to listen to the word of God and its implications

    - Presentation of a lectionary/Bible

  - Promise of the community to catechumen

  - Promise of God to catechumen

- Announcements/questions

- Prayer and conclusion

The rite of acceptance is a threshold rite. It carries those who participate in the rite from one state to another. Before the rite, Teresa was an inquirer; afterward she is a catechumen. The rite is also a bridge from the past to the future. At the Thursday evening preparation session, Alice wisely helped Teresa and the others see that the rite was celebrating the growth that had already occurred in their lives. This helped to reduce their anxiety so they could approach the rite more confidently. Again, for people from an oral culture, this is very important. As a threshold rite however, it also sends Teresa and the others into an unknown future. Teresa has never been a cate- chumen before and has never belonged to a church community. She has never publicly declared her relationship to God, Christ and the church.

Teresa begins her new life as a catechumen with a mystagogical cate- chesis of the rite. In the mystagogical session, Alice helps Teresa transition into her new life by remembering the rite and connecting the issues of God, Jesus, church family, the bible and prayer to the rite. This mystagogical process is very important for Teresa because she is about to embark on a new phase of her initiation journey. A sense of continuity will be important for her as she takes her first steps into her future as a catechumen.

RITE OF WELCOMING THE CANDIDATES

Joan and her children are ready to celebrate the rite of welcoming on the Twenty-second Sunday in Ordinary Time. Again, the women of the parish have prepared a reception in their honor and, again, the organist reviews the ritual music, which is the same as it was for Teresa's rite, before the liturgy begins. Joan Burnett and her children meet Pauline and Jim Schneider and their children in front of the church where they spend a few minutes visiting. When they are ready, the Burnetts go in and sit in the same pew with the Schneiders. Joan's parents have come at the invitation of their daughter. Father Dan welcomes them before the liturgy begins and again invites the parishioners to participate in the rite as enthusiastically as possible.

Once the processional with lectionary and ministers and the opening hymn are finished, Father Dan invites the Burnetts to come forward with the Schneiders. They come to the front of the church and the pastor asks them to step into the sanctuary near the baptismal font and turn around to face the assembly.[17] Keith, now on crutches, is assisted into the sanctuary by Jim Schneider and his older son. Father Dan steps into the main aisle and the acolyte with the processional crucifix stands nearby. As with Teresa, the sponsors are invited to introduce the three candidates. Pauline introduces Joan and then Jim introduces Keith and Sue. As they introduce the Burnetts, Pauline mentions that Joan is baptized in the Methodist Church and Jim mentions that Keith and Sue were baptized at infancy in the Catholic church.

As each responds to the three questions at the beginning of the rite, Father Dan places the processional crucifix before them and ties their first response to the image of Christ crucified, noting that they are making a promise to a deeper commitment to Christ in light of their privileged status as baptized Christians. The community is asked to give a sign of its support and then the signing of the forehead follows. The sponsors dip their hands into the blessed water of the font and sign the forehead of all three candi- dates while Father Dan makes the sign of the cross over all of them, saying, "Receive the cross on your forehead as a reminder of your baptism into Christ."[18] The lectionary is brought over from the ambo and opened before the Burnetts. Father Dan invites them to place their hand on the lectionary as he addresses each of them, tying their initial responses at the beginning of the liturgy, as he did with Teresa three weeks earlier, to the word of God. After the homily, the parishioners rise to make the profession of faith[19] and the intercessions follow. The lector includes the extra intercessions on behalf of the new candidates. Father Dan concludes the rite by extending his hands over the three candidates and praying the prayer over the candidates. Father Dan invites a round of applause from the assembly and then invites the two families to return to their places in the midst of the assembly for the rest of the liturgy, as recommended in the rite.[20] They attend the reception after the Mass and participate in the mystagogical session as Teresa did three weeks earlier. They are given a crucifix and a lectionary.

Some Final Observations

The rite of acceptance into the order of catechumens and the rite of welcoming the candidates may be celebrated more than once in a given year.[21] In most rural and small-town parishes there may be no need to celebrate these rites more than once a year because there may be no inquirers to celebrate them.

There is no specific time of the year, such as the First Sunday of Advent, when the rites must be celebrated. If an inquirer, whether baptized or not, is ready to be received or welcomed in October or February, it may be scheduled during those times of the year.

In the past, those who have become members of the Catholic church from other Christian religions have been referred to as "converts." National Statute 2 states very clearly that the term convert is reserved for those who are unbaptized and who are converting from unbelief to Christian belief. Teresa is a convert; Joan is not.

Sometimes questions arise about the validity of someone's baptism. See Appendixes 14, 15 and 16 for information on this question.

As a catechumen, Teresa has some rights and privileges[22] since she is now part of the household of Christ. She may be married in the church.[23] She may also receive Christian burial should she die as a catechumen.

Notes

[1]See RCIA, 47, which explains all the benefits catechumens enjoy once they have celebrated this rite.

[2]See RCIA, 50 and 52, for the unbaptized and RCIA, 418 and 419. It is clear that there is some leeway in formulating the initial questions to suit the circumstances and people celebrating this rite. In the case of both the unbaptized and the baptized their intention is to make or renew a promise and through it to become a catechumen or a candidate. Promise making is serious business among oral people and asking for God's divine help and the community's support is very meaningful for them. Hence, the suggested questions here may be more appropriate to help oral people, both the candidates and the community, understand what is going on at the beginning of the rite than the ones suggested in the ritual text.

[3]RCIA, 49, invites the presider to introduce the liturgy to the assembly.

[4]RCIA, 48, prefers that those who are to become catechumens actually gather outside the church so that their entrance may ritualize the threshold dynamic more powerfully. However,

in its pastoral wisdom, the same paragraph allows for other choices to be made regarding the location for the reception of those who are to become catechumens. Since Teresa has already crossed the threshold many times, it did not seem as important that she ritually cross it today. Standing inside the doors of the church seems to convey a similar dynamic.

[5]See RCIA, 50.

[6]See RCIA, 52, invites the presider to shape the intention of the petitioner based on the answers received from the individual in the opening dialogue. It is always to end with a question asking the petitioner if he or she is ready to begin this journey. The use of the processional crucifix is a way of enhancing the words of the rite with a symbol that focuses the significance of the words in a very concrete manner. Its use is entirely optional.

[7]RCIA, 53, asks for a promise from the sponsor and assembly and concludes with a prayer addressed to God, which seals the catechumen's promise ("I am").

[8]RCIA, 55, states that when the candidates are few in number, the presider traces the first cross on the catechumen. If there are larger numbers of catechumens, the sponsor may trace the first cross on the forehead of the catechumen while the presider makes the sign of the cross over the group.

[9]RCIA, 56, asks that either the sponsor or the catechist sign the senses while the presider states the words.

[10]RCIA, 64, provides an optional presentation of a Bible. Since the lectionary from which everyone hears the word of God on Sunday is the symbol of that word for the community at worship, the stronger presentation may be as described. A Bible or lectionary may be given to the catechumens after the liturgy for weekly and personal use. The words chosen by the presider recapitulated the words spoken by the catechumen at the beginning of the rite.

[11]RCIA, 67, recommends that the catechumens be dismissed at this time in the eucharistic liturgy. It is permissible for them to remain for the rest of the liturgy when serious reasons warrant. This is the case at St. Al's because no catechist is available to go with Teresa at this point in the liturgy. Dismissing her with no one to accompany her would be an act of inhospitality.

[12]These terms are borrowed and slightly adapted from an article by Kathleen Hughes, "Acceptance into the Order of Catechumens," found in *Celebrating the Rites of Adult Initiation: Pastoral Reflections*, pp. 1–14. Chicago: Liturgy Training Publications, 1992.

[13]RCIA, 45.

[14]RCIA, 74, offers the option of presenting a cross during the rite. Father Dan incorporated one in the ritual. Here, Alice gives Teresa a crucifix so that she may have a symbol in her home to remind her of the importance of the death and resurrection of Jesus.

[15]There are many versions one might give to a catechumen. Popular ones include *Living the Word* published by World Library Publications and *At Home with the Word* from Liturgy Training Publications.

[16]RCIA, 64, provides for the optional presentation of a bible as part of the liturgy. To draw attention to the lectionary, Father Dan and Alice decided to present a paperback lectionary to Teresa during the reflection session that took place after the rite of acceptance.

[17]RCIA, 416–417, states that the baptized candidates are to be seated among the parishioners at the beginning of the liturgy and are invited forward when it is time to celebrate the first part of the rite.

[18]RCIA, 422, indicates that the presider makes the sign of the cross over the candidates while a sponsor traces the cross on the forehead. The use of water in this signing is a pastoral adaptation (not found in the rite) to emphasize the baptism of those who are preparing for reception into full communion.

[19]See RCIA, 429.

[20]RCIA, 432, indicates that candidates are not to be dismissed at the conclusion of the rite if the liturgy of the eucharist follows.

[21]See RCIA, 18 and 414.

[22]See RCIA, 47.

[23]See the *Rite of Marriage*, 55–66.

Chapter 4

The Period of the Catechumenate

This chapter will examine:

- how to adapt the catechumenate to people from an oral culture

- the components of initiation catechesis

- why the catechetical sessions of this period should be connected to the Sunday liturgy of the word

- the importance of dismissing catechumens and candidates after the homily

- how to prepare and facilitate catechetical sessions during this period

- how to use the minor rites during this period

- how to discern readiness for the rite of election.

Now that they have pledged to date each other exclusively, Joe and Maria began to spend much more time with each other outside of dating. She went over to his place, and occasionally he dropped by her family's home. As the amount of time they spent with each other increased, they began to learn more and more about each other.

Maria learned that Joe was a churchgoer, an experience she was not exposed to during her childhood. She began going to church with Joe at his invitation. Initially, the order of worship was unfamiliar to her but eventually she got accustomed to it with Joe's help. The other members of the church seemed friendly and always made her feel welcome both at church and during the week. Joe discovered that Maria grew up in a home where

Boy meets girl/ First dates	Commitment to go steady	**Building the relationship Meeting the family Learning the traditions**	Engagement	Pre-Cana/ Marriage prep	Wedding	Honeymoon/ First year of marriage
Precatechumenate	Rite of Acceptance into Order of Catechumens	**Catechumenate**	Rite of Election	Purification and enlightenment	Sacraments of initiation	Mystagogy

praying was important but in a style much more spontaneous than he was used to.

Maria was invited to Joe's family home for dinner one Sunday. They spent several hours with the Werner family. Joe's siblings—Albert, Conrad, Freddy and Tracy—were there. Maria was struck by the tidiness of the Werner home and how quiet it was in comparison to hers. There was plenty of food, although the cuisine was quite different from that served at her house. She had her first taste of sauerkraut. Joe's parents asked her all kinds of questions and Freddy, the young teenager, teased Joe about getting married.

Maria stopped by Joe's store one Friday evening near closing time. As they were about to leave the store, Joe mentioned that he had to make a stop at Charlie Baker's home to deliver some items Charlie needed. He asked Maria if she would mind going with him. She said she wouldn't mind at all.

Mr. Baker was a retired farmer and a widower who had suffered a stroke. He walked with great difficulty. Joe brought the few items Charlie had ordered by telephone into the house. It was somewhat run down and needed cleaning. Joe put the items away and sat down to visit with Charlie. Maria joined in the conversation. About an hour into their conversation, Joe asked Charlie why he had ordered plumbing materials for a toilet. Charlie said that his toilet was not shutting off and that probably the rubber ring in the toilet plunger had begun to wear out and needed replacing. Joe asked how he was going to replace the defective part; Charlie said his son was coming to visit in a week and would fix it along with a number of other things on a repair list Charlie had made. Joe volunteered to stop by the next day and fix the toilet. Charlie demurred at first but Joe mentioned that he would be wasting water, so Charlie accepted his offer. They set up the time, and Maria and Joe left to go to dinner. Maria was impressed by Joe's generosity. Over time she would come to know that he was also generous with his time in helping many others.

Maria had Joe over to her home several times. The first time, Joe was a bit intimidated by the number of people at Maria's home. In addition to her mother and three siblings, Maria's maternal grandmother and several aunts and uncles were there, not to mention her many cousins. Although Maria's family was poor, the meal was like a banquet and there was much laughter and banter among the family members. It was very noisy compared to his parents' home. At other times there were fewer people, but generally on the weekends the extended Marino family was present. They teased Maria about having a non-Italian boyfriend and commented on how beautiful their children would be. Joe took it all in good humor and enjoyed becoming acquainted with a group of people he had previously not known. Life seemed very alive in Maria's home!

Their relationship continued to grow over the months. Joe learned Italian Christmas customs, and Maria learned how to make sauerkraut from Joe's mother. When they went out, it was more and more often without other couples. They continued to learn about each other and were falling more deeply in love. They eventually began to talk about what life would be like if they were married to each other and found that as they explored those ideas they had much in common. After a year of dating, Joe proposed to Maria and she accepted.

THE CATECHUMENATE PERIOD

The period of the catechumenate is to the process of initiation what the developing bond between Joe and Maria is to a relationship. Joe and Maria are deepening their relationship. During this time of courtship, they meet each other's families and learn the values and traditions of those families. Maria is learning about Sunday worship and is witnessing how Joe cares for others. These are similar to the tasks of the catechumenate period. Paragraph 75 of the RCIA identifies the four goals of this period as becoming acquainted with the major teachings of the church, learning the Christian way of life in the midst of a community, learning to pray and worship and learning the life of discipleship.

As Joe and Maria become acquainted with the traditions and stories of each other and their respective families, so do the catechumens and uncatechized candidates become acquainted with the major teachings of the church during this period. Like our unmarried couple that learns about love and family life from their families and friends, the catechumens and candidates learn how to live the Christian life in the midst of a faith community and with the help of other members of the parish during this period. Just as Maria learns about Sunday worship from Joe and he learns to pray more spontaneously from her, those participating in this period of initiation learn more and more about how to pray, both alone and with a community. Finally, Maria learns of Joe's generosity to others and he learns of her deep love and devotion to her younger siblings. Likewise, the catechumens and candidates discover that discipleship is a constitutive part of the life of a Catholic Christian.

CATECHESIS, COMMUNITY, WORSHIP AND DISCIPLESHIP IN A RURAL SETTING

Just as one learns how to camp by camping, catechumens and candidates learn to be Catholic Christians by living like Catholic Christians. This sort of apprenticeship model summarizes how rural catechumens and candidates are best formed during this period. Someone has described apprenticeship this way: First I do and you watch. Second, we do together. Third, you do and I help. Finally, you do and I watch. Forming catechumens and candidates in an experiential and practical way rather than a more introspective and analytical way is more appropriate with rural people. Experts on rural culture remind us that formation for the Christian life is more effective in this setting when the emphasis is placed more on the behavioral than the intellectual.

The rite itself endorses this approach. Paragraph 75 of the RCIA makes it clear that catechumens and uncatechized candidates learn best about liturgy and worship by participating weekly in the liturgy of the word at Sunday Mass rather than by reading about it. Catholic Christians sit beside them in the church and show them how to worship by worshiping beside them, showing them the location of the hymns and the ordinaries of the introductory rites (such as the "Lord have mercy" and the "Glory to God") in the hymnal. Remember how Joe and Maria mentored each other about this part of their lives. He brought her to the church and companioned her through the liturgy and she taught him to pray spontaneously by her example.

There is a story told about a rural catechumen who wanted to know about the rosary. The well-intentioned, college-educated catechist responded by explaining the history of the rosary, the spirituality associated with it, and the 15 mysteries. The catechumen politely thanked the catechist for the explanation. The next day the catechumen's sponsor, a rural woman who was present at the session, stopped by to visit her friend. In the course of their conversation, the Catholic woman asked her friend if she still wanted to know something about the rosary. Her friend indicated she did, so the woman opened her purse, pulled out a rosary, and placing the rosary in the catechumen's hand showed her how to make the sign of the cross with the crucifix and then, using the beads, prayed the Our Father, the Hail Mary and the Glory Be with her. Both the catechist and the sponsor answered the woman's question, but the sponsor gave a better and more enduring response to the rural catechumen. It was practical and experiential.

The catechumens and candidates experience community by being with a worshiping community on Sunday and being associated with members of the community (such as sponsors and catechists) in a variety of ways during this period. The importance of relationship in rural society is echoed by paragraph 75 of the RCIA, which recommends that members of the community help the catechumens and candidates by good example and support. That good example and support might occur off the church property. A rural Catholic might call or visit a catechumen as a sign of friendship and encouragement. Catechumens and candidates could be invited to a social event being held by the parish or to the home of a Catholic family where people are gathering to discuss the Bible or the readings from the previous Sunday. Because rural people frequently see their church community as their second family, they are quite comfortable welcoming and assisting the catechumens and candidates when they come to Mass. After all, these people are part of the family. Maria experienced this sense of family at Joe's church and during the week when she ran into members of the parish.

Discipleship is not simply spoken about. Rather, catechumens and candidates should be apprenticed into discipleship by the example of parishioners during this period. Paragraph 75 says that a change of conduct should be a consequence of this period of formation. For some rural people the change may be from bad behavior to good. In other situations it may be from inertia to activity. For example, a rural Catholic who volunteers at a local migrant-farmer health clinic might invite the catechumens and candidates to accompany her in order to get acquainted with Catholics from another country who now live in the local community. This "fieldtrip" might challenge preconceived ideas the catechumen or candidate might have about the poor and foreigners and/or motivate them to become involved as a volunteer.

During a catechetical session in this period, wise catechists will regularly surround the church's teachings with stories that reinforce the point and with examples from daily life that show how the teaching is lived or explain it in a way that is meaningful for rural people.

THE THREE FORMATION SETTINGS OF THE CATECHUMENATE PERIOD

All four components of paragraph 75 of the RCIA should be incorporated into the catechumenate period in the three settings where formation occurs.

The Sunday Liturgy

The parish Sunday liturgy is considered the first of these. There the catechumens and candidates experience liturgical worship in the midst of a community who learns about its faith and is invited to live that faith as disciples in the coming week. Beginning with the rite of acceptance into the order of catechumens that Teresa celebrated (or the rite of welcoming the candidates for those who are baptized yet uncatechized, like Joan), the process of initiation presumes that the Sunday liturgy is the starting point for all further formation. Note in paragraph 75.1 of the RCIA that the catechesis of this period is to be "accommodated to the liturgical year and solidly supported by celebrations of the word." This means that weekly catechumenate sessions should be built upon the liturgy of the word of Sundays and holy days. Why? Because the church believes that, in the liturgy itself, people encounter the God who is continuously revealing divine love, truth and wisdom to them. The liturgy makes God and God's grace visible and tangible to them. It makes present and real for people the grace of God that is always already around them but that is frequently missed.[1]

The Catechetical Session

The catechetical session that follows the liturgy is the second formation session. Grace is made visible and tangible through this experience as well. The catechumens and candidates gather with a catechist, somewhere on the church property or in someone's home, to explore more deeply both the beliefs of the church that emerge from the liturgy recently celebrated and the call to discipleship that emerges from both the liturgical worship and the catechetical session. Teresa and Joan will meet with Bill or Alice (or both) for their catechetical session after Mass and the fellowship hour are concluded. They will reflect on what they experienced at the Mass and look more deeply into its meaning for their daily lives.

Life

The third formation session is experienced in the day-to-day life of the catechumen and candidate as they attempt to integrate what they learned in the other two sessions. Additional grace is made visible and tangible when they practice what they have both experienced in the liturgy and reflected on it their catechetical session. Let us take the example of one Sunday to illustrate these three formation moments.

An Example

Recall the gospel from Matthew on the Twenty-fifth Sunday in Ordinary Time, Year A, in which the estate owner hires workers throughout the day and ends up paying the same daily wage to everyone, regardless of whether they worked for 12 hours or one. Rural people who make their living off the land will be fascinated to hear what this story is all about. It is a story with many layers of meaning. Among its many meanings is how different God's ways are from our ways. No one in his or her right mind would pay a worker who labored for one hour the same amount of money owed to one who worked for 12. Yet the estate owner, a symbol of God, does. It is a reminder that God's logic, built on love, is quite different from human logic, built on fairness. Second, it is a story about the incredible generosity of God, a generosity that is not dependent on when one shows up in the course of life to follow the Lord. In the story, the wage is symbolic of eternal life. The scoundrel in his sixties who awakens to God's love and is converted to this love receives the same gift of heaven as the person baptized in infancy who has never strayed from the path. Finally, it is a story about grace, which might also be defined as God's love. The wage given to the workers is also the gift of God's endless love made available to all without discrimination.

In the first formation setting, the liturgy of the word at church, Teresa, Joan and her children gather with all the faithful of St. Al's to praise God through their worship. The opening song of the Mass is "Amazing Grace." The penitential rite proclaims the timeless gift of God's grace made visible through Christ to the world:

You came to gather the nations into the peace of God's kingdom,
Lord have mercy.

You come in word and sacrament to strengthen us in holiness,
Christ have mercy.

You will come again with salvation for all your people,
Lord have mercy.

The first reading from Isaiah reminds the listener not only are God's ways different than the ways of human beings, they are also vastly superior to them. Psalm 145 proclaims the greatness of God in song. The homily explains how the word of God and the eucharist are perpetual sources of grace. The first eucharistic prayer for Masses of reconciliation further illustrates this notion of God's "graceful" ways by proclaiming that "time and time again we broke your covenant but you did not abandon us. Instead, through your Son, you bound yourself even more closely to the human family by a bond that can never be broken." Then there is the gift of holy communion itself in which the members of the parish receive the gift of God's generosity, grace made visible in bread and wine. Since there is only one Mass at St. Al's, Bill and Alice Smith, the catechists, stay for the entire Mass. This means that Teresa, Joan and her children are not dismissed after the homily as recommended by the ritual text.[2] Because they remain until the end of the Mass, they have an opportunity to experience grace made visible and tangible throughout the entire liturgy.

Following the Mass and fellowship hour, Teresa and Joan gather with Bill for their catechetical session in the living room of the rectory while Joan's children attend the Sunday school program with their peers. This second formation setting will give Teresa and Joan another opportunity to experience grace as they reflect upon what they experienced at the Mass and interact with Bill. He takes the three points Father Dan made at the beginning of his homily about God (God's ways are not our ways, God's generosity, and grace) and tells stories to illustrate these points.

To illustrate that God's ways are not like that of humans, they have a humorous exchange about things that would not exist in the world if they were God. Among their selections they mention things like mosquitoes, flies and weeds. Examples of God's generosity include sunsets, the stars on a clear summer night and the birth of a child. Bill then speaks about grace for a few minutes and together they silently think about how they might become more aware of how grace is always already present in their lives. The conclude by singing a few verses of "Amazing Grace."

Joan's children have spent some of their time during the Sunday school session reflecting on the Sunday liturgy and scriptures they just participated in. They too share faith and learn from their catechists how they might experience God's grace more consciously.

As they depart for home, Teresa, Joan and her children enter the third formation setting: their world. Throughout the week they will have opportunities to practice becoming aware of God's grace all around them and to help others become more aware of that grace, especially those who might not find much grace in their life or who are in need of some generosity. For Teresa this will be her mother, who is crippled with arthritis. For Joan it will be her husband, who is underemployed. For Joan's children it will be with classmates in school who are not popular or well liked.

EVALUATING THIS MODEL OF FORMATION

All three settings are to be connected to one another during this period of formation. The catechetical sessions of this period, the second formation setting, build on the liturgical celebration that preceded them and call the participants to make connections between their day-to-day life and what they experienced in both the liturgy and catechetical sessions. Catechetical sessions that are divorced from the Sunday celebration of the liturgy of the word or do not regularly invite catechumens and candidates to discipleship are not faithful to the vision of the rite.

Some initiation ministers have expressed concern about the adequacy of this liturgy-catechesis-discipleship model of formation, fearing that the catechumens and candidates do not receive an appropriate acquaintance with the dogmas and precepts of the church. There are three responses to this concern. First, it seems clear that the church in its wisdom has stated in paragraph 75 of the RCIA that a catechetical session accommodated to the liturgical year and supported by liturgical celebrations of the word of God is the normative model. The model of catechesis here is initiation catechesis and not religious education. The hope of the church in this model is that the newly initiated will see the intrinsic connection between liturgy and discipleship and will become so motivated as a result of their formation that they want to explore their faith more once they have been initiated. The church seems to be saying that as important as knowing doctrine is, it must be experienced in the context of worship, community and service during the formation period of catechumens and uncatechized candidates.

Second, National Statutes 6 and 31 state that in the United States the length of time in the periods of the catechumenate and of purification and enlightenment should extend for at least 12 months for catechumens and uncatechized candidates. The entire mystery of Christ is revealed over the course of a liturgical year.[3] This means that the major teachings of the church are experienced in the course of a liturgical year. Appendix 4 gives an overview of church teaching that unfolds over the course of the three liturgical cycles.

Third, from time to time issues arise from the catechumens and candidates that are not connected to what the church is inviting all its members to reflect upon at worship. Because of this, a supplemental session may be beneficial from time to time. But these sessions are viewed as something occasional and purposefully separate from the catechesis that is normally connected to the Sunday liturgy. For example, in the course of a catechetical session one Sunday, Teresa asked about the many objects and furnishings in the church. She wanted to know more about them. Joan agreed that she was curious about them also. So Bill arranged for Father Dan to give Teresa, Joan and her children a walking tour of the church one Saturday morning. To help them, Father Dan gave them a piece of paper describing the objects and furnishings in simple terms (for example, altar: the table around which the people gather with their priest to celebrate the holy eucharist).

Preparing the Catechetical Session

Bill Smith is the catechist for the coming Sunday, the Second Sunday in Ordinary Time, Year A. Using his Catechumenate Session Preparation Form (see Appendix 5), he begins his preparation. He begins by noting the feast, liturgical year and date of the session at the top of the page. Then he writes down the scriptures assigned for the day in "Box 1: Scripture Passages for the Sunday/Feast" (see the completed form on page 72). He then reads the passages aloud. He does this because he knows he gets more out of the readings when he actually hears the words of scripture rather than reading them silently in his head. He writes down his first impressions on a piece of paper. Next he sits in silence with these passages for a few minutes to listen for additional insights. He jots down these insights and then goes to a scripture commentary to read what the scholars have written about the passages, writing down the significant points that strike him. Next, he refers to other resources for suggestions on catechetical topics.[4] See Appendix 4 for a sample list of topics.

He is struck by the fact that God had a purpose for the servant (in the book of Isaiah) from the time he was in his mother's womb. He is also struck by the proximity of this reading to the anniversary of Roe versus Wade, the United States Supreme Court ruling on abortion, and how the Catholic church is engaged in efforts to reverse this decision. He notes this focus in "Box 4: RCIA, 75.1: Suitable Catechesis/Doctrine."

After writing down the focus of the catechetical session, he considers the points he wants to make about life before birth and abortion, drawing from a number of resources he keeps on hand to help him with his preparation (See Appendix 6 for some recommended resources). He reads paragraphs 355–368, 2258 and 2270–2275 in the *Catechism of the Catholic Church* and two pamphlets ("Gospel of Life: An Abbreviated Version" and "Abortion: What the Church Teaches") from his *Catholic Update* binder.[5] After reading these resources, Bill decides on three points for his session with Teresa and Joan: 1) the dignity of humans, created in the image of God at the time of conception; 2) God alone is the Lord of life and no one has the right to destroy innocent human life; and 3) the inalienable right of every innocent human individual to life. Based on these three points, Bill wants to teach that abortion is morally wrong. He makes a few notes from his reading of these materials on the paper he used for his scripture reflections. He also notes these three points in Box 4.

Bill, like his wife Alice, also knows that rural people view life more experientially than theoretically and so he thinks about a way to relate the teaching of the church on abortion to the daily life of Teresa and Joan. He thinks of how much excitement there is in a rural community every year over the two or three babies that are born or the way news spreads about the birth of livestock. He also thinks of how corn seed could be used as an analogy for God's designs for everything in creation. He notes these in "Box 3: Setting up the catechesis/doctrine: experiences from daily life."

He also wants to connect all this to the community of St. Al's so that Teresa and Joan see how the parish engages life issues. He notes that there is

A Harvest for God: Christian Initiation in the Rural and Small-Town Parish

a pro-life committee and decides to ask someone from the committee to attend the session with Teresa and Joan. He is aware that there will be a Mass in the church followed by a rosary before the image of Mary and the Christ Child on January 22 (the anniversary of the Supreme Court decision) and notes that perhaps Teresa and Joan should be invited to this experience of worship. He jots these thoughts down in "Box 5: RCIA, 75.2: Christian Way of Life in Community."

Bill wants them to see how Catholic Christians demonstrate their commitment to life issues, so he asks Alice and Father Dan what ideas he could offer for consideration for this session. Father Dan mentions that a group from the parish will go to the state capitol building for a pro-life rally on January 22. Alice observes that pregnancies and births are frequent topics of conversation in the community. She mentioned that many in the community send cards, call or stop by to visit both newborn and mother. She suggested Bill encourage them to consider writing, calling or visiting a mother and her newborn.

Bill wants to incorporate prayer into his session. The Hail Mary, with its reference to Jesus as the blessed fruit of Mary's womb, seems a natural choice for the end of the session. He writes this down in "Box 7: Prayer from the Treasury of the Church." He wants a bridge between the liturgy (the first formation moment) and the catechetical session (the second formation moment), so he calls Father Dan and the parish organist to see what is being planned for Sunday's Mass. Father Dan tells Bill that the pro-life committee is distributing holy cards before Mass with a prayer for life on the back and that the parishioners will be encouraged to pray this prayer at home during the week, especially on January 22. The organist tells Bill that she is planning to use "Yahweh, I Know You Are Near" for the responsorial psalm. Bill notes these points in "Box 2: RCIA, 75.3: Prayer/music/symbols."

Finally, in order to present the teaching of the church on abortion, Bill organizes the comments he wrote down from his reading of the scriptures, the commentaries and the catechetical resources he consulted in preparation for his session. He thinks of ways to illustrate his points in a way that will help Teresa and Joan and notes these on his paper also.

THE CATECHUMENATE SESSION

After Mass, Teresa, Joan and Pauline, Joan's sponsor, spend time visiting with the parishioners in the fellowship hall and enjoying a hot cup of coffee on a cold January day. Phyllis, Teresa's sponsor, has a sick child at home and feels it is important for her to return to relieve her husband, who had stayed home to care for the boy, so she leaves as soon as possible. At the designated time, about 20 minutes after the conclusion of Mass, Joan's children go with their peers to their Sunday school session and the three women walk over to Father Dan's home.

Bill had already gone over to set up the kitchen table for their session. He has placed a lectionary and a lighted candle on the table. Maxine Wells, chairperson of the parish pro-life committee, has accompanied Bill to the

CATECHUMENATE SESSION PREPARATION FORM

Sunday/Feast: *Second Sunday in Ordinary Time* Cycle: *A* Date: *January 20*

1. Scriptural passages for the Sunday/feast.

    Isaiah 49:3, 5–6   Psalm 40   1 Corinthians 1:1–3   John 1:29–34

2. RCIA, 75.3: Prayer/music/symbols connected to the liturgy of the word.

    Lectionary with Readings
    Song: Yahweh I Know You Are Near (Psalm 139)
    Madonna & Child Holy Cards from Pro-Life Committee

3. Setting up the catechesis/doctrine: Experiences from daily life.

    A. Birth of a child; birth of animal/livestock: Description
    B. Planting seeds that will become crops: from conception to birth
    C. What is my purpose in life? Discussion

4. RCIA, 75.1: Suitable catechesis/doctrine connected to the liturgy of the word.

    FOCUS: Isaiah 49:3, 5–6. God has a design for everyone before birth. Roe versus Wade (January 22) and Pro-Life Agenda of the Catholic Church.

    POINTS TO COVER: 1) the dignity of humans, created in the image of God at the time of conception; 2) God alone is the Lord of life and no one has the right to destroy innocent human life; and 3) the inalienable right of every innocent human individual to life.

    CONCLUSION: Abortion is morally wrong

5. RCIA, 75.2: Christian way of life in community connected to liturgy of the word.

    A. Pro-Life Committee of Parish-Call Maxine Wells and invite a member to the session.
    B. Parish Mass/Rosary on January 22 at St. Al's at 7:30 AM.

6. RCIA, 75.4: Works of mercy/outreach/witness that emerges from the liturgy of the word.

    A. Visit/Call/Write someone who is expecting/adopting a child and thank them for choosing life.
    B. Go to Pro-Life Rally at State Capitol on January 22.

7. Prayer from the treasury of the church (including minor rites from RCIA text).

    A. The Hail Mary

house and has brought with her some of the prayer cards they had distributed before Mass. Bill also has brought some hymnals from church and placed them on the chairs around the table.

As the three women come into the kitchen, Bill introduces them to Maxine and tells them she was invited to this session to talk a little bit about the pro-life committee. Both Teresa and Joan know Maxine because everyone knows everyone else in a small town like Oakville. As a matter of fact, Joan and Maxine are distant cousins. They spend a few minutes visiting and, when everyone seems ready, Bill invites the women to close their eyes and picture in their mind the scripture he is about to read. He picks up the lectionary and reads the gospel. When he finishes he invites the women to describe what they saw.

Joan remembers her image of John the Baptist from the previous week's gospel and describes his scraggly beard and his funny clothes. Pauline describes the picture she has of Jesus who has this kind of glow about him. She sees the glow as a depiction of the Holy Spirit and talks about a saintly elderly neighbor whom she thinks has a similar glow about her. Teresa chimes in that she too pictured Jesus but that she saw him walking along the Jordan River (something she remembered from the previous week's discussion) toward John the Baptist. Bill gives a brief explanation of the passage explaining that when John the evangelist wrote his gospel there were some who thought John the Baptist was the Messiah. He then says that John the evangelist corrected this erroneous belief by having the Baptist testify that Jesus is the "Lamb of God" and the "Son of God."

They repeat the process, this time reading the passage from Isaiah. After a few moments of silence following the reading, Teresa says that she has no picture in her mind but that someone in the reading is going to do something very important for God. Joan and Maxine agree. Bill explain briefly that in this passage Isaiah is speaking about a special servant of God's who will not only bring the Jewish people back to Israel from their exile in Babylon but will also lead people throughout the world to God. Bill says a little bit about how Christians identify this servant of God as Jesus. Then he rereads the place in the passage that says, "Now the Lord has spoken who formed me as his servant from the womb, that Jacob may be brought back to him and Israel gathered to him." Afterwards, he says that the group is going to discuss how God is involved in life even before someone is born.

He describes the birth of his first child and the joy it brought to his wife, him, their parents and extended family. Joan and Maxine immediately agree and then talk about the almost indescribable joy they experienced when their children were born. They also note that Jane Franklin is pregnant and expecting her fourth child in May. They tell Teresa that she will know this joy when it is her turn to have a child. Bill then tells a story about the journey of corn from planting to the dinner table. He describes the planting, the fertilizing, the waiting, the development of the ears, the harvesting and the cooking of fresh corn for dinner. They all can identify with the story for they all have had experience with crops.

Bill concludes the story of the corn by saying that the purpose of the journey of the corn is to nourish people and livestock. He then says that the journey of human life is similar; God has a purpose for us from the moment we are conceived in our mother's wombs. He tells them that he believes the purpose of his life is to be a husband, a father and a good Christian. He asks the four women if they have ever thought about the purpose of their lives. Teresa says that she never really has. As a young woman, she says she assumes she will get married at some point in time and will probably have some children. Pauline says that she thinks her purpose is to be married to her husband and to raise good Christian children. Joan humorously says she thinks her purpose is to keep everyone organized and that God has put her in the midst of some of the most disorganized people in the world to provide her with opportunities to fulfill her purpose! Then she illustrates her point by telling a story about how at the beginning of her marriage she had to organize her husband's unpaid bills because her husband, who is hopelessly disorganized, was on the verge of major financial disaster because he couldn't keep track of his bills.

Bill asks the group to pick up the hymnal and turn to the responsorial psalm. Together they sing the refrain and each takes a turn reading a verse between the sung refrain. Bill then explains that some of the verses speak of the love of God for everyone from the moment of conception and repeats those verses so that they may hear them again. From there he begins to explain that Catholic Christians believe that all people are important and precious in the eyes of God from the moment of conception. He says that everyone is made in the image and likeness of God from the moment of conception and because of this everyone must always be respected from the moment of conception because of the One in whose image and likeness they have been created. He goes on to speak about the church's tradition of respect for all innocent life, including the unborn, and that everyone, from the moment of conception, has a right to life. He also mentions that God has a plan for everyone and everything from the moment of creation. He says that abortion transfers the unfolding of that plan from the hands of God to human hands and that this is not our power to possess. He then concludes that the Catholic church has taught for a very long time that abortion is a moral violation of these beliefs about life and its purpose and therefore forbidden.

After this, Bill asks Teresa and Joan to sit quietly for a few moments and think about something this teaching has done to affirm, inform, inspire or challenge them. Joan is the first to speak. She says that she has always believed in her heart that abortion was wrong but that she was glad to have some understanding why her heart was telling her the truth. Teresa, the catechumen, says that she is again amazed how involved God is in our lives and that she is making a deeper connection between God and her value as a human being.

Bill then invites Maxine to tell the three women about the pro-life committee at St. Al's. Maxine tells them that they are a small group of people who do what they can to promote the pro-life, womb-to-tomb teachings of the church. In the area of abortion, they organize a Mass and rosary at the church on January 22, the anniversary of Roe versus Wade. They distribute and keep holy cards with a prayer for life in the church throughout the year.

They also organize a group that travels to the state capitol on January 22 to participate in a rally for life. They place an ad in the telephone directory for counseling services during a pregnancy. She noted that their group meets about five or six times a year and at every meeting they spend time praying together for life in all its forms. After Maxine explains what the members of her group do, she invites Teresa and Joan to participate in one or more things her committee sponsors.

Bill then invites Teresa and Joan to take out their small notebooks in which they write a few comments from their weekly sessions. He asks them to sit silently for a few minutes to consider one practical way God might be inviting them to respect life. They sit still for a bit and then write a few private lines in their notebook. Teresa notes for herself that she wants to begin saying prayers of gratitude to God for being so involved in everyone's life, especially hers. She also notes that she wants to go visit Jane, her pregnant neighbor. Joan writes "Go to Mass on January 22" in her notebook. When they are finished, Bill invites them to pray the "Hail Mary," which he has on a prayer card for them, and the prayer for life that Maxine has on her prayer cards. After cleaning up behind themselves, they give each other a hug and go home.

Notice the many rural-friendly ways Bill catechized. It began with the fellowship hour after Mass. Bill did not exclude Teresa and Joan from this experience of community. He also made sure there was time for the members of the initiation group to catch up on news and to visit before starting the session. As they begin their initial reflection on the lectionary passages, Bill did not ask them to follow along in a Bible, lectionary or handout. Rather, he invited them to close their eyes and allow the proclaimed word to touch their inner lives. As Bill explains the scriptures, he keeps his explanations simple and concrete. He avoids speculative thinking and fancy words that are frequently of little interest to oral people. As he prepares to enter the central component of the catechetical session, he tells them what they are going to do (a good adult education technique) before starting. He then uses practical examples well known in the rural world to get them thinking about the proposed topic as a way to prepare them to hear the church teaching in a more effective manner. His teaching is simple, straightforward and logical. Because he knows that oral people make sense of the world in which they live in light of its consistency with the past, he notes the long history associated with the church teaching. He is also aware of the fact that rural people have a strong belief in the power of God and emphasizes this in the course of his presentation. He shows respect for Teresa and Joan by asking them to name what they found helpful and then invites them to name one concrete way they can integrate the teaching with their daily life.

The Question of Dismissal

Anecdotal evidence indicates that the majority of rural parishes that have some process for the initiation of adults do not dismiss their catechumens and uncatechized candidates after the homily as recommended in the rite.[6] The rite notes that for practical or pastoral reasons dismissal may not be advisable. There are many reasons why dismissal, while ideal, may not be practical in a rural or small-town parish. Sometimes in smaller communities there are no meeting facilities apart from the church building that would allow the catechumens and candidates the privacy they need for their session. Sometimes there is only one parish Mass and the one or two initiation catechists do not want to miss the liturgy of the eucharist, especially communion. Sometimes the priest is the catechist and for obvious reasons cannot leave the Mass early! Sometimes a catechist is not available on Sunday for catechesis and must meet some other day of the week. Consequently, dismissal might be viewed as inhospitable if a catechumen or uncatechized candidate is dismissed and has nowhere to go and nothing to do but get in the car and leave before the community finishes its worship. Finally, in rural and small-town communities, almost everyone knows everyone else. In a culture where relationship is so important, dismissal may be viewed as a bit peculiar.

Some rural and small-town parishes have multiple liturgies and facilities that make it possible to consider dismissal. Dismissal is preferred, and if a parish can do it, it should. If not, the parish must work within its own realities and do the best it can.

Structure of a Catechetical Session with and without Dismissal

There are two general models that may be utilized for the catechetical session during the catechumenate period: the unified model and the two-part model. At St. Al's, Father Dan has decided, after consultation with the initiation catechists, to omit the dismissal since there is only one parish Mass on Sunday. As a result of this decision, they use the unified model to guide them. It appears in Appendix 7. In the next town, St. Joseph's parish incorporates the dismissal into their initiation process because they have facilities, multiple liturgies and several catechists. Their session will look a little different from the one used at St. Al's. They use the two-part model and the structure of their sessions appears in Appendix 8. Those who do not dismiss and conduct a catechetical session on another day of the week may find the unified model helpful. Those who dismiss after the homily but conduct a catechetical session on another day of the week may find the two-part model more appropriate.

Minor Rites during the Catechumenate Period

The ritual book offers some simple liturgies that may be used during this part of the formation process. They are found in paragraphs 90–103 of the RCIA. The liturgies are grouped into three sections: minor exorcisms of the catechumens, blessings of the catechumens and anointing of the catechumens. With the exception of the minor rite of anointing, a qualified lay

A Harvest for God: Christian Initiation in the Rural and Small-Town Parish

catechist may lead all the other rites.[7] They may be celebrated after the homily in the liturgy of the word or at the end of a catechetical session.

Evidence from rural communities seems to indicate that these minor rites are rarely celebrated, frequently because initiation ministers are unaware of their existence. Rural initiation ministers are encouraged to include these rites in the catechumenate period. Those who have used them generally insert them at the end of a catechetical session where prayer might normally occur. Presuming that catechumens are in this period of formation for a minimum of 12 months, it makes sense to utilize these rites to assist them during this long period of formation.

Recall what was said earlier about the power that rituals have to make God's grace visible and tangible for us. Celebrating these minor rites strengthen, encourage and sometimes heal catechumens. If they are growing and experiencing conversion during their formation, they will need the grace that is available to them through these rites, which both heals past pains and strengthens for future conversion.

Let us see how this occurs in the life of Teresa, the catechumen at St. Al's. As we saw earlier, Teresa has some unresolved issues concerning the premature death of her father. Over the course of the catechumenate period, Teresa may reach a point where she seeks God's help to resolve further the issues between her father and her. Bill, aware of this issue in Teresa's life, may see an opportunity to celebrate the minor rite of exorcism in the context of an upcoming catechetical session based on a gospel passage in which Jesus heals someone. He reviews the texts in the ritual book and thinks that RCIA, 94h, might be an appropriate exorcism prayer for the occasion. So he prepares for this brief rite just in case Teresa accepts his invitation to celebrate it at the end of their catechetical session.

DISCERNMENT FOR ELECTION

Teresa and Joan have been in the catechumenate period for almost 14 months. Both have been regular in their attendance of the catechetical sessions and the Sunday eucharist. There have been a few weeks when the group did not meet for their catechetical session because of bad weather and a few times when Teresa or Joan needed to be held excused because of sickness, vacation or last minute transportation problems. By and large, however, they have been faithful participants in this period of formation. Lent is approaching in about six weeks and Bill mentions one Sunday at the end of a catechetical session that an opportunity is approaching for them to consider whether or not they are ready to be initiated. Bill is favorably impressed with both women and thinks they are ready but realizes that Teresa and Joan must be of the same opinion. He asks them to think about it and tells them that he will follow up with a telephone call later in the week to learn of their decision. To help them with their discernment, Bill hands out a piece of paper with a guide for discernment, giving it to Teresa, Joan and their sponsors (see pages 78–79 and Appendix 9). He tells Teresa and Joan that the outline will give them a way to determine their readiness and will help Phyllis

DISCERNMENT GUIDE FOR BAPTISM OR RECEPTION INTO FULL COMMUNION

You have traveled many miles on your faith journey with us. We are excited by the growth you have experienced. You have indicated your readiness for baptism or reception into full communion. To help you in this final discernment for readiness, you will find some reflection questions below. Please think about these in preparation for your conversation with your sponsor, catechist, and me in the near future. We look forward to meeting with you. Sincerely, Father Dan.

A. Tell about an experience or experiences you have had that have helped you grow in your awareness of God's love for you. Some suggestions to trigger your memory follow.

- An experience of God through prayer and/or worship

- An awareness of Christ's death on the cross as an expression of his love for you

- A spiritual healing from God

- A gift of inner peace from God

- An experience of God's love through a parishioner or group of parishioners

- Some other experience?

B. Once we experience one of these divine encounters, we want to deepen our relationship with God. So we look for opportunities to meet and spend time with God. Frequently, we want to express our gratitude to God for loving us so much. So we find ways to say "thank you" by serving God and others. Sometimes we want to share what we have received from God with others. So we tell others about God and Jesus. Tell us about some of these experiences since you started coming to our church. Some suggestions to trigger your memory follow.

1. Prayer/Worship	2. Community
a. What is it like coming to St. Al's on Sunday to worship God with us? b. What is speaking and listening to God in private prayer like for you?	a. What has it been like becoming part of our church family? b. Tell us about some of the parishioners you have met or gotten to know better.
3. Tradition	**4. Service**
a. Please tell us some important things you have learned about God, Christ, the Catholic church and Christian life while with us. b. Please tell us a scripture story you have heard at St. Al's that has been helpful for you?	a. Has your commitment to discipleship grown since you began to spend time with us? If so, could you tell us about it? b. Have you told anyone about the good things happening in your life since you began to spend time with us? If so, could you tell us about it?

and Pauline participate in a future conversation should Teresa and Joan decide they are ready.

After passing out the paper, Bill reviews it and asks if they have any questions. Teresa wants to know if she has to talk about everything listed on the sheet if she thinks she is ready for initiation. Bill tells her that the sheet is a guideline and is meant only to help her recall the important memories she would like to share. He tells her that she might tell Father Dan and him how she has grown in her awareness of God's love for her, using one or more of the prompts under letter A, and then mention one thing in response to the four points under letter B, namely, prayer/worship, community, tradition and service. He suggests that Teresa and Joan chat with their sponsors as an initial part of their discernment. Phyllis and Pauline readily agree and they set up a time to chat with Teresa and Joan before Bill will call them regarding their readiness for initiation.

Later in the week, Bill calls each woman and learns that they would like to be initiated at the coming celebration of the Easter Vigil. He arranges for Joan and her sponsor Pauline to meet with Father Dan and him at his home the following week. He arranges the same kind of gathering for Teresa and her sponsor Phyllis for a later night in the same week.

Joan and Pauline stop by the Smiths' place on the appointed evening. As always, Alice has prepared a little something to eat and has the coffee pot ready. They spend some time visiting and talking about the latest news of the community, especially the heart attack of Mrs. Schmelzer, an elderly parishioner of St. Al's. Father Dan arrives a few minutes late due to a visit he needed to make with a parishioner on his way out to the Smiths' place. After some time Bill suggests that they go into the living room. They adjourn to the living room and Father Dan, at Bill's suggestion, begins by reading Psalm 139. Then he offers a prayer of thanks to God for the gift of Joan and asks the Holy Spirit to be with all of them as they visit.

He and the Smiths talk about the joy Joan has brought to so many of the people of the parish since she started coming. They mention that many parishioners have enjoyed getting to know Joan, especially during the fellowship hour after Mass. They all comment on her great sense of humor. They praise her for her faithful presence at Sunday Mass and the inquisitive minds of her children. Bill comments on how insightful she is during their catechetical sessions. Pauline speaks up, telling how helpful Joan had been with the School Auction and how she has grown in her friendship with Joan.

Joan is a little embarrassed by all the accolades and expresses her appreciation for all Father Dan, the Smiths and Pauline have done for her over the last 18 months. She tells them how much they and the parishioners of St. Al's have restored her confidence in a church community and that she often comments on this to her elderly parents and her husband. She tells them that John, her husband, has begun asking the children about their Sunday School lessons and has been seen a time or two reading their religion workbooks. She wonders aloud if God might be doing something in his life. They all agree that time will tell and encourage her to keep doing what she and her children are doing.

Joan tells them that she feels at home at St. Al's. She tells them she was nervous at first, especially when it came to knowing when to stand, sit and kneel during the liturgy, but that Pauline had been very helpful to her, especially when she was trying to follow the order of worship in the hymnal. She comments on the crucifix in the church and how it has become such a powerful reminder to her of the love of Christ for her and everyone. She recalls how she learned about Jesus as a child in her Methodist church and how her understanding of Jesus has become much more mature since participating in the parish initiation process. She speaks a little about Teresa and how lovely a young person she is and how much she has grown since they first met each other.

As she recalls the many ways in which she has grown in her faith, she notes particularly her appreciation for the word of God, her awareness of the connection between holy communion and discipleship, the gift of forgiveness in the sacrament of reconciliation, and the intercessory role of Mary and the saints. She tells them that on the way home from church she and her children talk about the word of God and what they learned that day and that in anticipation of the coming Sunday, they sit down together and read aloud the scriptural passages they will hear at the church. She comments on the way Father Dan in his preaching and Bill in his teaching both reinforce the connection between receiving the body of Christ in holy communion and becoming the body of Christ for others. She tells them she is making a more conscious decision to act as a disciple of Christ in her day-to-day life, especially with her family and her neighbors. She confesses that she still gossips too much but that she is working on it. Lastly, she expresses her appreciation for the role of Mary and the saints as intercessors for her. She tells them she has enjoyed getting to know more about Mary and finds as a mother and wife that she asks Mary for inspiration as she tries to live her life as a good mother and wife.

She tells them how much her children have grown in their faith since coming to St. Al's and how much she appreciates the values they are learning from their catechists. She concludes by telling them a story about how Sue, her third grader, has become good friends with a new Hispanic girl in her class who speaks very little English. Joan wonders aloud if her daughter would have made friends with this foreigner before she started coming to St. Al's. She tells them that Claudia, Sue's new friend, is coming over this coming Saturday and how much she is looking forward to having her in their home. She plans to bring Claudia to Mass with them on Sunday.

After everyone has spoken, Father Dan asks Joan if she is ready to become a member of the Catholic church. Joan answers affirmatively and Father Dan tells her about the rite of sending. They spend a little time talking about this ceremony and the one she will be invited to attend with the bishop on the First Sunday of Lent. Bill tells Joan and Pauline about the preparation they will make in a few weeks for these ceremonies and then congratulates Joan. The rest follow suit. Bill then asks Joan about her children and their readiness for confirmation and holy eucharist. She tells the group that she believes they are ready. Father Dan tells Joan that he would like to visit with her children, Keith and Sue, and their catechists in the near future. They set a tentative date for the children to meet with Father Dan and their catechists.

To conclude their gathering they pray in thanksgiving, and after a little more to eat and drink, everyone departs for home. As soon as Joan gets home, she calls Teresa to tell her the good news and to assure her that it wasn't at all painful!

Teresa's visit goes as smoothly as Joan's. For her the most significant experiences during her formation have been her awareness of God's profound love for her and the healing that has occurred within her over the death of her father. She too comments on the role the church community has played in making her feel welcome, the important things she has learned about the Christian faith, and her awareness of the connection between what they do in church on Sunday morning and what they do the rest of the week.

As Lent approaches, Father Dan announces that Teresa, Joan and her children will be initiated at the coming celebration of the Easter Vigil. The parishioners applaud at the end of the announcement and congratulations are extended to the four during the fellowship hour after Mass. In a few weeks, they will celebrate the parish rite of sending and a second ceremony with the bishop of their diocese.

Notes

[1] See "Making Priesthood Possible" by Michael Himes in *Church* 5:3 (Fall, 1989) for a further description of grace in the life of liturgy and sacraments.

[2] See RCIA, 75.3 and 83.2.

[3] See the *Constitution on the Sacred Liturgy,* 102.

[4] One of the best commentaries in plain English is *Footprints on the Mountain* (Paulist Press, 1994) by Roland Faley.

[5] *Catholic Update* is published by St. Anthony Messenger Press.

[6] See RCIA, 75.3 and 83.2.

[7] See RCIA, 91, 96, 16 and 12.

Chapter 5

The Rites of Sending and Election

This chapter will explore:

- how to celebrate these rites in a rural-friendly manner

- how to prepare rural catechumens, candidates and community for these rites

- how to conduct a mystagogical catechesis on these rites in a rural-friendly manner

- the structure of the rites of sending and election

- the ritual differences in these rites for catechumens and baptized candidates.

Since the time Joe and Maria agreed to date only each other over a year ago, their relationship has blossomed. They have gotten to know each other quite well by walking in each other's world. They have gotten to know each other's families and their respective traditions. Maria has learned how important serving others and having a relationship with God are to Joe, and she has begun to incorporate some of those practices into her own life. Joe has grown in his admiration for Maria's family, a family who knows how to enjoy life despite economic hardship. They have fallen deeply in love with each other.

Joe and Maria go to Springfield for dinner one Saturday evening in late October. Joe has made a reservation at the best restaurant in town, a little place known for their Italian food. They enjoy their evening, sipping wine, eating good food, and chatting with each other about a variety of things. After placing their order for dessert, Joe turns to Maria and tells her how much he loves her and how she has brought a sense of completeness to his life. He tells her about the many things she does that bring joy to his life.

Boy Meets girl/ First dates	Commitment to go steady	Building the relationship Meeting the family Learning the traditions	Engagement	Pre-Cana/ Marriage prep	Wedding	Honeymoon/ First year of marriage
Precatechumenate	Rite of Acceptance into Order of Catechumens	Catechumenate	Rite of Election	Purification and enlightenment	Sacraments of initiation	Mystagogy

She tells Joe that her feelings for him are the same and that she has not known such happiness in all her life. Taking her hand, Joe looks into her eyes and asks if she will marry him. With tears welling up in her eyes, she looks into his and says yes. Then they kiss each other. Joe reaches into his jacket pocket and pulls out a small box containing an engagement ring. He presents it to Maria and places it on her ring finger. She kisses him again. Joe then looks toward the kitchen and gives a prearranged nod to the waiter, who brings a bottle of champagne and two glasses to the table. After the champagne is poured, Joe offers a toast to their future as husband and wife.

Two other diners from Oakville who know Joe and Maria, Jim and Sylvia Kelsey, stop by the table before leaving the restaurant to speak with them. They are delighted to learn of the engagement. Upon her return to Oakville, Sylvia makes a few phone calls to her friends, telling them the good news.

When Joe and Maria arrive for Mass the next morning, many parishioners come up to the couple and offer their congratulations on their engagement. Joe's pastor also seeks them out, offers them congratulations and asks if they have set a date. Maria tells him they really haven't had time to discuss it with each other but that a date in the spring might be possible. He tells them there are no other weddings scheduled until late June and that except for Easter weekend the church is available in the spring if they wish to celebrate their wedding there. The pastor embraces Maria and offers his hand in congratulations to Joe before heading off to prepare for Mass. Before he leaves, he asks if he might announce the good news to the parishioners. They observe that probably everyone in the parish already knows the news. Nevertheless, they agree to let the pastor formally announce their engagement during Mass. Such is life in a small town.

INTRODUCTION TO THE RITES OF SENDING AND ELECTION

Joe's proposal to become engaged to Maria must be seen in relationship to what the engagement itself anticipates: marriage. In the same way, the rite of election must be seen in light of what it anticipates: the celebration of the sacraments of initiation. The rite of election is celebrated because the catechumens and the local church community have mutually discerned that the catechumens are ready to be initiated. This initiation will follow some six weeks after the rite of election. In the same way, Joe and Maria have mutually discerned that they are ready to be joined to each other in matrimony. The celebration of their marriage will follow some six months after they become officially engaged.

Joe proposes marriage to Maria because they have established a solid commitment with each other that has grown and deepened since that evening many months ago when they promised to date only each other. They are now ready to make their initial commitment a permanent one and are ready to undertake the intense preparation required to cross the threshold into marriage. In the same way, the catechumens' relationship with the local parish has deepened to such an extent that it is seen as a solid one in the eyes of both the catechumens and the community. Together they have discerned that the catechumens are ready to undertake the final, intensive preparation that leads to the waters of baptism and the other initiation sacraments. The catechumens have become acquainted with the major teachings of the church, learned the Christian way of life in the midst of a community, learned how to pray and worship, and begun to live as disciples.

The engagement ring symbolizes Joe and Maria's engagement. In a similar way, the catechumens' name in the book of the elect symbolizes their betrothal to Christ. After the proposal, Joe and Maria announce that they are an engaged couple. After the rite of election, the church announces that the catechumens are now "the elect."

The "engagement rite" for those catechumens ready for initiation is normally celebrated in two parts. The first is the rite of sending of the catechumens for election (usually called the rite of sending) at the parish, and the second is the rite of election, a diocesan celebration. Let us look at the diocesan rite first.

The Rite of Election

The rite of election is for the unbaptized (see RCIA, 129–137). In the United States, it is generally celebrated as a diocesan rite around the First Sunday of Lent. A bishop or his delegate usually presides over this diocesan rite. When it is impossible to join the diocesan celebration of the rite, the local parish may celebrate it. Regardless of where it is celebrated, it ordinarily should not be omitted for the catechumens except under extraordinary circumstances[1] or in danger of death.[2]

The rite of calling the candidates to continuing conversion (see RCIA, 450–458) is a parallel rite for those baptized individuals who began the initiation process as uncatechized Christians and who are now ready to come into full communion with the Catholic church and/or to complete their initiation through the reception of confirmation and holy eucharist. Unlike the rite of election, the normal setting for this rite is the parish unless there are catechumens who are also ready to celebrate the rite of election.[3]

When both catechumens and previously uncatechized candidates are preparing for the celebration of the sacraments of initiation at the upcoming Easter Vigil, a combined rite of election and calling may be used (see RCIA, 550–561). It is recommended that this combined rite be celebrated at the diocesan level and only at the parish level when necessary.[4] These three rites are identified below.

Three Rites of Election and/or Call to Continuing Conversion

1. Rite of Election: unbaptized only

2. Rite of Calling the Candidate to Continuing Conversion: Uncatechized baptized only

3. Combined rites of election and calling the candidate: unbaptized and uncatechized baptized

---

The Rite of Sending

The rite of election is the second of the two-part "engagement rite" for catechumens who are ready to be initiated. The first of this two-part ritual is called the rite of sending. In the United States, a parish rite of sending may precede a diocesan celebration of the rite of election or the combined rite with both catechumens and baptized candidates. This parish rite has been developed to emphasize the importance of the local parish in the discernment for readiness to celebrate the diocesan rite of election.[5] This rite offers the local parish the "opportunity to express its approval of the catechumens and to send them forth to the celebration of election assured of the parish's care and support."[6] Because baptized, uncatechized candidates are also going through the initiation process in the parish, a parish rite of sending rite has been developed for them (RCIA, 434–445) as well as a combined rite (RCIA, 530–546). These three parish rites are identified below.

Three Parish Rites of Sending

1. Rite of Sending Catechumens for Election: unbaptized only

2. Rite of Sending Candidates for Recogniton by the Bishop and for the Call to Continuing Conversion: uncatechized baptized only

3. Combined rites of sending for catechumens/candidates: unbaptized and uncatechized baptized

---

The parish rite of sending is simple in its structure. After the homily, the catechumens and/or candidates who will go to the diocesan celebration of the rite of election are presented to the pastor and parishioners of the parish. Testimony given by godparents or sponsors regarding their readiness for the sacraments of initiation follows. The assembly may then be invited to express its approval of the catechumens and/or candidates. Depending on the policy of the diocese, catechumens may then be invited to sign the book of the elect. Following this, intercessions for the catechumens and candidates and a prayer over them occurs. Finally, they are dismissed if this is pastorally feasible.

The combined parish rite follows this structure:

- Proclamation of scripture and homily

- Presentation of catechumens

- Testimony by the godparents

- Affirmation by the assembly (optional but recommended)

- Signing of the book of the elect by the catechumens (diocesan policies vary)

- Presentation of the candidates

- Testimony by the sponsors

- Affirmation by the assembly (optional but recommended)

- Intercessions for catechumens and/or candidates

- Prayer over catechumens and/or candidates

- Dismissal of catechumens and/or candidates (depending on local circumstances).

PREPARING FOR THE CELEBRATION OF THE COMBINED RITE OF SENDING AT ST. AL'S

Teresa, Joan and Joan's children have been in the catechumenate period of their formation for about 16 months.[7] After their discernment evening with Father Dan, Bill Smith and their sponsors (described in the previous chapter), these two women and two children are declared ready for initiation. It is now time to celebrate their readiness ritually and to ask both the parishioners of St. Al's and the bishop of the diocese to affirm their readiness for initiation. Because St. Al's has only one weekend Mass, a combined rite of sending will be celebrated.

Bishop Reese will preside over a diocesan celebration of the rite of election and call to continuing conversion at the cathedral at 3:00 in the afternoon on the First Sunday of Lent. Father Dan decides to celebrate the rite of sending at the Sunday morning Mass on the same day and contacts the chair of the Women's Sodality to ask for a light reception after the liturgy.

Rehearsal

As he did with the rite of acceptance for Teresa and the rite of welcome for Joan and her children, Father Dan meets with their sponsors at the church on the Saturday afternoon before the combined rite of sending will be celebrated to show them where they will stand and what they will do and say. At the conclusion of the rehearsal, Father Dan thanks them for coming and reminds them to be at the church by 9:45 on Sunday morning to welcome and seat the four candidates and their guests.

Preparation Session for the Catechumen, the Candidates and Their Sponsors

Because it is February and the children are in school, the Smiths invite Teresa, Joan and her children, and their sponsors to their home on the Saturday morning before the rite of sending for a session to prepare them for the rite. Joan and Pauline appreciate that Alice is avoiding both a school night and night driving in possible bad weather as she schedules this preparation session. The children had hoped it would be scheduled on a school night so that they might get out of some homework! They gather at the Smith's around 10:00 in the morning and are welcomed with hot coffee, hot chocolate and hot ham biscuits. After a time for the adults to visit and the children to run outside in the yard, Alice gathers everyone into the living room, where a Bible and a burning candle are already on the coffee table.

She begins the session by telling them that they are going to be invited to remember some important events in their lives and that remembering these events will prepare them to celebrate the rite of sending on Sunday. She tells them that remembering is very important. It's important to remember things about God, about Jesus, and about one's personal life.

With this introduction, Alice then invites them to be still and to remember a time when someone stood up for them. The group sits quietly for a few moments as they call an example to mind. Teresa is the first to speak and tells the group about a time when she was having trouble finding a job after she graduated from high school. After several rejections, she went to see her favorite high school teacher, Mrs. Johnson, and told her how frustrating it was to find a job. Her teacher was very sympathetic and told her the next time she applied for a job to ask her prospective employer to call her for a recommendation before deciding whether or not to hire Teresa. Sure enough, when she applied for her next job and mentioned that Mrs. Johnson would vouch for her, she got the job. Little Sue told a story about the time when she was in the first grade and a second grader started picking on her during recess. She said that her brother stood up for her and told his fellow second grader, who was bigger than Keith, to leave his sister alone.

Alice then directed them to the next point. She asked them to remember someone who gave them permission to do something important and to describe the important thing they were given permission to do. After a few moments of silence, Joan speaks and says that her story was not directly about her, but it affected her. She then tells the story of how her husband John had to come and ask Joan's father for permission to marry her because he knew if her father did not approve, they would not get married. She remembers how nervous John was when he came to visit because he was not sure how her father was going to react to his request. Pauline then recalls when she asked her parents for permission to get a driver's license. She remembers that her father was a bit skeptical about giving her permission to drive when she was only 15 years old but that her mother had convinced her father that it would be good because then she could help take some of her brothers and sisters to their different activities after school and on weekends, thereby freeing her mother to do other things.

Alice then asks them to remember a time when someone said they were ready to finish one thing and move on to something bigger and more challenging. Louis, the sixth-grade son of Pauline and Jim, recalls when his dad told him he was old enough to stop feeding the chickens in the back yard and to start milking the cows. He remembers how grown up he felt when his father told him this and when he showed him how to milk the cows. Then with a grin on his face he also noted that his father conveniently forgot to tell him about the challenge of getting up so early to milk the cows! They all laughed when he said this, including Louis' father Jim. Joan spoke next and told the group how having their first child was like moving to something bigger and more challenging. Before Keith was born, John and she had a lot of time for each other and had fewer responsibilities. When Keith was born, all that changed.

Finally, Alice says she wants to tell them a story. She continues, saying:

One day a chicken and a pig are walking in the barnyard. The chicken says to the pig, "You know, those people who live in the big house are very nice to us. They feed us every day and make sure we are protected when the weather is bad or cold. Don't you think it would be good idea if we did something nice for them?"

The pig agreed saying, "Yes, I think that would be a good idea. What should we do?"

The chicken said, "I was thinking we should give them something."

The pig agreed saying, "Yes, I think that would be a good idea. What should we give them?"

The chicken said, "I was thinking we should give them bacon and eggs."

At that, the pig stopped dead in his tracks and said, "No way! For you that's only a little inconvenience, but for me it's a total commitment!"

They all laugh, especially the children. Afterwards, Alice invites them to remember a time when they made a total commitment to something, one they could not go back on once they had made it. Sue speaks first and remembers when her father told her she was ready to start riding her bicycle without training wheels. She tells them she told her father that she was afraid she would lose her balance and fall down and hurt herself and that she didn't want the wheels taken off. She told them that her daddy said it was her decision but that all her friends would think she was acting like a big girl if she started riding her bicycle without training wheels. Sue said that she thought and thought about it until one day she saw her friend Alison riding without training wheels. With that she asked her father to take the wheels off and to teach her how to balance herself on the two-wheeler. She concludes by saying, "And I've never gone back to training wheels!"

Teresa then says that she thinks what she's doing in the catechumenate is similar. She says that she feels like she's made a total commitment to be baptized and live her life as a Catholic Christian and that she cannot go back on her decision, even though some of her best friends cannot understand why she would make such a decision.

Alice seizes the moment and says that this is exactly what they are celebrating tomorrow. They have come to the moment when they are ready to make a total commitment. For Teresa it will be to die with Christ in baptism and to be confirmed and receive holy eucharist. For Joan it will be to make a profession of faith thereby becoming a member of the Catholic church and to be confirmed and receive holy eucharist. For Keith and Sue it will be to receive confirmation and to share in holy communion for the first time as Catholics. She tells them that it is a total commitment and that the two rites they will celebrate the next day are a public affirmation by the church that they are ready to make this commitment in six weeks at the Easter Vigil.

She also notes that Teresa will indicate her desire for baptism by signing a book. Writing her name in this book says that she wants to be declared ready for baptism in the eyes of God. Alice tells the group that the bishop, acting in the name of God, will declare Teresa ready for baptism by what is called an "act of election." She goes on to say that because Joan and her children are already baptized, they do not need to be declared "elect" as a step prior to receiving the other sacraments of initiation. Therefore they do not need to sign a book. Their presence and the word of their sponsors will be sufficient.

She goes on to tell them that in both celebrations their sponsors will stand up for them and declare before Father Dan, the parishioners of St. Al's and Bishop Reese that they are ready to make this commitment. As an aside she looks as Teresa, Joan, and Joan's children and says, "And the best part is, you don't have to say anything. Your sponsors are going to vouch for you just like Mrs. Johnson vouched for you, Teresa, and your brother stood up for you, Sue." She mentions that the sponsors will be asked a few questions about their candidate's readiness in both ceremonies based on the discernment they did a few weeks ago with the Father Dan, Bill and their sponsor. She then tells the sponsors that Father Dan will go over the questions with them at the rehearsal later that afternoon.

Next she tells them that in these two ceremonies they will be given permission to be initiated. The bishop gives this permission during the ceremony at the cathedral. She explains, however, that before the bishop authorizes their initiation, he wants assurances from the local parish that the candidates are ready. Therefore, the first ceremony is celebrated so that the parish may formally endorse the readiness of the candidates. She concludes by telling them that the reason they may be endorsed by the parish and authorized by the bishop is because Father Dan, their catechists and their sponsors believe they are ready to face the challenges that will come with initiation into the Catholic church.

She reminds the sponsors (and everyone else present) of the afternoon rehearsal, about coming early to the church on Sunday morning, coming to the reception after the ceremony at St. Al's and carpooling to the cathedral for the afternoon ceremony. She asks if there are any questions. They want to know more about the ceremony at the cathedral. Alice tells them that it will be similar to the one at the church but that there will be several hundred people like themselves from throughout the diocese who will be asking Bishop Reese for permission to be initiated at the upcoming Easter Vigil. She tells them that she will explain more about the cathedral rite when they get together on Tuesday evening to reflect on the two rites. With no other questions coming forth, they conclude their session with a prayer and go their separate ways.

Analysis of the Preparation Session

Alice always prepares catechumens, candidates and their sponsors for the major rites of Christian initiation so they do not come to the rites in the dark. To do so would be especially difficult for indigenous rural people. She does not rehearse the rite with them; she simply places the rite in the context of similar events they have experienced in the past so that they will have some idea what they will be celebrating without the need to rehearse it. Father Dan actually rehearses the rite but only with the sponsors.

As she did with the rite of acceptance and the rite of welcome, Alice gathers those who will celebrate the rite of sending and takes them through a guided reflection to prepare them. Again, going into an unknown experience is a bit more intimidating for people from rural society than it is for those from an urban one. Because the past has such high value in the lives of people from the countryside, Alice wisely develops a preparation session that incorporates a process of remembering past events and connects them to the upcoming, unknown rite.

The heart of her process, the central meaning of the rites of sending and election, has four points that fit into a larger format:

- Hospitality and informal conversation

- In the rites of sending/election:

  - Someone stands up and vouches for you (sponsor/godparent)

  - Someone gives you permission to advance (parish/bishop)

  - You advance to something important (initiation)

  - You prepare (Lent) to make an important, irreversible commitment (initiation)

- Brief explanation of two rites

- Announcements and other information about the rites

- Other questions

- Prayer and conclusion

Alice knows that relationships are important in the rural world. Consequently, she wants the group to consider all the relationships that will be affirmed in these rites: sponsors, catechists, parishioners, pastor and bishop. She leads them to this awareness by inviting them to recall a relationship where someone vouched or stood up for them and then shows how the same thing occurs in the two rites. Because life is still lived more hierarchically in the rural world than in an urban one, people in positions of authority tend to be valued, sought and obeyed. Consider the importance of the parish matriarch or patriarch or of an elderly grandparent. Alice wisely takes some time to emphasize the importance of the bishop as someone who authorizes them to move forward at this important moment in their lives. Because big decisions tend to be made in consultation with one's elders in rural society, Alice incorporates this dynamic into her preparation session, showing how sponsors, parishioners, pastor and bishop are consulted in the major commitment they are about to make.

In addition, she speaks to Teresa of the importance of God electing her for baptism. God is important in rural society because there is so much in rural life that is beyond anyone's control and because there are so many problems in life that only God can rectify. That God would declare Teresa ready for baptism by the "act of election" proclaimed by the bishop will have significant meaning for her.

Finally, Alice does all of this in the context of storytelling and analogies, common ways of communicating experience in rural society.

Celebrating the Rite of Sending at St. Al's

It is a chilly February morning that greets everyone heading to St. Al's for Sunday Mass. No one is hanging around outside the front doors of the church for conversation. It's too cold! Phyllis and the Schneiders are waiting for Teresa and the Burnetts inside the church near the door. As the candidates arrive with their guests, Phyllis and the Schneiders welcome them and escort them to their usual places in the body of the church. Father Dan takes a moment to speak with Teresa, the Burnetts and their guests before going to the front of the church to welcome everyone. He reminds the parishioners that there will be a special ceremony after the homily for Teresa, Joan, Keith and Sue to celebrate their readiness for the sacraments of baptism, confirmation and holy eucharist at the upcoming celebration of the Easter Vigil. He invites them to listen carefully to what is said during the rite and to participate enthusiastically in the celebration. He walks down the aisle to the door, the organist announces the opening hymn and the liturgy begins.

After the homily, Father Dan invites Bill Smith to come forward and address the community. Bill walks into the sanctuary and, using paragraph 537 of the RCIA as his model,[8] he says the following:

> Father Dan, parishioners of St. Al's and guests, for many months, Teresa Phelps has been on a spiritual journey with us. We will celebrate the great Easter Vigil in six weeks and Teresa believes she is ready to be initiated through the sacraments of baptism, confirmation and holy eucharist at that time.
>
> She asks us to affirm her decision and to send her forth with our blessings and prayers to the rite of election celebrated this afternoon at the cathedral by Bishop Reese.

Father Dan invites Teresa forward with her sponsor Phyllis, who leads her to the front of the church where they turn and face the assembly. Father Dan steps out into the main aisle facing Teresa. Father Dan does not ask Phyllis to introduce Teresa as she did at the rite of acceptance since everyone now knows her. Father Dan addresses the assembly and Teresa. Using paragraph 538 of the RCIA as his model, he says the following:

> Parishioners of St. Al's and guests, Teresa has been preparing for this day for a long time and believes she is ready to celebrate the rite of election with Bishop Reese and to be chosen by God through Bishop Reese for the sacraments of baptism, confirmation and holy eucharist. Her sponsor and catechists have determined that she is ready to make this commitment. I now ask Phyllis, her sponsor, to place her hand on Teresa's shoulder and vouch for her.
>
> Phyllis, has Teresa taken her formation in the gospel and in the Catholic way of life seriously? Has she?

Phyllis responds, "She has." Father Dan continues.

Phyllis, has Teresa given evidence of her conversion by the way she lives her life? Has she?

Phyllis again responds, "She has." Father Dan continues.

Phyllis, do you judge her to be ready to be presented to Bishop Reese for the rite of election? Do you?

Phyllis responds, "I do." Father Dan then addresses the parishioners.

Parishioners of St. Al's, I ask you, do you approve that we send Teresa to the rite of election this afternoon so that God, through Bishop Reese, may choose her for baptism, confirmation and holy eucharist at the next celebration of the Easter Vigil? Do you?

The parishioners respond, "We do." Then Father Dan says:

Then I invite you to stand and affirm Teresa by a round of applause.

The parishioners stand and offer a round of applause. When they are finished, he addresses Teresa:

Teresa, Phyllis has vouched for you and people of St. Al's affirm your decision. We recommend you to the bishop, who, in the name of God, will call you to the Easter sacraments. May God bring to completion the good work he has begun in you.

Father Dan then invites Phyllis to take Teresa to the side of the sanctuary. Father Dan then invites Bill to address the community again. Bill says:

Father Dan, parishioners of St. Al's and guests, for many months, Joan, Keith, and Sue Burnett have also been on a spiritual journey with us. We will celebrate the great Easter Vigil in six weeks and the Burnetts believe they are ready to celebrate the sacraments of confirmation and holy eucharist with us at that time. In addition, Joan believes she is ready to make a profession of faith and become a member of the Roman Catholic church. They ask us to affirm their decision and to send them forth with our blessings and prayers so that Bishop Reese may call them to celebrate these sacraments at the upcoming Easter Vigil.

Father Dan invites the Burnetts forward with their sponsors, the Schneiders. They lead the Burnetts to the front of the church, where they turn and face the assembly. Father Dan then addresses the assembly and the candidates. Using paragraph 541 of the RCIA as his model,[9] he says the following:

Parishioners of St. Al's and guests, Joan, Keith and Sue, already one with us because they are baptized, have asked to participate fully in the sacramental life of our church. Their sponsors and catechists have determined that they are ready to make this commitment. During the many months they have been on their spiritual journey, they have listened to the scriptures with us on Sunday morning, worshiped with us on a regular basis, become a part of our parish community, grown in their knowledge of our Catholic faith, and grown in their commitment to follow Jesus as his disciples.

But rather than take my word for this, I ask their sponsors, Pauline and Jim, to place their hand on the Burnetts' shoulders and vouch for them.

Pauline, as God is your witness and as Joan's sponsor, do you affirm that she has grown in the way I just described and do you affirm that she is ready to be received into full communion with the Catholic church? Do you?

Pauline says, "I do." Father Dan continues.

Jim, as God is your witness, do you affirm that Keith and Sue have grown in the way I just described and do you affirm that they are ready to be confirmed and receive holy eucharist? Do you?

He answers, "I do." Father Dan then addresses the parishioners.

Parishioners of St. Al's, I ask you, do you approve that we send Joan to Bishop Reese so that he may give her permission to enter the Catholic church and send the three of them to the bishop so that he may call them to celebrate confirmation and holy eucharist at the upcoming Easter Vigil? Do you?

The parishioners respond, "We do." Father Dan then says:

Then I invite you to stand and affirm them by a round of applause.

The parishioners stand and offer a hearty round of applause. When they are finished he invites them to be seated and then addresses the Burnetts.

Joan, Keith and Sue, your sponsors have vouched for you and this entire community has spoken in your favor. The church, in the name of Christ, accepts their testimony and sends you to Bishop Reese who will exhort you to live in deeper conformity to the life of Christ and call you to the celebration of confirmation and holy eucharist at the next Easter Vigil.

Father Dan invites Teresa and Phyllis to join the Burnetts and Schneiders at the front of the sanctuary and invites Bill to lead the intercessions, which include special petitions for the four going to the cathedral later that day. At the conclusion of the intercessions, Father Dan invites the sponsors again to place their hands on their candidates' shoulders while he extends hands over them and offers the "prayer over the catechumens and candidates." At the conclusion of the prayer, he invites the sponsors to congratulate the four candidates. They all return to their seats in the body of the church. After Mass concludes, a light reception in the church takes place, after which Teresa, Phyllis, the Burnetts, the Schneiders, Father Dan and the Smiths go to a local diner for lunch and then on to the cathedral for the afternoon rite.

ANALYSIS OF THE RITE OF SENDING FROM THE PERSPECTIVE OF ORAL CULTURE

The rite of sending is a fairly straightforward liturgy. Father Dan and the Smiths incorporated a few rural dynamics as they planned the celebration. First, they were sensitive to the importance that belonging to a community has for rural people. Consequently, the affirmation of the assembly became an indispensable part of the rite, although the ritual text states that it is optional.[10] The support of the community and the affirmation of their sponsors will be important as they go to the bishop, who will choose them for the sacraments of initiation in the name of God and the church. It is reassuring for the candidates to know that they go to this high official of the church with the support of their local parish community and sponsors. Consequently, ritualizing this affirmation is very important in the rite of sending.

Second, putting in a good word for someone is an important feature of rural society (just as putting in a bad word is). Everyone talks about everyone else. It is a form of communication common to the rural world, and rural people accept it as a normal part of life. Consequently, speaking well of someone, especially in public, is highly valued. That the sponsors publicly vouch for the candidates, and that the community affirms them through applause, is much appreciated by rural candidates.

While speaking well of someone in public is a value that rural people hold, speaking well of someone in great detail is not. Rural people are particularly sensitive about being perceived as a show off. Sometimes it is the practice of urban/suburban churches to personalize the testimony offered by the sponsors and occasionally by the assembly as well in the celebration of the rite of sending. In large parish communities where people frequently do not know the candidates personally, there may be some wisdom in asking the sponsors to offer more personalized testimony on behalf of the people they are sponsoring. This becomes a form of evangelization and allows the assembly to become better acquainted with candidates they probably do not know. This approach is not recommended in rural communities where everyone knows just about everyone else. The parishioners of St. Al's know Teresa and the Burnetts. They know if they've been worshiping on a regular basis and if they've become part of the parish community. The community knows if they've been acting increasingly as disciples of the Lord because they have seen them in the course of daily life. Describing these personal details in a public setting is unnecessary and unwanted.

Rural catechumens and candidates would probably be mortified if information of a personal nature regarding their faith journey were vocalized in a public rite of the church. People in the parish know about them already so it looks like bragging if it is articulated in detail in a church ceremony. In addition, the prospect of describing someone else's life in detail in a public setting would be awkward and uncomfortable for sponsors who themselves come out of oral culture. Knowing this, Father Dan uses the questions found in the ritual text[11] by which the sponsors vouch for the candidates through the simple response of "I do" or "He/she has."

DIOCESAN CELEBRATION OF THE RITE OF ELECTION

The group from St. Al's arrives at the cathedral around 2:30 in the afternoon. With the exception of Father Dan and the Smiths, this is the first time most of the group has been inside the cathedral. The first-timers are impressed with the majestic architecture of the building. Ministers of hospitality greet them, ask for the name of their parish and town, and invite them to sit as a group in the part of the church designated for their deanery. As the hour draws near to begin the liturgy, the first-timers are amazed to see such a large crowd gathering. Father Dan had mentioned to them at lunch that there would be about a thousand people from all over the diocese present for the liturgy and that about half of them would be catechumens and candidates.

A few minutes before the liturgy is to begin, the rector of the cathedral welcomes everyone and then a cantor leads them in a brief music rehearsal. The organist then plays a brief prelude followed by the opening hymn. The ministers process to the sanctuary. Bishop Reese is last in the procession. He is a distinguished-looking man in his late sixties. He wears the liturgical vesture of a bishop and carries his crosier, the sign of his authority. Before the liturgy begins, he adds his welcome to that of the rector.

Those present hear the word of God proclaimed and the bishop gives a strong homily.[12] Here are a few excerpts from his homily.

> My dear catechumens, the church rejoices that you have come this far on your faith journey, that you want to die with Christ in the waters of baptism so as to rise with him. One of my greatest joys as bishop is to witness this day, for today your godparents testify that you are ready to die and rise with Christ. They will stand before me in a few moments and declare that you have grown sufficiently in your relationship with God, Christ, and the church to be baptized. I am proud of you and for the progress you have made in your faith journey.

Today is a day of transition in your lives. In a few minutes, in the name of God, I will declare you "elect." This means that you will be different after this liturgical celebration than you were before it began. We rejoice in what God has accomplished in your lives.

While we celebrate today what God has begun in your lives and how you have responded to that grace, we also call you into a season of intense spiritual preparation for baptism. In 40 days you will die and rise with Christ in the waters of baptism. What does that mean? First, it means that in the waters of baptism you will die to sin. Are you ready to die to sin? Are you really ready to die to sin? Are you ready to die to every power and authority over you except Jesus Christ and his gospel? Are you ready to die to every empty promise, glamour and evil work of Satan? Are you ready to reject Satan, sin and those things that bring death into our world? We give you 40 days to prepare to say "yes" to these questions.

Do not enter these waters frivolously. Use your 40 days well. During this time you might wish to keep this analogy in mind. If your doctor said you had but 40 days to prepare for your death, what might you do during that time? Would you take a close look at the life you have lived? Would you mend some relationship? Would you seek or offer forgiveness and reconciliation? Would you put your affairs in order? Ponder some of these questions during your 40 days of preparation.

Candidates, first of all, I express my thanks to whoever brought you to the waters of baptism. If you can still speak with them, thank them for this wonderful gift they made possible for you to receive.

Your sponsors will testify in a few moments that you are ready to make a deeper commitment to your Christian faith in union with the Catholic church. They too will declare that you have deepened your commitment to Christ. I rejoice to hear this news also.

I also bring you a word of challenge. We, the baptized, are being called to a 40-day journey of purification, repentance and grace. The truth is, we have not always said "no" to sin and evil; we have not always lived as men, women and children transformed in Christ's resurrection. Sometimes we have allowed that grace to lie dormant in our hearts. To the extent that it has, I charge you to pray, fast and give alms. Repent and be reconciled to God and neighbor.

The waters you prepare for are the tears of repentance. Hopefully these tears will lead you to the sacrament of reconciliation so that your hearts will be prepared to receive confirmation and holy eucharist in the near future.

My dear catechumens and candidates, this is a great day in your lives and in the life of the church. Let us support one another in prayer and by example as we plunge ourselves into the mystery of Lent and, in the near future, the sacraments of baptism, confirmation and holy eucharist.

After the homily, the diocesan director of liturgy goes to the lectern and addresses the bishop and the assembly. At the conclusion of her comments she asks that the catechumens—those seeking baptism, confirmation and holy eucharist—stand as their parish is announced. When Teresa hears her parish name, she stands. After all the catechumens are standing, the bishop invites the godparents to stand and to place their hand on the shoulder of the person they are sponsoring. Using the words found in paragraph 552b of the RCIA, he then asks the godparents to vouch for their catechumens. He does not ask the entire assembly to vouch for the group of catechumens since those gathered do not know all of them. After receiving the affirmation of the godparents, the bishop asks the catechumens directly if they wish to receive the sacraments of initiation. They affirm their desire and the bishop invites them to offer their names for enrollment.

The director of liturgy invites everyone to be seated and asks that the pastor or delegate from each parish rise when his or her parish is announced, taking the parish book of the elect to the lectern nearest them in the aisle (five were put in place after the homily) for the catechumens from their parish to sign. She asks the catechumens to rise when their names are called, bow their head to the bishop and follow their pastor or delegate to the lectern to sign the book of the elect. She then invites representatives from each parish to come forward as a group to the two microphones to announce the name(s) of those from their parish who will be elected. Bill Smith goes forward along with the representatives from about 65 parishes. When it is Bill's turn, he identifies the parish and town and announces Teresa's name. She rises, acknowledges Bishop Reese with a slight bow of her head and follows Father Dan to the lectern where she signs her name in the book of the elect. After finishing, they return to their seats.

Once everyone has signed their books, the bishop takes a moment to explain the reason why the catechumens have signed this book. Then he invites the catechumens to stand and declares them, in the name of God, to be members of the elect. He then invites the godparents to stand and places the elect into their care, asking them to offer some gesture of care to the one they are sponsoring while the community offers a round of applause. There are many hugs and a few handshakes. After the applause ends, the elect and their godparents are invited to have a seat.

The diocesan liturgy director again addresses the bishop and the assembly. She notes that the next group in the celebration is baptized and that by their baptism have already been elected by God. At the conclusion of her remarks, she invites the candidates for full communion and those who will be confirmed and receive holy eucharist for the first time to stand as their names are announced, to bow their head in acknowledgement of the bishop and to remain in their places. Parish representatives are called forward to the microphones again. Joan and her children rise when Bill identifies their parish and announces their names.

After all the candidates are named, the bishop invites the sponsors for these candidates to stand and to place their hands on the shoulders of those they are sponsoring. Using the words found in paragraph 556b of the RCIA, he asks the sponsors to vouch for their candidates. He omits the question to the assembly for the same reason he omitted it earlier in the celebration. Bishop Reese then recognizes their desire for confirmation and holy eucharist and grants them permission to make their final preparations for these sacraments. He then invites the sponsors to offer some gesture of care to the one they are sponsoring while the community offers a round of applause. Again there are hugs and handshakes and, after the applause ends, all are invited to stand for the intercessions and the prayer over the elect and candidates. A reception is announced, and the liturgy concludes with a final blessing and closing song. After the reception, the group from St. Al's drives back to Clarkville, talking nonstop about their day.

Mystagogical Catechesis on the Rites of Sending and Election

Teresa, the Burnetts and their sponsors come to Alice and Bill Smith's home on the Tuesday evening after the rite of election, as previously agreed. After the usual chatting and eating, Alice invites the group into her living room and tells them they are going to spend a little time reflecting on the two celebrations from the previous Sunday. She notes that they have already done some reflecting on the rites during their travel to and from the cathedral and have undoubtedly spoken about it with others since returning to Clarkville. Everyone agrees!

She asks them to become quiet and to listen as she briefly reviews the two rites with them. After a few moments of silence, Alice begins to describe the major elements of the rite of sending. She recalls the chilly morning and the children's excitement before the liturgy. She recalls an image from each of the three readings and the main idea of Father Dan's homily. Then she reminds them of Teresa's invitation to the front of the church and how Phyllis, with her hand on Teresa's shoulder, vouched for her and the community, through voice and applause, affirmed her. She then calls to mind how the same was done for the Burnetts. She describes Father Dan praying over them, the lovely reception after the Mass and the lunch at Carson's Café.

She then moves to the rite of election. She recalls the magnificent cathedral and the majestic organ and the many people who filled the church. She describes Bishop Reese, carrying his crosier and wearing his miter. She recalls a few words of his homily and how all the sponsors again vouched for the catechumens before the bishop. She remembers how they were invited to sign the book of the elect and how Bishop Reese solemnly proclaimed the catechumens the elect of God, accompanied by embraces and applause.

She tells of Bill announcing the names of the Burnetts, Joan, Keith and Sue, and how the bishop again asked the sponsors to vouch for the candidates.

She then recalls how Bishop Reese confirmed their desire to celebrate confirmation and holy eucharist and how the whole church again applauded as they were congratulated by their sponsors.

Having recalled the two rites, Alice asks them, "As you remember these two liturgies, what memories stand out for you?" She invites Teresa and the Burnetts to speak first. Joan is the first to respond and says that she was very comforted by the support she felt from both Pauline and the parishioners of St. Al's. She mentions how great it felt to have Pauline's hand on her shoulder as she was testifying on her behalf, especially at the parish ceremony where she was a little nervous. The others quickly agreed. Keith spoke next, commenting on the beautiful cathedral, the large crowd and the bishop. He said that he didn't realize what a big deal all this was until he experienced the ceremony at the cathedral. Sue liked hearing her name announced in the cathedral, and the applause made her feel very good. Teresa said she was blown away by the whole experience. She particularly remembers signing her name in the book of the elect and the solemn way Bishop Reese proclaimed her and all the other catechumens to be the elect of God.

Phyllis was impressed with the people from all over the diocese who were present for the ceremony at the cathedral. She said that it really inspired her that so many people were preparing to be initiated into the church. Pauline recalled the homily, especially the part where Bishop Reese reminded her that the baptized have not always said "no" to sin and evil, and how Lent was a time to shed the tears of repentance. She said it was a great way to begin Lent and to begin thinking about celebrating the sacrament of reconciliation before Easter. Teresa chimed in and said that the bishop's homily really hit her when he said she had 40 days to get ready to die. She said that she had never really thought about baptism in that way, but it really made sense. She said she had a few things to review in her life in preparation for her baptism in light of his comments.

Alice said that they remembered a lot about the two liturgies and that based on what they said they had gotten the purpose of the celebrations. She recalled the sponsors' testimony and the affirmation of the parishioners and says how important other people are on someone's faith journey and how all the parishioners have a responsibility to support and vouch for the spiritual growth in each other's lives. She told them that this is part of the responsibility baptized people have. She said that it is so important that the bishop could not accept the word of the catechumens and candidates alone before announcing his decision to authorize them to celebrate the sacraments of initiation. She said that the bishop depends on the help and insights of his people in order to make important decisions, especially ones where he is acting in the name of God.

She then spoke further of the bishop. She recalled Keith's comments about him and asked them if they had any idea why they went to the cathedral to celebrate the second ceremony. Louis wondered if it had something to do with the fact that he's in charge of the diocese. Alice affirmed his insight and went on to say the bishop's role in the cathedral rite is very important. She said that the bishop is the visible sign of unity of the whole diocese and is a symbol of the unity we have with other Catholics all over the

A Harvest for God: Christian Initiation in the Rural and Small-Town Parish

world because of his unity with the pope and the other bishops of the world. She said that in churches all over the world last Sunday, thousands and thousands of catechumens and candidates were called to the initiation sacraments by bishops.

Alice then looked at Teresa and told her that Catholics believe that God's love and grace are communicated to us in visible ways so that we will know how much God loves us. She went on to say that when she signed the book of the elect, she was declaring to God and to the world in a visible way that she wanted God to give her the grace of baptism. She then said that Bishop Reese, acting as God's visible representative to Teresa and the other catechumens, declared in God's name that she and the others were worthy to receive this grace by dying and rising with Christ in the waters of baptism so that they could live forever as God's children and as Jesus' sisters and brothers. Alice reiterates that God declares Teresa worthy in this rite and asks Teresa how she feels about that. Teresa's eyes become a little moist and she tells the group that it feels wonderful.

Joan asks why she and the other candidates didn't sign the book. Alice explains that because they are baptized, they are already worthy in the eyes of God. She goes on to explain a little more about the importance of their baptism. Joan notes that she wouldn't mind signing something as a public declaration of her desire to become a Roman Catholic. Alice responds that she will have an opportunity to make such a public declaration at the Easter Vigil when she makes a profession of faith in the Roman Catholic Church.

Alice tells them that they will celebrate a special rite at Mass next Sunday: the presentation of the creed. She notes that although Joan and her children are baptized in denominations that profess a creed they never received any formation or instruction on it.[13] Therefore they will join Teresa in its presentation at Mass next Sunday. She reminds the sponsors of a short rehearsal at 9:30 on Sunday morning with Father Dan in preparation for the rite. They conclude with prayer and everyone returns to their homes.

Analysis of the Mystagogical Catechesis Session

Because some time had elapsed between the rites of sending and election and the session for mystagogical catechesis, Alice used a simple process to recall the two rites. Using a sheet of paper on which she has written some of the key elements, words, music and gestures of the two rites, she recalls them so as to refresh the memories of those who participated in them. This is a particularly important yet simple technique to use when time passes between the actual celebration of a rite and a mystagogical catechesis on the rite.

Having triggered their memories, she asks them to speak about their memories of the two rites. The participants recall many elements. Alice has a master list of possible choices they might recall and checks them off in her head as the participants remember the two rites. After the participants have concluded their reflections, Alice continues the reflection by pondering the meaning of the testimony of the sponsors, the affirmation of the parishioners, the role and symbol of the bishop, the importance of the book of the elect and other elements with the participants.

As we have already seen, a sense of belonging is particularly important for rural people. The testimony of their sponsors, the affirmation of the parishioners and the proclamation of the bishop foster trust and assurance in people from rural society and give them a further sense of belonging and identity, important qualities in the lives of rural people. Teresa and the Burnetts experienced these things in both rites.

Because rural people do not often feel connected to the larger world, it is particularly important that they participate in the diocesan rite of election. This celebration will help people from the countryside realize that they belong to something much bigger than a parish and that this bigger church does care for them (something they do not always experience).

Relationship with God is highly valued in rural society. Teresa was affirmed in the importance of her relationship in the eyes of God by the ritual elements of signing the book of the elect and the act of election by the bishop.

The format Alice followed is summarized below.

- Welcome and brief explanation of session

- Remembering the rites:

  - Recalling key elements, words, music, gestures of the rites

  - Prompt: "What memories stand out for you from these liturgies?"

- Checklist of elements and their meanings:

  - Testimony of sponsors: someone vouches for growth/conversion in catechumen/candidate

  - Affirmation of parishioners: catechumens/candidates belong

  - Calling of names: catechumens/candidates are personally known by God and the community

  - Signing the book of the elect: catechumen is worthy in eyes of God

  - Diocesan celebration: belonging to something bigger than parish

  - Role of bishop:

    - Sign of unity of diocese and with universal church

    - Acts in name of God

- Rite is threshold into lenten preparation for initiation sacraments

  - The elect prepare for waters of baptism

  - The candidates prepare for the tears of repentance (reconciliation)

- Announcements/questions

- Prayer and conclusion

Notes

[1]RCIA, 332, states that exceptional circumstances include such things as sickness, old age, change of residence and long absence for travel.

[2]RCIA, 370–374, explains these circumstances.

[3]RCIA, 447–448.

[4]RCIA, 548, indicates that the bishop or his delegate normally presides for this rite, although RCIA, 449, provides some leeway for parish celebrations.

[5]See RCIA, 107, 435 and 531, which describe the purpose of a parish Rite of Sending for catechumens and/or candidates.

[6]RCIA, 107.

[7]Recall that National Statute 6 asks catechumens (and uncatechized candidates) to be in formation at least 12 months between the time they celebrate the rite of acceptance/welcome and the time they are initiated. RCIA, 401–402, implies a similar period of time for those who begin the process as baptized but uncatechized individuals.

[8]There is some flexibility built into this introduction so that the speaker may modify the text to make it as appropriate as possible for the occasion. If the speaker prepares different words, it should follow the general ideas contained in the ritual text.

[9]The ritual text allows the presider to modify his words to the assembly.

[10]See RCIA, 112, 440, 538 and 541, where this option is noted.

[11]See RCIA, 112, 440, 538 and 541, to see the specific questions that are asked.

[12]What follows is inspired by a model homily written by Joanna Case for a publication given to participants in the Beginnings and Beyond Institute. It is used with her permission.

[13]See National Statute 31, which states that baptized candidates who have receive no Christian instruction or formation may celebrate this rite with the unbaptized. Because Joan's formation was nominal and ended when she was a small child, Alice, after speaking with Joan, has decided to include her in the ritual celebration. Keith and Sue have had no instruction on the creed.

Chapter 6

The Period of Purification and Enlightenment

This chapter will explore:

- the structure of the scrutiny rites and the presentation rites (Creed and Lord's Prayer)

- how to celebrate these rites in a rural-friendly manner

- how to prepare rural elect, candidates and community for these rites

- how to conduct a mystagogical catechesis on these rites in a rural-friendly manner

- how catechesis during this period of formation is different from the catechesis of the previous two periods

- the ritual differences in these rites for the elect and baptized candidates.

Life has become unexpectedly busy for Joe and Maria since they announced their engagement. They shared the news with their families and after several discussions set a tentative wedding date for late April. Joe remembered his pastor saying that the church was free on every Saturday in the spring except Easter weekend and the Kiwanis Club hall, of which Joe is a member, was available every Saturday in April also. Having confirmed these facts, Joe called his pastor to set the date and to set up a meeting to discuss the Pre-Cana program of the parish.

At Joe and Maria's first appointment with Father John, the pastor, he asks them to tell him all about their plans and the details of their engagement. Maria shows Father John her engagement ring and tells him about their

Boy meets girl/ First dates	Commitment to go steady	Building the relationship Meeting the family Learning the traditions	Engagement	**Pre-Cana/ Marriage prep**	Wedding	Honeymoon/ First year of marriage
Precatechumenate	Rite of Acceptance into Order of Catechumens	Catechumenate	Rite of Election	**Purification and enlightenment**	Sacraments of initiation	Mystagogy

evening in the restaurant. After hearing this story and offering his congratulations again, Father John explains the marriage preparation process. He tells them about the paperwork they will need to complete, some conversations they will have with him about the sacrament of matrimony and the wedding ceremony, a retreat they will be invited to make, and some conversations they will have with a married couple in the parish. At the end of the conversation, they schedule the next meeting.

At the next meeting Father John begins by asking them to tell him about their individual stories as well as their story as a couple. He hears about their families. He knows Joe's family quite well and is happy to learn more about Maria's. He spends the remainder of this session speaking about marriage in terms of forming a new family in the context of biological and church families. During the following session, he asks them to speak about their spiritual lives, both as individuals and as a couple. In this context, he explains what sacramental marriage means for Catholics as an irrevocable bond between the bride and the groom and between God and the couple. Maria has many questions and is impressed with the seriousness with which the Catholic church takes marriage. They meet a few more times to discuss nuts and bolts issues concerning the ceremony and the documentation that must be completed and provided in preparation for their wedding.

Joe and Maria are invited to attend a weekend retreat sponsored by the diocese for engaged couples. They find the weekend to be enlightening. They learn more about the importance of spirituality in their relationship and they learn many practical things about day-to-day life as a married couple. As part of the weekend they complete a premarital inventory that will be scored and sent to Father John. They find the weekend enriching, and it confirms the path they have chosen to follow. They also learn that married life is not always easy and they have a couple of serious discussions about some things about which they disagree.

After the retreat, Father John invites them to meet with the Ralph and Louise Henderson, a couple married almost 30 years, for some follow-up sessions. He has given the results of the premarital inventory to this seasoned couple, who in turn sit down with Joe and Maria to review it with them. Joe and Maria enjoy their time with the Hendersons. Ralph and Louise tell them many stories about married life and as they review the inventory, Joe and Maria are pleased to learn that they agree on many things that will be important in married life, such as a desire for children, how to handle their finances, careers, and their relationship with their extended families. They are also made aware of the fact that they disagree with each other on a few things, some of which are very important in married life, such as decision making, use of alcohol and the religion of their children. The Hendersons spend a few evenings reviewing these issues with Joe and Maria, who are encouraged by the support and affirmation they receive from all those helping them to prepare for marriage. They also struggle with some issues on which they don't see eye to eye. Some of these struggles they discuss between themselves and some they discuss with the Hendersons, who listen patiently and offer a bit of wisdom that they have obtained over 30 years of marriage.

The preparations include the wedding ceremony. They meet with the organist to select music and decide who will serve as ministers in the ceremony. Bridal showers are held for Maria by her friends and family. Plans for the reception are put in place. A wedding party is selected from among their friends and relatives, gowns and tuxedos are ordered, photographs are taken, invitations are sent out, the honeymoon is planned, and the happy couple finds that before they know it, their wedding is just a few days away.

INTRODUCTION TO THE PERIOD OF PURIFICATION AND ENLIGHTENMENT

It has been said that a wedding is for a day and a marriage is for a lifetime. While the details connected with a wedding ceremony are many and important, those connected with helping the couple prepare to live the rest of their lives together are far more important. Joe and Maria have many details to attend to in preparation for the day when they will celebrate the sacrament of holy matrimony, but the preparations they make for married life during this time are far more important.

In an analogous way, this is what the period of purification and enlightenment does. Teresa is preparing to die and rise with Christ, with all that this dying and rising means. While it will be important to discuss what she will wear for her baptism, how her hair should be styled and who she should invite as guests, dying and rising with Christ in the waters of baptism and the implications of that bath are far more important. Remember the rite of election when Bishop Reese challenged the catechumens to prepare themselves to die to sin to every power and authority over them except Christ and his gospel so that they might rise as a transformed people permanently configured to Christ and his way of life. This will require some intense spiritual preparation and ongoing purification in the weeks leading up to baptism. Without this preparation and purification, Teresa may experience the waters of baptism as a nice ritual that brings her into a special relationship with Christ and the church, but it will not be experienced as the pivotal experience of her entire life.

Joe and Maria will meet with Father John and the Hendersons to engage in several conversations about married life. They will discover the many things they share in common and those areas about married life where they are in agreement. They will also discover that there are things they do not agree on and a few obstacles they will have to face in order for their lives as a married couple to grow and deepen. This is what the elect and the candidates are about during this period of formation.

Joe and Maria are enlightened about their relationship as a couple during their Pre-Cana program. They discover what is good about their relationship and receive affirmation from Father John, the retreat leaders and the Hendersons. They also discover what needs more growth and perhaps even change in their relationship. Those who lead them through this preparation process also bring these issues to the couple's attention, but they also discover these areas of growth and development for themselves through their own reflection on the issues they discuss during this period of time.

In the same way, the elect and candidates are called to an intense preparation for the initiation sacraments. Paragraph 138 of the RCIA tells us that this preparation period is of an intensely spiritual nature and consists "more in interior reflection than in catechetical instruction."[1] This interior reflection, done with other elect and candidates, catechists, parish leaders and a faith community, is meant to help the elect and candidates purify their hearts and minds through an examination of their consciences and through acts of penance as well as to enlighten them to a deeper awareness of Christ as their savior. This is why this period of formation is referred to as that of purification and enlightenment.

The process of both purification and enlightenment is experienced in the three scrutiny rites designed for this period.[2] In addition, the presentation of both the creed and the Lord's Prayer is for the enlightenment of the elect and those candidates who began the process uncatechized and with no formation in the Christian life.[3] This period, which coincides with Lent, is not a time to complete whatever topics have not yet been covered in preparation for initiation. The holistic formation envisioned during the catechumenate period comes to a close with the celebration of the rite of election. The rite of election is a public declaration that the catechumens and candidates are ready to proceed to the sacraments of initiation at the end of Lent. If they are not ready, they should not celebrate this rite. Rather, they should remain in the catechumenate period until such time as they are determined to be ready for the final, intensely spiritual focus of the period of purification and enlightenment.

This period of spiritual purification and enlightenment is experienced primarily in the three scrutiny rites and the two presentation rites. Consequently, the catechesis of this period is based on these liturgical rites and is similar to the mystagogical catechesis described for the rite of acceptance and the rite of election in earlier chapters. Just as Father John, the retreat leaders and the Hendersons help Joe and Maria prepare for their lives as a married couple, initiation ministers do the same with the elect and the candidates who are preparing to celebrate the sacraments of initiation.

THE SPIRITUAL FOCUS OF THIS PERIOD

For Teresa and the Burnetts, the focus of this period is primarily on sin and grace.[4] Teresa will prepare to die to sin so as to be joined to Christ through the waters of baptism while the Burnetts will be invited to consider how, as baptized Christians, they have lived as people already joined to Christ but who have allowed the covenantal bond they enjoy with Christ to become weakened through sin. Teresa's journey is to the waters of baptism while the Burnetts' journey is to the tears of repentance that will lead them to the sacrament of reconciliation. If these are their respective destinations, then it is essential that an extended reflection on sin become part of their spiritual preparation during this period.

This will not be as simple as it might first appear. There are many difficulties associated with addressing sin in rural society. Before addressing those difficulties, it will be important to examine not only what needs to be understood about sin, but also what needs to be understood about grace. John Paul II has described sin on two levels: personal and social. We will begin with a brief overview of sin, both personal and social, and will conclude with a brief overview of grace. Following this overview, the difficulties associated with addressing sin in rural society will be described.

Personal Sin

John Paul II describes six types of personal sin. The first kind of personal sin is described as an act or omission that fails to respect or enhance human dignity. For example, if a husband commits adultery, the dignity of his wife and their life as a married couple is seriously compromised.

The second kind is an act or omission that exploits someone else's diminished human dignity for personal interest or gain. For example, the co-worker who learns about this husband's infidelity and uses that information to blackmail him in order to advance in his job commits this type of sin.

The third kind of personal sin is a failure to avoid, eliminate or at least limit a sinful act because of laziness, fear, indifference or secret complicity. For example, a group of employees gathers for lunch and someone in the group tells a racist joke. One person in the group is offended by the joke but out of fear of being ridiculed by the group says nothing.

The fourth is sidestepping the effort necessary to address a sinful situation because of the inconvenience it will generate. For example, an employee learns that her supervisor is stealing from the company. She knows the thievery to be true but says nothing to her supervisor's boss because it will create tension between her supervisor and her. Addressing the problem might even jeopardize her job. Therefore she says nothing and allows the stealing to continue.

The fifth kind of personal sin is doing nothing about a sinful situation because it is seemingly impossible to change the situation. For example, in the case of the racist joke another person in the same group decides to say nothing because he is convinced the man who told the joke has been a racist all his life and will never change.

The sixth category is rationalizing why one cannot address a situation where human dignity is diminished. For example, a man who learns of his co-worker's marital infidelity may justify his silence about the sin by concluding that the man's wife deserves it because she is bossy.

Social Sin

John Paul II also addressed the reality of social sin. Social sin results from groups of people who fail to respect or enhance the human dignity of other groups of people in society. Social sin exists when one group of people oppresses another group. What makes this different from personal sin is that groups of people commit the sin and groups of people are oppressed by the sin. Frequently, the sin is not even perceived as a sin. Those committing it are frequently oblivious to the fact that it is a sin because it has become an acceptable (and sometimes legal) behavior by the group.

The story of the man born blind (John 9:1–41) is an example of this. In this story, the religious leaders collectively oppress the man born blind who is healed by Jesus on the Sabbath. Their religion taught them that everyone born blind is steeped in sin. When the man who can now see challenges their collective religious belief forbidding healing on the Sabbath, they rely on the religious belief that the man is a sinner from birth and that therefore they do not have to listen to his challenge to their beliefs. Their beliefs precluded them from seeing a different truth.

Perhaps a contemporary example may further help to illustrate what the pope is describing. The farming industry in the United States is dependent on migrant labor. Without it, the farming industry could not function as it does. These men and women come to the United States because their labor is needed and because there is an opportunity to earn a living wage to support their families. Poverty in their native countries motivates many migrant laborers to seek work in the United States in order to survive or to have a better life. However, immigration laws in the United States make it difficult for these men and women to enter and/or work here legally or to travel back and forth from their native lands for seasonal work. As a result, they live in fear and sometimes are taken advantage of by employers.

Agribusiness and some private farmers need workers. As the proverb goes, necessity is the mother of invention. Out of necessity, migrant laborers are hired, often illegally, to get the job done. Unfortunately in more than a few agribusinesses, profits often determine the bottom line in the areas of wages, benefits and working conditions. As a result, illegal migrant laborers may work under oppressive conditions because their alternative is no work at all or deportation.

Rural farmers, often dependent on migrant labor, may also act prejudicially against these migrant laborers because they are racially, ethnically, linguistically and culturally different from the local farmers.

When these factors are at work, social sin is committed, according to John Paul II.

Grace

Balancing any discussion of sin is a discussion of grace. The period of purification and enlightenment is built on this premise. There is a fundamental belief in the Catholic tradition that ours is a grace-filled world. Among the many definitions of grace, "God's love" is perhaps the most significant. It is manifested in many ways. One of the most important aspects of grace is that it is unmerited. We do nothing to earn it. Dennis the Menace is describing unmerited grace when he tells Joey something important about Mrs. Wilson: "She gives you a cookie because she's nice, not because you're nice." It is God's nature to give us grace. The only thing we must do is accept it. Mrs. Wilson can offer cookies all day long, but until Joey accepts one and eats it, the effects of the cookie are nonexistent. Helping rural elect and candidates ponder this truth is one of the tasks of this period of formation. As they ponder this great truth, it will enable them to acknowledge and respond to the lenten call to conversion and repentance.

Another kind of grace from God might be described as "Genesis grace." This too tells us something of fundamental importance about God. Genesis grace means that all of creation is fundamentally good because God is the author of all creation. If we read the creation stories at the beginning of the book of Genesis we will see that everything God creates is deemed "good" or "very good." This is as true of God's creative acts today as it was at the beginning of creation. Someone has described Genesis grace at work in our lives this way: "The grace of God means something like this: Here's your life. You might never have been, but you are because the party wouldn't have been complete without you."[5] In rural society, where low self-esteem is more prevalent than in other societies, speaking of Genesis grace as part of the lenten journey will be important if rural people are also being invited to explore the reality of sin in their lives.

Central to the period of purification and enlightenment is the fact that the elect and candidates are preparing for the sacraments of initiation. Baptism confers grace upon the one who is baptized. In traditional language we refer to this grace as sanctifying grace. Someone once identified this sanctifying grace as "Calvary grace": When humanity showed it was incapable of getting back to Genesis grace, out of a superabundance of love, God sent Jesus to take on himself on the cross the sins of all humans for all time in order that all of creation might be truly and irrevocably redeemed. The fruit of this grace is the conquest of all sin and evil, even death. The following story aptly describes this kind of grace that Teresa is preparing to receive at the Easter Vigil.

> This is a true story. In Europe, after World War II, there were a number of initiatives to heal some of the wounds that had occurred. One was through cultural exchanges.
>
> There was one particular French village where, during the war, the Resistance Movement was active. In reprisal, the local Nazi commander randomly executed a number of the villagers, amongst whom were a large number of children.
>
> Following the war, a German choir was to make a tour of this village on one of these cultural exchanges. The village leaders scheduled the arrival of this German choir. What they did not know, however,

was that this was a children's choir. Nor did the German leaders know the history of this particular village now empty of children.

When the choir arrived, it so struck the villagers to see these children that they became outraged and all their grief and pain that had been buried came to the surface. And they began to riot. The local police had to intervene, lest the children be harmed. So the children were quickly hustled back on to the buses and the buses were escorted out of town.

After things calmed down, the village leadership asked, "What have we done here? This is awful. We must do something." So they worked for a whole year with the villagers to try to help them heal some of their feelings.

The village made the decision to invite the children's choir back. When the day came and the children arrived, the villagers had arranged that the first meeting of the choir would be in the village church. Everyone from the village was in the church when the children arrived. As they began, the leader of the children's choir stood up and said that they had brought a gift with them for the village.

The mayor of the village took the gift and opened it. Inside the box was a chalice. On the base of the chalice was inscribed, "Some sins only this blood can heal."[6]

The sanctifying grace Teresa will receive in baptism might also be described as Calvary grace. During the period of purification and enlightenment, Teresa and the candidates will be well served if they are provided with an opportunity to ponder this gift. For Teresa it is a gift to anticipate; for the Burnetts and all the faithful it is a gift to be remembered.

The last kind of grace to be considered during this period of formation might be described as "Kingdom grace." This grace was inaugurated by the incarnation of Jesus and is continually unleashed by the power of the Holy Spirit and the acts of discipleship by Jesus' followers. It is a grace that says that nothing will prevent God from winning the ultimate victory over sin, evil and death. It is a grace that Teresa and the Burnetts have been learning to embrace during the catechumenate period and that they will be charged with unleashing through the power of the Holy Spirit after the Easter Vigil. This story offers an example of this kind of grace.

The high school senior was undergoing cancer therapy. On top of the crushing fear and daily nausea, he suffered the added indignity of losing all his hair. Still, when the day came that his therapy ended, he headed back to school. When he walked through the door that first morning, there were all of his friends with shining bald heads. They had, every one of them, shaved their scalps clean. They could not take away his cancer, but they could relieve his shame. And so with a special and—as always—surprising grace, they welcomed him with laughter and with baldness.[7]

Kingdom grace proclaims that no matter how bad things get, God's grace is always more powerful. Someone has said it this way: In an election in which the choices are sin and grace, grace will ultimately win 51 percent of the vote. This does not mean that sin cannot take the lead during the balloting or even win the primaries. It means that in the final outcome grace will always win. In any discussion of sin, especially in a rural setting, it will be important to keep grace as a counterpoint to it. Keeping grace consciously before rural people will give them the courage they sometimes need to move away from sin. It plays into their belief of a powerful God who, while in relationship with them transcendentally, shows his great love for them through Jesus Christ and who allows them to share in that love (grace) through the sacraments and the word of God.

Difficulties Associated with Addressing Sin in Rural Society

Discussing sin, reflecting on one's sinful behavior and converting away from sin are difficult things to do in the rural world. Part of the problem stems from the fact that indigenous oral people are not inherently reflective. They tend to live life more reflexively and habitually, primarily from the gut and not so much in the mind. Therefore discussing and reflecting on sin is not something that will come naturally to many rural people. They can do all this, but it will need to proceed carefully.

Additionally, rural people are more accepting of the imperfect because frequently this is the best that can be achieved in their limited world. This does not mean that rural people do not care about the moral life. Indeed, they care about it very much. But they are also more understanding when people do not achieve moral perfection, because perfection is not a goal in rural life. Life is messy. When someone is acting immorally or is simply acting in an inappropriate manner, rural people will address the issue. Those in relationship with the offenders (which could be nearly everyone in a rural community, if you combine those who are related to the offenders by blood or marriage) will confront them, particularly if their behavior is bringing shame on the family name. They do this primarily through telling a story with a moral, gossiping or threatening ostracism.

Discussing Sin in the Rural World

Sin exists in the rural world as much as it does anywhere else. Rural people can hear exhortations to individual repentance and conversion as long as the one exhorting has moral authority in their eyes and exhorts in a way that is rural-sensitive. An elderly, indigenous member of the community generally possesses this ability. An elderly fisherman was once asked what advice he would offer a young man for living a moral life. His response was, "Don't cuss; don't carouse; go to church." Rural people will respect these words

A Harvest for God: Christian Initiation in the Rural and Small-Town Parish

because they are clear, unambiguous and easily remembered. If a member of this man's family develops a problem with cursing, the fisherman may find a time when he can tell a story about someone who gets into trouble for cursing. He will tell the story when the offender is present within a group of people so that the offender will not be directly confronted but will still get the point. This is a rural-friendly manner of addressing sin.

A priest or religious sister also has this authority, at least initially, provided they exercise it in a rural-sensitive manner. If they lose it, it is frequently because they pushed too directly or quickly for change in general, or tried to get the people to address social sins in a manner that is beyond their ability.

Calling rural people to repentance and conversion is only half the challenge. Getting them to do something about it is the other. Rural people can hear the call to conversion but for a variety of reasons often feel powerless to do anything about it. This has to do with the connection between moral issues and relationship. Moral issues are viewed through the lens of relationship, and relationship exerts a very powerful influence on morality. In a world where relationships tend to be few in number and lifelong, rural people are afraid that confronting sin will upset and even jeopardize the stability of their relationships, even if the relationship is dysfunctional!

The wife of an unfaithful husband will be more tolerant of her unfaithful spouse than her suburban counterpart might be because as the old saying goes, "A bird in the hand is worth two in the bush." Because the possibilities for finding a spouse is limited to begin with, an unfaithful husband is considered better than no husband at all. In addition, shame will be brought to the family name—both the husband's family and the wife's—if there is a divorce. Consequently, the unfaithful rural husband stands a better chance of remaining married than his urban counterpart.

Conversion by its nature involves change, and change upsets the status quo. In a world where maintenance is more important than change, keeping things calm is more important than stirring them up; where life is viewed as unchanging, confronting sin must be done carefully. Pressure is applied, almost subconsciously, to keep everything in place, even sin, because of the fears associated with the unknown consequences of change. Change is, therefore, a great challenge for rural people. This is not to say that change does not happen. It will simply take longer and will tend to move in small, incremental steps over a long period of time. Therefore, addressing sin is more likely to succeed if the process is more like that of water dripping on a rock than of a stream raging through a riverbed.

THE RITE OF SCRUTINY AT ST. AL'S

Joe and Maria, our engaged couple, take some time during their immediate preparation for sacramental marriage to explore all that is strong in their relationship but they also are invited to consider all that remains weak, perhaps even sinful, in their relationship. The pre-marriage program has affirmed them in the many areas where they are strong and has also placed before them opportunities to discuss and reflect upon those areas that could harm their life as a married couple if left unattended. The retreat leaders, the Hendersons and their pastor all act as agents of grace for them during this time, helping them look at their weaknesses so that they may discover ways to reduce their influence in their married life. In a similar way, this is what the scrutiny rites do.

Within the period of purification and enlightenment three scrutiny rites are to be celebrated. So serious are these rites that only with the permission of the local bishop may a parish be dispensed from one or, in exceptional circumstances, two of these celebrations when there are elect preparing for baptism at the coming celebration of the Easter Vigil.[8] The three celebrations of this rite invite the elect to an experience of self-searching and repentance regarding sin in preparation for baptism. These three celebrations are intended to "uncover, then heal all that is weak, defective, or sinful in the hearts of the elect; to bring out, then strengthen all that is upright, strong, and good."[9] Because they are preparing to die with Christ in the waters of baptism and be forever joined to him, the scrutiny rites are intended to help the elect "deepen their resolve to hold fast to Christ and to carry out their decision to love God above all."[10] In other words, this is serious business!

The rite of scrutiny is celebrated three times so that the elect may be "instructed gradually about the mystery of sin . . . and thus saved from its present and future consequences."[11] But as each rite focuses on sin, grace accompanies it. In the first scrutiny rite, the grace for the Samaritan woman at the well is found in Christ who is the living water; in the second, the grace for the man born blind is in Christ who is the light of the world; and in the third, the grace for Lazarus is in Christ who is the resurrection and the life.[12] For the Samaritan woman the grace is forgiveness; for the man born blind the grace is healing; and for Lazarus the grace is liberation and life.

The scrutiny rites are for the elect, the unbaptized, only. There is a parallel rite for candidates called the penitential rite (RCIA, 459–472). The rites may not be combined and the candidates may not celebrate the rite of scrutiny along with the elect. The significant reason for the separation has to do with the status of the candidates as baptized Christians. The ritual language of the rite of scrutiny clearly anticipates baptism. The purpose of the penitential rite is to help prepare the candidates for the celebration of the sacrament of reconciliation. This rite is optional whereas the scrutiny rites are not. Frequently in rural parishes, the penitential rite for the candidates is omitted due to the fact that many candidates participate in a lenten penance service in which they experience a penitential rite and celebrate the sacrament of reconciliation in one service. Since the elect do not celebrate sacramental reconciliation prior to their baptism (because they receive sacramental forgiveness in the waters of baptism), the scrutiny rites are indispensable in preparing the elect for the profound experience of baptism and the other sacraments of initiation.

Preparation for the First Scrutiny

Because the parish is fortunate to have an unbaptized adult seeking initiation at the next Easter Vigil, the first scrutiny is scheduled for the Third

Sunday of Lent at St. Al's as recommended by the rite.[13] On the Friday evening prior to the celebration of the rite, the parishioners are invited to a traditional celebration of the stations of the cross at 6:30 in the evening. Following this lenten devotion, they are invited to the parish hall for a lenten soup supper. At the conclusion of the meal, Father Dan reminds the parishioners that they are invited to remain as Teresa, the Burnetts and their sponsors make some preparations in anticipation of the celebration of the first scrutiny. He had announced this the previous Sunday and had encouraged the parishioners to consider attending this preparation as part of their lenten commitments.

About a dozen parishioners join Father Dan and those to be initiated for the session. Using a format he will repeat the next two Fridays in anticipation of the other scrutiny rites, Father Dan begins by telling them about a retreat he made before his ordination. He describes the place he went, how long the retreat lasted, who directed him and what he did during the retreat. Most importantly, he tells them that he went on the retreat to make final spiritual preparations for his ordination and that he could not have been ordained without this spiritual preparation. He tells them that during the retreat he discussed with his spiritual director his joy about being ordained a priest as well as a sense of unworthiness, because he was not perfect. He told them that he confessed his sins to the retreat master because he felt it was important that he come to his ordination without any obstacles in the way. Father Dan concluded the story by telling them that he left the retreat with a feeling of assurance that God was with him as he prepared to be ordained.

Father Dan then compares his retreat experience to what Teresa and the Burnetts are doing in anticipation of the Easter Vigil when they will celebrate the sacraments of initiation. He tells them that everyone in the parish is called to do the same thing as they prepare to recommit themselves to God and Christ at the Easter weekend Masses, to recall how they have been faithful as well as unfaithful to God. He tells them that Teresa and the Burnetts are making spiritual preparation to receive the sacraments of initiation and that part of their preparation involves a reflection on the role sin has played in their lives. He tells them that Teresa is preparing to be baptized and, that in order for her to be ready for this incredible gift from God, she will participate in three rituals in which she asks God to help her be aware of her sins but also, more importantly, of God's profound love for her. He tells them that the Burnetts and all the parishioners will gather around Teresa to pray for her during these three rites.

Having set the context of the scrutiny rites, Father Dan opens a lectionary to the story of Jesus' encounter with the Samaritan woman at the well (John 4:5–42). Before he reads the passage, he invites the group to place themselves into the story as observers and to pay close attention to the sights, sounds, feelings, smells and tastes in the story. Then he reads the story to them.

When he finishes, he pauses for a few moments and then asks the group what they saw, heard, felt, smelled or tasted. Responses begin slowly, but eventually people describe a well and a thirsty man without a bucket and a woman who has one. Someone hears a little sarcasm in the woman's voice as she responds to Jesus' request for a drink. Another person says she felt embarrassed for the woman when Jesus told her she had five husbands and a live-in boyfriend (and added that she should have been embarrassed!). Keith said the story made him thirsty.

Father Dan next takes out a sheet of paper that contains the intercessions that will be used in the First Scrutiny rite (RCIA, 153b). He tells them that in the rite on Sunday they will be making petitions to God on Teresa's behalf and that he wants them to hear these petitions ahead of time. He then says that following each petition there will be a reflection question for them to think and pray about. He tells them that their reflections will be personal and private and that they should get comfortable so that they can both hear and reflect on the questions without falling asleep!

Once they are ready, he tells the group that he will read the petition once, followed by silence. Then he will read the petition a second time. After the second reading, he tells them he will be silent for 30 seconds, during which they are invited simply to consider the petition at its face value. He concludes by telling them that after the 30 seconds of silence he will lead them through a guided reflection.

He reads the first petition: "That, like the woman of Samaria, the elect may review their lives before Christ and acknowledge their sins." He pauses for a few moments, repeats the petition, and tells those gathered to listen to the petition in their heart and their head. They sit silently for about 30 seconds. Then Father Dan reads the reflection based on the petition from the "Preparation Guide for the First Scrutiny" (see Appendix 10). When he finishes reading it he invites them to be silent for two minutes and call to mind their sins. They sit in silence for two full minutes and then he moves to the second petition, following the same procedure as given for the first petition until he has worked through all the petitions and reflections.

About 40 minutes after they began the guided reflection, they are finished. The entire session lasted a little less than an hour. Father Dan thanks everyone for coming, reminds Teresa's sponsor, Phyllis, to stay after the session for a few minutes, ends with a prayer and tells everyone to drive carefully as they return to their homes. As the participants make their way to their cars, Father Dan and Phyllis walk next door to the church. He takes about 10 minutes to explain the logistics for the rite of scrutiny they will celebrate at the 10:00 Mass on Sunday morning. He tells her that the other two scrutiny celebrations are exactly the same as the first and that therefore there will be no need for further rehearsals until they do the walk-through for the Easter Vigil.

The parishioners will be invited to join Teresa, the Burnetts and their sponsors for the next two Friday evenings to go through the guided reflections for the remaining scrutiny rites. They will follow the models found in Appendixes 11 and 12. The next Friday there are about 20 parishioners present for the reflection session, and the following Friday there are about 15. Father Dan tells the parishioners and the Burnetts that these reflections are an excellent way to prepare for the sacrament of reconciliation.

The parish will not celebrate the penitential rite for the Burnetts. There are several reasons for this decision. First, there is only one Mass at St. Al's.

Father Dan thinks it will be overwhelming to spend four Sundays in a row celebrating both the penitential rite and the three scrutiny rites. He believes the guided reflection and the three scrutiny rites will provide ample opportunities for the Burnetts to prepare for the sacrament of reconciliation. He also knows that the Burnetts will attend the parish lenten penance service and that it will include a penitential rite. Since the penitential rite is optional, he decides in light of the circumstances in the parish to omit it. In the future, if there are candidates but no elect, or if he is in a parish with multiple weekend Masses, he will schedule a celebration of the penitential rite during one of the Sundays of Lent.

Analysis of the Preparation Session

Getting rural people to speak openly about sin, especially their own, is very difficult. Nevertheless, Father Dan wants the lenten season to be a time for his parishioners to think about their sins so that God's grace may help them to repent of them and they may experience the grace of forgiveness. Having the good fortune of an elect in the parish, he decides to invite the parishioners to participate with Teresa in the preparation session for each scrutiny rite. He chooses a time when parishioners will already be at the parish (since many come from several miles away) to schedule this preparation session. Tying it to a traditional event in Lent that attracts parishioners makes it possible for more parishioners to participate in the preparation session.

In designing the session, Father Dan turns to the intercessions of the scrutiny rites. He figures that it might be beneficial for both the elect and the baptized not only to hear the intercessions before the actual celebration of the rite but also to reflect on the meaning of those intercessions, since reflection does not come as quickly to oral people as it might for those who live life daily in the midst of literate culture where reflection is more commonplace.

Turning to the intercessions that are assigned for the first scrutiny, he selects a few that can be connected explicitly with the gospel. He does this because he knows that rural people will enjoy the story-like nature of the gospel. He also knows that if he can connect the intercessions to the scripture passage, they will be more likely to remember the intercessions and connect them to their own lives. He develops some reflection questions to go with these intercessions, tying them explicitly to the gospel to reinforce their impact (see "Preparation Guide for the First Scrutiny," Appendix 10). Because of the importance rural people place on relationship with God and the power of God, the pastor tries to frame some of the reflection questions in such a way that they may use the occasion to strengthen their relationship with God or to invoke God for help.

Because rural people are not generally open to an explicit discussion on sin in a public setting, Father Dan has decided that the preparation session will be more private than conversational in style. The participants will not be sharing their thoughts with each other, nor will they be writing anything down on a piece of paper. To do so would guarantee fewer participants at future reflection sessions, which is something Father Dan wants to avoid.

The Celebration of the First Scrutiny at St. Al's

Phyllis meets Teresa at the doors of the church on the morning of the Third Sunday of Lent, and they go to their regular place in the assembly. The Burnetts take their places in the pews with the Schneiders. The parishioners hear the familiar story of the Samaritan woman at the well, and Father Dan gives a strong homily on how sin parches one's life and how the grace of God's forgiveness replenishes it. He then tells the assembly that they will be celebrating a scrutiny rite today (and the next two Sundays) in order to help Teresa prepare for baptism. He tells them that the rite will help Teresa become aware not only of sin but also of the love of God. He concludes by telling them that as the baptized their responsibility is to pray for Teresa and for all the elect throughout the world who are preparing for baptism.

Having finished his remarks, Father Dan invites Teresa to come forward with her sponsor, Phyllis. Phyllis leads Teresa to the front of the church to the foot of the sanctuary. Father Dan, standing between them and the altar, invites everyone to pray in silence that Teresa will not only become aware of her sins but more importantly be given a spirit of repentance that will help her as she prepares to be baptized in the waters of forgiveness. Father Dan asks Phyllis to place her hand on Teresa's shoulder, and then invites the assembly to bow their heads in silence for about a minute. Then Father Dan invites the lector to read the intercessions taken from the rite.[14] At the end of the intercessions, Father Dan prays the prayer of exorcism (RCIA, 154b), addressing the first part of the prayer to God the Father. At the conclusion of the prayer, he approaches Teresa and lays hands on her in silence. Following this, he concludes the prayer, addressing the third part of the prayer to Jesus. Teresa is invited to stand; Phyllis helps her up. They are invited to return to their places in the body of the church since Teresa will not be dismissed. The Mass continues with the preparation of the gifts.[15]

Analysis of the Rite of Scrutiny from the Oral Perspective

The rite of scrutiny is very simple and straightforward. Following the homily, the rite consists of four elements: an invitation to silent prayer, intercessions for the elect, the prayer of exorcism and dismissal (recommended but optional). Wisely, Father Dan took a few moments to explain the rite and the assembly's role in it before beginning. It has been a couple of years since the parish had an adult preparing for baptism. The pastor knows that rural people are more uncomfortable with change in their liturgy than their urban counterparts, so he explains the rite and their role in it in order to help them embrace it more readily.

He is aware of a practice common in cities and suburbs in which the intercessions are sometimes replaced with a list of sins that are recited or sung in litany style. He knows that this kind of explicit naming of sins will generate much distress among his rural parishioners, so he wisely avoids this adaptation and stays with the intercessions provided by the ritual text. He reviews these texts and selects from the options provided, carefully changing a word here or there to make the prayer more accessible to his parishioners.

Because of the power of story in oral culture and the nature of the scrutiny gospel, he divides the parts of the gospel and invites a few lectors to join him in its proclamation so that it comes across more story-like. He is also careful to connect his homily to the gospel and to tie it to the rite so that Teresa and the parishioners will see more clearly the connections between the gospel and the rite in light of Lent.

Mystagogical Catechesis on the First Scrutiny

The parish has chosen to omit refreshments after Mass as part of their lenten discipline, but the adult parishioners are invited to the parish hall for a lenten series of adult education sessions on the Ten Commandments. Teresa, Joan and their sponsors go with Alice to the pastor's home for a reflection on the rite that was just celebrated. After they settle in at the kitchen table, Alice tells them they are going to spend a few minutes reflecting on the rite they just celebrated in the church.

Alice asks the women to close their eyes for a few moments. When they are quiet, she asks them to remember the ceremony they just celebrated in the church and tells them she will give them a minute to recall it. At the conclusion of this quiet time, Alice says, "What do you remember?" Then quickly she adds, "It's all right if you remember something that was not particularly pleasant."

Joan speaks first. She remembers everyone bowing their heads while Teresa knelt. She says that she felt united with Teresa in the time of silence. She went on to say that as the intercessions were being read she remembered some of the sins she thought about during the preparation session and how she needed to pray for John, her non-practicing Catholic husband. Teresa speaks next and tells everyone she was very nervous going up to the front of the church because she didn't know what was going to happen. She looks at Phyllis and tells her she was particularly happy that she was beside her the whole time and felt okay once Phyllis placed her hand on her shoulder. She tells them that she really felt the presence of the community praying with and for her and that when Father Dan placed his hands on top of her head, it felt like God was touching her.

Pauline also comments on the intercessions and says how glad she was that she had gone to the Friday night session to reflect on them. She says that she felt she was really asking God to help her with her sins and difficulties during the intercessions. Alice comments on the connection between the gospel story, the homily and the ritual and recalls a couple of places where the images of the woman at the well, water, sin and forgiveness kept coming together.

As they finish their recollections, Alice asks them what this ritual said about sin. Phyllis says that sin is real and that it can turn us into dry, parched people. She says, as an aside, that she knows a few people who strike her as dried up. Alice asks her why she thinks they're dried up. Phyllis sits quietly for a few moments and then says that in one situation it's because of bitterness and in another it's because of resentment. Alice quickly asks Phyllis what she thinks these people and anyone else who is dried up need in order to be refreshed. Phyllis says that she thinks they need what the Samaritan woman needed: someone to be their friend and perhaps a kick in the pants! The group chuckles at this response. Alice asks Phyllis if God might be calling her to be a friend of one of these people. Phyllis looks at Alice, purses her lips just a little and says, "Probably."

Alice then smiles and says that this may be how grace is meant to work for those who are dried up. God send gifts of refreshment through people, a kind word, friendship, generosity, acceptance, so that people will not become permanently dried up. God does not want us to live like parched, dried up people. So God sends us his love like the water he sent to the Jewish people in the desert that they heard about in the first reading, like the water that Jesus gave the Samaritan woman. Alice continues to explain the gift of grace that God continually sends into the midst of sin, noting how they experienced it in the liturgy through the gospel story they heard, the good news Father Dan preached about forgiveness, their praying together the scrutiny rite. She also noted that God might be calling them to share this grace with others, especially those who are dried up for whatever reason.

Alice refers to the laying on of hands that Teresa recalled. She tells the group that Teresa was being scrutinized during the rite, not by the parishioners and Father Dan but by God. She then recalls the exorcism prayer and tells them it has three parts: the first part addressed to God the Father, the second to the Holy Spirit and the third to Jesus. She tells them that when Father Dan laid his hands on Teresa's head, he was calling down the Holy Spirit upon her. She continues by saying that the Trinity was scrutinizing Teresa to help loosen any sin in her life so that it might more easily be washed away in the waters of baptism.

Alice takes a few minutes to speak a little more about the reality of sin and grace, reminding them that while becoming aware of sin is a part—sometimes a painful part—of the process of repentance, God's offer of forgiveness is more important. Teresa responds by telling the group that she became aware during the preparation session of the fact that she has allowed other things and people to substitute for God. She says that when she became aware of it, she felt badly, but that when Father Dan laid his hands on her head, she felt God's understanding and forgiveness. Alice confirms this and says that she will receive this forgiveness in the waters of baptism.

As they bring their session to a close, Alice reminds them of the preparation session on Friday evening for the next scrutiny rite and passes out her famous index cards with an Act of Contrition she has typed on it from the rite of penance. They pray the prayer together and, after a few minutes of informal conversation, they leave for home.

Analysis of the Mystagogical Catechesis Session

Alice has again used a simple format to help the group recall and reflect on the rite they just celebrated. She invited them to remember the liturgy by sitting quietly for a minute and then asked them to describe their memory, giving them permission to describe an unpleasant memory if one emerged during their recollection. This permission is important because sometimes people have some unpleasant experiences as they remember the reality of sin in their lives. Having permission to remember may help someone to talk about it as part of the process of healing and forgiveness. Usually this will not be discussed during the session. If the rural elect (and others involved in the mystagogical reflection) sense that the catechist is trustworthy, they may summon the courage to speak privately to him or her about the unpleasant memory.

The group collectively remembers most of the significant points and figures out their significance. Alice has a master list of points that might be covered and mentally checks them off as the conversation unfolds. The points are as follows:

- reality of sin

- God always offers grace to us: forgiveness, healing, liberation

- the community prays and supports the elect

- the Holy Trinity scrutinizes

- the word of God teaches us about sin and grace

- the community intercedes to God for help.

As the group explores these issues based on their experience of them in the rite, Alice adds a comment here or there to embellish the point, as was the case in explaining how the Holy Trinity scrutinizes in this rite. She will use the same format for all three scrutiny rites. Alice is careful not to get too personal regarding sin, whether it is the sin of a member of the group or someone outside of it. If someone mentions a sin (for example, bitterness, resentment, substituting God with people or things), she listens and then invites them to consider how God's grace might be bringing something good out of it. By doing this, she connect the person to grace without ignoring the sin but also without intimidating the sinner.

THE PRESENTATION RITES

Joe and Maria have learned a lot more about each other and what married life will probably be like during their pre-marriage program. Particularly important has been the discussion between them and their pastor about the theology of Christian marriage and the insights they have gained from the Hendersons. In a similar way, the elect receive the Creed and the Lord's Prayer as they enter the final weeks of preparation for initiation. These texts express the "heart of the church's faith and prayer"[16] and are normally presented during the period of purification and enlightenment because it is the belief of the church that the elect are now ready to be entrusted with these important texts that encapsulate the essential beliefs of Christianity.

These two texts contain the essential elements of the Christian tradition. Tradition is lived in people and written down on paper. When it comes time for the elect to receive the Creed and the Lord's Prayer, the rite says that they are to be presented verbally. In oral culture, this will be particularly important. Sometimes parishes have handed on the creed and the Lord's Prayer by presenting a scroll containing these words during the rite. Nowhere in the rite is this indicated. Perhaps at the reflection session following each presentation rite a scroll or plaque containing the words of the creed and the Lord's Prayer may be given to the elect for further reflection, but not during the presentation rite itself.

Some have wondered if it might ever be appropriate to present the creed and the Lord's Prayer to those already baptized. National Statute 31 clearly says that only those candidates who have received no Christian instruction or formation prior to beginning the parish initiation process may celebrate these rites. If they do, the texts of the prayers in the rites will need to be expanded to reflect the presence of baptized candidates in the rite (for example, RCIA, 161 and 182). Teresa and the Burnett children are qualified to participate in these rites. Joan has had some formation as a child baptized and formed in the Methodist tradition until she was approximately 10 years old. She would be omitted from these celebrations but could certainly participate in the mystagogical catechesis that follows.

Celebrating the Presentation of the Lord's Prayer at St. Al's

On Tuesday of the First Week of Lent, the church assigns the Lord's Prayer (Matthew 6:7–15) as the gospel of the day. During the Tuesdays of Lent, St. Al's celebrates the eucharistic liturgy at 6:30 in the evening as part of its lenten Mass schedule. Teresa, Keith and Sue are invited to this Mass. Their sponsors arrive a little early to receive a brief instruction on the logistics of the rite. Unlike Sunday Mass, they sit in the front pew on the ambo side of the church, with each sponsor sitting beside their candidate. The Mass proceeds as normal. At the time of the gospel, Father Dan proclaims the Lord's Prayer as prescribed for that day. Before he proclaims the text, he invites the sponsors to place their hand on the shoulder of the person they are sponsoring. After the proclamation, all are seated and Father Dan gives an extended homily on the importance of prayer and the Lord's Prayer as a model for all prayer. After the homily, he invites everyone to stand and invites the sponsors to place their hands once again on the shoulders of those they are sponsoring. He then prays the text of paragraph 182 of the RCIA with a brief modification for Keith and Sue, who are baptized.[17] They remain for the rest of Mass.

Mystagogical Catechesis on the Presentation of the Lord's Prayer

Teresa, the Burnetts and their sponsors adjourn to the pastor's home with Father Dan, who will guide their reflection session. After they are settled in, the pastor invites them to take a few moments in silence to remember the liturgy they just experienced. They sit quietly for about a minute. Father Dan asks them what they remember about the celebration. Teresa speaks first and mentions that she never realized that the Lord's Prayer is found in Matthew's gospel. She then says that she appreciated Father Dan's emphasis on prayer as a conversation between God and the person praying, and how important it was to listen. She mentioned that this is an area where she needs to grow because she does most of the talking during prayer. Joan mentions that she heard the Lord's Prayer in a way she had never heard it before. She comments on the part of the prayer that asks God to forgive the person praying the prayer in the same way the person praying the prayer forgives others. She mentions that made her feel a little uneasy because she has prayed those words without realizing what she was saying.

Father Dan takes the opportunity to comment on how important it is to mean what you pray. He asks them if they can say the Lord's Prayer. Teresa, Keith and Sue answer affirmatively since they have been exposed to it for many months during Mass at St. Al's. Joan and the sponsors indicate that they have known it for many years. He asks them to go over the prayer together, line by line, so that they may further reflect on what the prayer is saying. He hands out a piece of paper with the Lord's Prayer printed in seven sections on it. He asks them to read the first part aloud, which they do.

"Our Father, who art in heaven, hallowed be thy name." Father Dan asks them what they think this line of the Lord's Prayer is saying. Sue answers that it is saying that God is in heaven and when she prays to God, she is praying to God who lives in heaven. Keith asks what the word *hallowed* means. Jim Schneider tells him it means "holy" and that the prayer says that we believe God is holy and therefore his name is holy and should always be used with great respect. Father Dan agrees and says that is what the second commandment is teaching when it says that we should never use God's name in a bad way. Father Dan also mentions that, by using the expression "Our Father," Jesus was saying two things: 1) that Jesus has a very close relationship with God and 2) that we share in that relationship. Father Dan tells them that if we translated the actual word Jesus used to address God it would be "Daddy." He says that this is a term we use only with our own fathers and that it is a term of love. Second, the fact that Jesus teaches his followers to refer to his "Daddy" as theirs also means that Jesus wants us to have a loving relationship with God just as he does. The pastor invites the group to say the line together.

Father Dan asks Keith to pray the next line: "Thy kingdom come." The pastor asks what they think this line is saying. Teresa suggests that it is asking God to bring his heavenly kingdom to earth. Father Dan asks what that kingdom would look like and how it would be different from the kingdoms on earth. Teresa says that there would be no more war and that everyone would live in harmony. Father Dan affirms her answer and asks the group to describe other ways the world would look differently if God's kingdom were present on earth. Louis Schneider says that there would be no more hunger in the world, and Ralph, his brother, says there would be no more sickness. Others offer images of the world and people where everyone is happy. Father Dan asks them to repeat the line together.

Father Dan asks Sue to read the next part of the prayer: "Thy will be done on earth as it is in heaven." He asks what they think this is saying. They are quiet for a few moments and then Phyllis says that it is asking God to help us do his will in the same way the saints and angels do God's will in heaven. Father Dan affirms this insight and asks why someone might ask God for this favor. Phyllis responds by suggesting that people don't always know what God's will is. She tells them about a time when she had to make a decision about her widowed mother who was no longer able to take care of herself and live in her home alone. Phyllis says that as the oldest child, she felt it was her responsibility to figure out what to do and that she was afraid she would do the wrong thing. So she asked God to help her know what his will was for her mother. She then discussed it with her siblings and remembered her brother telling her that the will of God was in the fourth commandment: Honor your mother and father. Phyllis concludes by saying that when her brother said this, she knew that God's will was for her mother to stay in her home and for one of her siblings to move in with her because that would be the best way to honor her mother. Fortunately, Phyllis' youngest sister was newly married and not yet settled into a new home. So Phyllis asked her mother and then her sister and brother-in-law about living in the family home. They agreed and now live together. Father Dan thanks Phyllis for her story and asks the group to repeat the line together.

Father Dan asks Ralph to read the next line: "Give us this day our daily bread." Again they are asked to consider what this petition is asking of God. Joan is the first to respond. She tells the group she heard a radio evangelist speak about this scripture passage one day and that she still remembers what he said. She says that he spoke about the request for daily bread as a request for God to provide those in need with the necessities of life. He told his listeners that in Jesus' day many people lived day to day and did not always know where their next meal was coming from. So the prayer was a request to God that the person praying be given what he or she needed to survive. She concludes by saying that she thinks the petition is asking her to trust that God will provide for her daily needs. The group spends a little time discussing what would be some contemporary examples of "daily bread." Pauline says that some days she thinks it might be patience, especially when her boys are being rowdy. The adults concur and Father Dan asks everyone to repeat the line from the prayer.

Father Dan invites Louis to read the next line: "And forgive us our trespasses as we forgive those who trespass against us." The pastor asks what trespass means. Louis responds that he has seen "No Trespassing" signs on the fences of some of his neighbors and knows that it means not to enter, and that if you do you can get into big trouble. He goes on to say that he thinks a trespass is doing something wrong that can get you into big trouble. Louis' father congratulates him on his answer. Father Dan then asks what the petition might be saying. Joan thinks it is asking God to forgive us when we do something wrong in the same way we forgive others when they do something wrong to us.

This generates a lot of discussion about the different situations in which someone can do something wrong and how difficult it is to forgive. Father Dan simply notes that Jesus forgave our sins on the cross while we were still sinners and recalled the part in the scriptures where Jesus forgives his executioners at the time of his crucifixion. The group agrees that this is a difficult petition. They repeat the petition together as they move to the next one.

Teresa is invited to offer the next petition. She reads, "And lead us not into temptation." Father Dan asks what a temptation is. Keith says it's when he comes home from school and finds that his mother has left a tray of freshly baked chocolate chip cookies on the kitchen counter with no one guarding them! Father Dan reminds them of the gospel from last Sunday in which Jesus is tempted by the devil. He tells them that Jesus was tempted, just like we're all tempted. He goes on to say that Jesus was able to resist the temptation. He tells them that the petitioners are asking God to protect them from temptation, and that when they are faced with temptation that they will not be faced with one that is too big for them to handle. They repeat the petition together.

Finally, Joan is asked to read the last petition: "But deliver us from evil." Father Dan asks if any of them have been in a bad situation that was not their fault. The group becomes quiet. Father Dan tells them a personal story. He tells them about a time when he was falsely blamed for stealing a pupil's watch when he was in high school and got into big trouble because of it. No matter what he said, no one believed him. He was punished by his father, put on restriction, and could not try out for the school wrestling team. It was the worst thing he ever had to endure. For six months he felt like a dark cloud was hanging over him. One day the student whose watch had disappeared came up to him and told him that he had found the watch in his gym locker and apologized for accusing him of stealing it from the bench where they were both changing clothes after gym class. The boy told the gym teacher and the principal, and Father Dan was exonerated. He said that he felt the dark cloud lift from him that day. He concludes by saying that this was an experience of evil in his life. It wasn't anyone's fault, but he still suffered. He then says that Jesus is teaching us that evil will sometimes come our way and that this petition is asking God to deliver us from evil when we are in the midst of it and when it looms ahead of us in the future. They repeat the final petition.

Father Dan asks the group to join together in praying the entire prayer slowly. They all pray the prayer. He gives them a nice scroll with the prayer on it and asks them to pray the prayer daily and spend some time thinking about the different petitions and what they mean. He tells them that Teresa, Keith and Sue will have the creed presented to them at Mass next Sunday in a simple ceremony. He tells Joan that she is excused from this ritual because of her upbringing in a denomination that professes the same creed. The sponsors are asked to be in church by 9:30 on Sunday morning for a brief rehearsal. The session ends and everyone departs for home.

Analysis of the Mystagogical Session

Father Dan uses stories and examples to illustrate his points and keeps the participants engaged by asking them to uncover the meaning of the Lord's Prayer by reflecting on the individual petitions. The session may unfold in several directions. This description takes the seven petitions and uses them as a springboard for conversation and reflection.

Celebrating the Presentation of the Creed at St. Al's

On the Second Sunday of Lent, those sponsoring Teresa, Keith and Sue arrive at the church at 9:30 in the morning. Father Dan briefly rehearses the rite they will celebrate at the morning Mass. Around 9:45 Teresa and the Burnetts arrive and are greeted by their sponsors. They sit in their regular places in the body of the church. Before Mass begins, Father Dan announces that there will be a short ritual celebrated after the homily for Teresa, Keith and Sue. He encourages the parishioners' enthusiastic response because they will be presenting the creed to these three today. The Mass begins in the usual way.

At the end of the homily, Father Dan explains that the heart of the Christian faith is expressed in the creed, and that for many months Teresa, Keith and Sue have been learning about these essentials of the faith. He tells the people that since these three will be celebrating the sacraments of initiation in a few weeks, they are ready to be entrusted with the creed and to reflect upon it in the coming weeks in preparation for the Easter Vigil when they will profess their belief in these essential teachings of the Christian faith. He reminds the assembly that they will join him in handing over the creed by standing and professing it with him in the presence of Teresa, Keith and Sue. He mentions that Joan will not celebrate this rite but will remain in the pews with the parishioners because she was baptized and raised in a denomination that professes the same creedal faith. Having made these remarks, he invites the three forward with their sponsors.

They take their places at the front of the church as Father Dan walks out into the main aisle and faces the three. He invites their sponsors to place their hands on their candidates' shoulders. He then addresses the three, using the words of RCIA, 160. As he concludes, he turns to the assembly, asks them to rise, and invites them to join him in presenting the creed to Teresa, Keith and Sue. Together they recite the Nicene Creed. At the end of the recitation, Father Dan prays over the three, slightly modifying the prayer contained in paragraph 161 of the RCIA in order to include Keith and Sue, who are baptized.[18] They are invited back to their pews and the Mass continues as usual. At the end of the Mass, the group heads over to the parish rectory, because refreshments are not offered during Lent.

Analysis of the Celebration of the Presentation of the Creed

Father Dan wisely offers a brief introduction on the ritual both before the Mass begins and immediately before the ritual is celebrated. Because the parishioners hand on the creed as part of the rite, Father Dan knows that it is important for them to understand both what they are doing and how they are to do it. He explains why Joan is omitted from the rite so that everyone may understand another common bond that exists between Catholicism and Methodism. Because the parishioners join with Father Dan in presenting the creed, he invites the three to face the entire assembly so that the handing over of the creed may be a more dynamic and convincing experience of faith for both the three who celebrate the rite and the assembly.

Mystagogical Catechesis on the Presentation of the Creed

As they had on the previous Tuesday evening, Teresa, the Burnetts and their sponsors go to the rectory after the conclusion of the Mass. Alice serves coffee and fruit juice as everyone spends a few minutes catching up on news and visiting with each other. When everyone seems ready, Alice invites everyone into the living room of the rectory for the catechetical session.

As she always does whenever there is an initiation ritual, she invites everyone to take a moment to become still. Then she asks everyone to take a few moments to remember the Mass they just concluded, especially the special rite after the homily. She gives them a minute and then asks them what struck them about the liturgy. Two things emerge. First, all three comment on the faces of the people and Father Dan as they were reciting the creed. Keith noticed that a few people were not saying the words, while Teresa noticed the warmth in the faces of several people. The second thing that is noticed is how the words of the creed are heard in a new way. Teresa observes that she has been hearing these words weekly for many months and that she has even begun to say the words silently to herself on Sunday. There was something different about the words today. They almost seemed alive to her. Alice smiles and tells her that the words were quite alive today because the words were given specifically to her and to the two children by a living community. She comments on the fact that the creed is a series of words that convey deep truths about the Christian faith, but unless they are believed by living people, they remain only words. She explains that the people in the pews, including Joan, handed something living to them. She said it is like the difference between seeing something in a catalogue and having it in your own hand. The picture is not as good as the real thing. In the same way, the words of the creed are valuable, but they become more valuable through the people who believe and profess those words.

She reminds them of Father Dan's words about their readiness to receive the creed because of their readiness for the sacraments of initiation. She says that there is more to this ritual than receiving a set of beliefs from a community. She tells them that they must be ready to profess their own belief in these words and be prepared to live by these words for the rest of their lives. She mentions that on the Saturday before Easter they will gather for a morning of reflection, and that on that day they will be asked to recite the creed in a small ceremony. She passes out a scroll on which is written the creed and tells them to spend the next few weeks reading, learning and remembering these words. She concludes by telling them that at the Easter Vigil they will profess their faith with this creed before they receive the sacraments of initiation.

Alice asks them if they have any questions they would like to ask about the creed during their time together. She gives them a few moments to look over the text and then asks them to read it aloud slowly with her. They do so. Following this recitation, she again asks if they have any questions. Teresa asks about the words, "begotten, not made." Alice tells the group this means that Jesus, although born in Bethlehem over 2,000 years ago, lived before he was born of Mary. In fact, the expression "begotten, not made" means two things: 1) that Jesus has lived forever, as long as God has lived, which is also forever, and 2) that Jesus was not created by God and is not inferior to God. Jesus has always existed. He came in human form when he was born of Mary, but before his human birth he existed with God and the Holy Spirit in heaven.

Joan expresses some curiosity about the phrase, "one, holy, catholic, and apostolic church." She remembers saying these words as a child in her Methodist church and wonders what the words mean, especially "catholic." Alice describes each word for a few minutes. She begins with the word "one." She tells the group that it is Christ's will that the church be one, just as Christ and God are one with each other. Using the image of a human person, she says that it is Christ's will that all Christians form one body with him as the head of the body. She tells them that the body has many different parts and that the parts don't do the same things. For example, the hands don't do the same thing as the stomach, but they are still part of one body. In the same way, Christ wants the entire Christian church to be united. She tells them that this is one of the reasons that Joan does not need to receive the creed. Her denomination, although separated from the Catholic church, believes in the same value of unity. She says that this is the hope of the Catholic church: that one day all the denominations will be reunited and that the Christian faith will be one.

Alice says that professing the church as "holy" means that God is at its heart. In this way, the church is always holy because God is always with the church. Alice notes, however, that the people are called to be holy, too.

She notes that, unfortunately, the people who make up the church are also sinners and that the church is always calling its members to pursue holiness so that the world will see by the holiness of the people the holiness of God.

The word *catholic* means "universal," Alice tells them. It is intended to describe the fact that the Christian church is meant to exist throughout the entire world over the course of human history since the time of Pentecost, when the church was born. She tells them that although they are separated in many ways, many of the Protestant denominations continue to use the term "catholic" in their creed to express the universality of the Christian faith despite the fact that the denominations are not united.

Finally, she tells them that the word "apostolic" means that the church is founded on the apostles and that the tradition handed down by the apostles continues to be handed down by the bishops, like Bishop Reese, who are successors of the apostles.

The group continues to chat about a few other parts of the creed. Alice concludes by telling them that the creed has been around since the year 325 and that a simpler version, the Apostles' Creed, has been around even longer. She tells them that when they recite the creed they join with millions of people who, over the course of almost 1,900 years, have professed their faith using these words. This impresses Keith.

As the session comes to a close, she asks them once again to recite the creed as a group. Slowly Alice leads them in the recitation. She especially commends Teresa, Keith and Sue to study and learn the text over the next few weeks. She asks Joan to help Keith and Sue. Alice tells them that there is another ceremony the next Sunday and that the preparation for it will be on Friday evening following the stations of the cross and the lenten soup supper. She asks if everyone can make it; all say they can. They end with a prayer and leave for their homes.

Analysis of the Catechetical Session

Alice remembers that rural people and children are not terribly interested in theological terms as they attempt to understand their faith. So she wisely avoids technical and "churchy" words that might seem strange to them. She uses the image of a product in a catalogue and the real thing to emphasis the difference between the tenets of faith printed on a piece of paper and lived faith based on those tenets. She uses the image of a body to help the group understand the concept of "one" in the four marks of the Christian faith. She shows ecumenical sensitivity as she describes "catholic" and makes the term "apostolic" real by using Bishop Reese as an example. Lastly, she makes the point that the creed is rooted to the past and that professing it today connects us to the past, something important for rural people.

Notes

[1] RCIA, 138.

[2] See RCIA, 139, 141 and 142, for a description of the scrutiny rites for both purification and enlightenment.

[3] See RCIA, 147– 149, for a description of the enlightenment these two presentations are meant to provide and National Statute #31 for a description of those baptized candidates who might be eligible to participate in these presentations and the circumstances that might suggest their participation in these two rites.

[4] What follows in this section is based on both training I have received and reading I have done on these topics. Some of the sources for this information have become blurred over time and I apologize to anyone whose work I may inadvertently omit crediting. Specific comments on sin are largely based on the Apostolic Letter of Pope John Paul II from the Synod on Reconciliation held in 1983 and synthesized for presentation by the Reverend Robert Duggan of the archdiocese of Washington. The comments on grace are largely my own but have taken shape through stories I received through the generosity of the Reverend John Durbin, a priest of the diocese of Raleigh, and extensive conversations with Joanna Case.

[5] Mary Fisher, *Sleep with the Angels,* Wakefield, Rhode Island: Moyer Bell Ltd., 1994, pp. 92–96.

[6] This story is credited to William McConville, OFM.

[7] Mary Fisher, *Sleep with the Angels,* 1994, pp. 92–96.

[8] RCIA, 20.

[9] RCIA, 141.

[10] Ibid.

[11] RCIA, 143.

[12] Ibid.

[13] RCIA, 146.

[14] RCIA, 153b.

[15] RCIA, 156, allows for the profession of faith and the prayers of the faithful to be omitted.

[16] RCIA, 147.

[17] Which will be required if National Statute 31 is used to justify the participation of people such as Keith and Sue in this rite.

[18] Ibid.

Chapter 7

The Easter Vigil: Celebrating the Sacraments of Initiation

This chapter will explore:

- how to prepare the elect and candidates spiritually for initiation using the preparation rites on Holy Saturday

- how to celebrate the initiation liturgy of the Easter Vigil, especially baptism by immersion, in a rural-friendly manner

- how to conduct a mystagogical catechesis on the sacraments of initiation.

The last weekend in April has arrived. On the evening before their wedding, Joe and Maria, accompanied by the wedding party, gather at the church for a rehearsal that will be followed by a dinner at the home of Joe's relatives. When everyone has arrived for the rehearsal, Father John asks those present to introduce themselves and to offer a wish, hope or dream for the couple, if they would like to. Several people respond to that invitation. One person wishes Joe and Maria a happy life as a couple while another hopes they will have many children! The matron of honor prays that they will always be best friends and will never go to bed angry at each other. Joe and Maria are quite moved by what they hear from their friends and relatives. Father John invites everyone to pray, asking God to bless not only this couple but all who will gather for this wonderful occasion.

Having completed the preliminaries for the rehearsal, Father John conducts a brief rehearsal for the wedding party so they'll know approximately where to stand and how to move as the celebration unfolds the next afternoon. At the conclusion of the rehearsal, he invites questions about the ceremony and asks those gathered for the rehearsal to enjoy their evening but not to celebrate excessively so that they may come to the wedding the next day able to participate fully in it.

Boy meets girl/ First dates	Commitment to go steady	Building the relationship Meeting the family Learning the traditions	Engagement	Pre-Cana/ Marriage prep	**Wedding**	Honeymoon/ First year of marriage
Precatechumenate	Rite of Acceptance into Order of Catechumens	Catechumenate	Rite of Election	Purification and enlightenment	**Sacraments of initiation**	Mystagogy

After the rehearsal, everyone proceeds to the home of Joe's Aunt Martha and Uncle David, where a bountiful meal has been prepared. Joe and Maria's families have already arrived by the time the couple gets there. Extra tables have been set up to accommodate everyone. Uncle David offers a blessing, and the father of the groom makes a toast. Then the meal begins! There is much conversation and laughter as they enjoy the evening. The traditional clinking of glasses occurs from time to time and subsides only when Joe and Maria kiss. Stories are told, more toasts are offered. As the evening concludes, Joe's mother Patricia offers a traditional blessing that has been in the groom's mother's family for several generations.

Joe arises the next morning and spends a little time in prayer as the day begins. He thanks God for bringing Maria into his life and asks God both to bless Maria and him and to help the day go smoothly. Maria also says a short prayer as she begins her day and then spends the next few hours getting ready for the wedding.

The wedding party and the groom arrive at the church about 45 minutes before the wedding. The guests arrive soon thereafter. A few minutes before noon, Maria arrives with her matron of honor and is escorted to the parish hall until it is time to begin the liturgy. At the appointed time, Maria's brother escorts her to the church and the procession begins. Down the aisle walk the groomsmen, the ring bearer, the best man and Joe, accompanied by his parents. Following them are the bridesmaids, the flower girl, the matron of honor and Maria, accompanied by her mother and brother. Once everyone is in place, the liturgy begins.

After the homily, Father John invites the couple with the best man and matron of honor to come to the front of the sanctuary, where Maria and Joe exchange their promises and rings. Joe and Maria receive the nuptial blessing and all exchange the sign of peace. Father John then concludes the liturgy, the couple kiss, and they walk down the aisle to begin their lives as husband and wife.

They go off to the Ruritan Hall for their reception, hosted by both families. There is much eating, drinking, dancing, toasting and storytelling, followed by the cutting of the cake and the first dance. It is a wonderful celebration that goes on for several hours. At the end of the reception, the couple returns to Joe's home to change clothes and then depart for their honeymoon in St. Louis.

A Harvest for God: Christian Initiation in the Rural and Small-Town Parish

INTRODUCTION TO THE CELEBRATION OF THE SACRAMENT OF INITIATION

The big moment has finally arrived for Teresa and the Burnetts. The Easter Triduum, the most important liturgical season of the year, has arrived. This is the annual commemoration of Christ's passion, death and resurrection, the heart of the entire Christian life, the event that forever changed the world.

The Triduum begins on the evening of Holy Thursday with the Mass of the Lord's Supper and extends until the evening of Easter Sunday. It may be understood as one liturgy spread out over three days.[1] Note that the Mass of the Lord's Supper does not conclude with a final blessing and dismissal, nor does the service of the Lord's Passion on Good Friday have a formal beginning or ending. The Easter Vigil does not have a normal beginning either. These three liturgies almost look as though they could be one liturgy with long pauses between them.

The culmination of the Triduum is the Easter Vigil, in which the sacraments of initiation are celebrated. Teresa will be washed in the waters of redemption, pardoned for her sins and adopted as a daughter of God during this liturgy. She and the Burnetts will be sealed by the Holy Spirit in Confirmation and welcomed to the eucharistic table for the first time.

While the heart of the Triduum is the Easter Vigil, it seems obvious that Teresa and the Burnetts should participate in the entire liturgical celebration of the season, beginning with the Mass of the Lord's Supper on Thursday evening. Father Dan is responsible for two church communities, St. Aloysius in Clarkville and St. Elizabeth in Bolton, some 12 miles away. It is the custom of these two parishes to share the liturgies of the Triduum. Traditionally, the Mass of the Lord's Supper is celebrated at St. Elizabeth's while the service of the Lord's Passion on Friday is celebrated at St. Al's. The parish with an adult to baptize hosts the Easter Vigil; when both have adults to baptize, the one with the most to be both baptized and received into full communion hosts the liturgy. This year, St. Al's will host the Easter Vigil because there are no adults being baptized at St. Elizabeth's.

The wedding liturgy is a peak moment for Joe and Maria. For Teresa and the Burnetts, the Triduum, culminating in the celebration of the sacraments of initiation at the Easter Vigil, is the moment they have awaited for many months. At their wedding, God will establish a marital covenant with this couple, and Joe and Maria will covenant themselves to God and to each other, establishing a bond that ends only in death. At the Easter Vigil, God will establish a baptismal covenant with Teresa, and Teresa will covenant herself to God, establishing a bond that never ends. In the same liturgy, the Burnetts and all the baptized present will reaffirm their baptismal bond.

The evening before their wedding, Joe and Maria come to the church to make final preparations. Their pastor conducts a rehearsal with those who will help them celebrate. Included in this rehearsal is prayer. At the rehearsal dinner is prayer, including a blessing offered by the parents at the end of the meal. On Saturday morning, both Joe and Maria pray as they start the day on which they will actually be married. In a similar way, Bill and Alice Smith invite Teresa, the Burnetts, the candidate from St. Elizabeth's and their sponsors to a morning of spiritual preparation on Holy Saturday. They used the ritual text (RCIA, 185–205) to shape the morning.

After they are initiated, Teresa and the Burnetts will be invited to continue the celebration through a reception in the parish hall. Later that week, they will gather to recall and reflect on the events of the Triduum, especially those celebrated at the Easter Vigil. Like Joe and Maria's wedding, the sacramental celebration of initiation will spill over into the events that follow afterwards, especially in the reception. As Joe and Maria will remember the highlights of their wedding while on their honeymoon, so too will the newly initiated take time to remember their initiation and continue the celebration.

SOME OBSERVATIONS ABOUT THE SACRED TRIDUUM IN RURAL COMMUNITIES

Increasingly, rural parishes share a sacramental minister. The pastor of one parish presides over the sacramental life of another. Sometimes permanent deacons, religious sisters or brothers, or other qualified lay people serve as pastoral leaders of these communities. Some describe these parishes as "yoked," and once in a while a joint celebration of some important occasion is recommended. The Sacred Triduum might be one such occasion. When there are people to initiate from more than one of these yoked parishes, a joint Easter Vigil may be celebrated. Occasionally, it is difficult or impossible for someone who is to be initiated to go to another parish for the Easter Vigil to celebrate sacramental initiation. Age, infirmity, distance, weather or even great discomfort with celebrating such a significant event in one's life in a strange building in the midst of unfamiliar people might merit the celebration of the sacraments of initiation on Easter Sunday or another Sunday in the Easter season.[2]

Because the Easter Vigil is the most important liturgical celebration of the year, every reasonable effort should be made to initiate at this liturgy. The other ritual elements of the Vigil, such as the fire that scatters the darkness of the night, the lighting of the paschal candle and the tapers held by the assembly, the Exsultet, the special readings and blessing of the water are powerful elements of the Vigil that contribute to the solemnity of this liturgy and its effect on the lives of those being initiated. When someone cannot be initiated at the Easter Vigil, everything should be done to make the initiation as significant as it would have been if it had occurred at the Easter Vigil.

PREPARING TO CELEBRATE THE SACRAMENTS OF INITIATION AT ST. AL'S

Bill and Alice Smith have invited Teresa, the Burnetts, Joseph Preston (the candidate from St. Elizabeth's) and their sponsors to a morning of reflection on Holy Saturday at St. Al's. Father Dan has graciously invited them to use his home for this occasion. As always, Alice has brought a little something for the group to drink but has not brought food to eat because the

A Harvest for God: Christian Initiation in the Rural and Small-Town Parish

elect and adult candidates are trying to observe a fast as part of their spiritual preparation.[3] After some time for the group to get acquainted with Joseph and his sponsor, the Smiths invite everyone to the living room. When everyone is settled, Alice tells a story.

> Several years ago I went on a trip with Bill to Washington, D.C. We had a wonderful time visiting the White House, the Capitol and all the monuments and museums. On our way back, we decided to visit Luray Caverns in the mountains of Virginia. The caverns were quite beautiful, and our tour guide told us some fascinating things about caverns. When we got to the deepest part of the cavern, the tour guide told us she wanted to give us a demonstration of how dark it is when there is absolutely no light. With that, she slowly began to turn down the amount of light provided by the many light bulbs placed throughout the large cavern in which we were standing.
>
> Suddenly, she turned off all the lights and we were in complete darkness. It was truly frightening. I had never been in such darkness in my whole life and began feeling very afraid. To make it worse, the tour guide imagined aloud what it must have been like for cave explorers who lost their source of light. I shivered to think of it. Just when I thought I might scream for the lights to be put back on, the tour guide lit a match. It was the most wonderful sight I've ever seen; I was amazed how much light it cast throughout the cavern. The tour guide told us that in total darkness, one match could cast a lot of light. She then turned the lights back on and guided us back to the surface. I was very happy to see the sun!

Alice then looked at everyone and asked them if they've ever had an experience of being in the dark and being afraid. All the children shook their heads up and down vigorously. Alice simply noted that in the Easter Vigil liturgy they will begin in the darkness of night near a bonfire and that they should pay attention to the way light is used in the ceremony.

Next, Alice tells them about a friend of hers who became very ill, was taken to the hospital and nearly died. She tells them this man could not take a bath or even be bathed because he was so ill. After nearly 20 days, he was finally strong enough to take a shower. A male nurse helped him into the shower, seated him on a shower stool, and turned on the water. The nurse said the man shouted in ecstasy as the water cascaded over his body and cried tears of joy. After his shower, the man told the nurse that he was never so glad to be clean as he was that day. He went on to say that he felt as though he was encrusted with death as he lingered near death's door and that the shower gave him his first real sense of hope that he might live. She concludes the story by telling them that this is what dying with Christ in the waters of baptism is all about and asks Teresa to remember this as she enters the waters later that night. She then turns to the others and suggests that they consider how they have been washed clean in their own baptism and how they will recommit themselves to live as cleansed people in the liturgy.

Next, Alice picks up the lectionary on the coffee table and asks Bill to read a pre-selected passage from it. Before he begins, Alice asks the group to picture the story in their minds as Bill reads the passage. Bill reads the first reading for the Fourth Sunday of Lent (Year A) about the anointing of David by Samuel (1 Samuel 16:1, 6–7, 10–13). When he has finished reading the text, he places the lectionary back on the table. Alice asks the group to describe the picture they have in their minds of David being anointed. Joe, the candidate from St. Elizabeth's, describes a teenager having oil poured over his head, and Teresa describes David's brothers and father watching this strange event happening in front of them.

Alice briefly describes what anointing was like in David's time and how anointing meant that David was chosen by God to become the next leader of the Jewish people. She tells Teresa and the candidates that they will be anointed with perfumed oil as part of the evening liturgy and encourages them to pay attention to everything going on around and within them as they are anointed with this special oil in the sacrament of confirmation.

She turns to the children and asks them to sit still for a few moments and think of one of the best meals they ever had in their lives. They are quiet for a short time, and then Keith speaks. He recalls going to his grandmother's home for Thanksgiving one year and describes in great detail all the wonderful foods that she served. Sue describes her eighth birthday party, where they had all her favorite foods and desserts. The Schneider boys recall their favorite meals, and even the adults get into describing a memorable meal. As they finish telling their stories, Alice tells them that at the end of the Easter Vigil ceremony they will all receive holy communion for the first time. She tells them that as happy as they were about their favorite meal, so their souls will be happy about this spiritual food they will receive tonight. She adds that, unlike a special meal that happens only once in a great while, this special meal is something they can receive every time they come to Mass beginning tonight.

After they have spent some time with these stories, Alice tells them that what they have done is to prepare for the wonderful experiences they will have tonight at the Easter Vigil. She refuses to give them more details about the liturgy but tells them to keep alert for all the ways their senses will be engaged during the ceremony. She tells them that Father Dan will pour some perfumed oil on the top of their heads and will rub some of it on their faces when he anoints them. She also tells them that they will be the first to receive holy communion, and that they should come forward when their sponsors indicate it is time to receive. She briefly shows them how to receive communion reverently. Alice then tells them that they will walk over to the church to see where the baptism will occur and Teresa will be shown where she will go to change her clothes after the baptism. Finally, she tells the sponsors that they will remain in the church for a brief rehearsal.

Having concluded her preparation session, Alice tells the group that they are going to have a short ceremony in the living room so that Teresa, Keith and Sue may return the creed they were given a few weeks earlier. The three have been preparing for this ceremony so they are not surprised by the announcement. Alice has been deputed to serve as a catechist by Bishop

Reese, so she will preside at this liturgy[4] since Father Dan is unavailable. A pamphlet with the order of worship is passed around to everyone.[5] After an opening song and greeting, Bill reads a passage from the Bible (1 Peter 1:17–21). Alice then offers a brief explanation of the text, noting that is was a primitive form of a profession of faith containing the basic beliefs of the early Christian community. At the conclusion of her comments, she invites Teresa, Keith and Sue to rise. She offers the prayer before the recitation (RCIA, 195) with a brief addition to the text to include the candidates and then asks the three to recite the creed. When they have completed the recitation, Alice prays the prayer of blessing (RCIA, 204). She adds a few words to this prayer asking God to bless the candidates also.

After the liturgy concludes, they clean up the living room and kitchen and adjourn to the church. Teresa and her sponsor are shown where the baptism will take place and where Teresa will go to change her clothes. Teresa receives an index card with a list of things, like a comb and a pocket mirror, to bring to the room where she will change clothes. Teresa and the candidates are reminded of their requested arrival time, shown where they will sit, and then excused. Bill takes the sponsors through a brief rehearsal so they will be more comfortable with the various parts of the initiation ritual. Remaining questions are answered and all leave for their homes to make their final preparations for the big night.

Analysis of the Preparation Session

As she has done in preparation for the other rites, Alice has gathered the elect, candidates and their sponsors in order to prepare them for the liturgy. As noted earlier, rural people find the unknown difficult, so Alice acquaints them with the rite by engaging them in storytelling around four components of the rite: light, water, oil and meal. The stories come from a variety of sources: Some are personal stories of the children, some are from Alice's personal life, and one is from scripture. She wisely focuses on stories of natural elements with which all can identify. She provides a few tips for them to remember as they experience the various rites and symbols of the liturgy to help them experience their initiation as fully as possible.

She has Teresa and the two children return the creed in preparation for the vigil liturgy. This is an especially important ritual for rural people because it provides them with an opportunity to recite the creed among friends and in an informal manner before they must profess their faith publicly and officially in front of a community of worshipers.

CELEBRATION OF THE EASTER VIGIL AT ST. AL'S

All have gathered outside the church, around the bonfire that lights up the evening sky. Before the liturgy begins, Teresa, the candidates and their sponsors show their guests where they will sit in the church once everyone comes inside and then lead them outside to meet those gathered around the fire. There is an air of excitement as all await the beginning of the liturgy. Father

Dan and the other ministers arrive from the church. He asks parishioners to introduce any guests they have brought and for visitors to identify themselves. Members of Teresa's family are acknowledged, as are the parishioners from St. Elizabeth's. Keith announces that his father John is present, and Joan identifies her parents as guests. Father Dan formally welcomes Joseph Preston, his family and his sponsor. He expresses his appreciation to the people of St. Elizabeth's who have come over for the liturgy and asks the people to greet those around them. Once all are greeted, Father Dan begins the liturgy by blessing the paschal candle and lighting it. From it, the tapers in the hands of the people are lit and the pastor intones, "Christ our Light," to which the people respond, "Thanks be to God." The procession of light moves towards the front doors of the church. At the doors, Father Dan again intones, "Christ our Light," to which the people respond, "Thanks be to God." All enter the church. Teresa, the Burnetts, Joe Preston, their sponsors and guests take their places in the midst of the assembly. Keith and Sue are fascinated by the faces that glow from the candlelight in the dark church. The Exsultet is sung and everyone is seated to hear the scripture readings and sing the responsorial psalms. The Gloria is sung, during which the servers turn on all the lights of the church and ring bells. They hear the passage from Romans, and then all rise to sing a glorious "Alleluia." The gospel follows and all are seated for the homily. Father Dan has chosen to do a story homily. It follows below:

> Centuries ago, it was known far and wide that a certain tribal leader was the greatest in all the tribes. When power was measured by proving superior physical strength, the most powerful tribe of all was the one that had the strongest leader.

> But this tribal leader was also known for his wisdom. In order to help his people live safely and peacefully, he carefully put laws into place guiding every aspect of tribal life. The leader enforced these laws strictly and had long ago acquired a reputation for uncompromising justice.

> In spite of the laws, there were problems. One day it came to the leader's attention that someone in the tribe was stealing. He called the people together and, with great sadness because of his love for them, said, "You know that the laws are for your protection, to help you live safely and in peace. This stealing must stop. We all have what we need. The penalty has been increased from 10 to 20 lashes from the whip for the person caught stealing."

> But the thefts continued. So the leader called the people together again and said, "Please, hear me. This must stop. It hurts us all and makes us feel badly about each other. The penalty has been increased to 30 lashes."

Still, the stealing continued. The leader gathered the people once more. "Please, I'm begging you. For *your* sake, this has to stop. The pain it is causing among us is too great. The penalty has been increased to 40 lashes from the whip."

The people knew of their leader's great love for them, but only the closet to him saw the single tear make its way slowly down his face as he dismissed the gathering. Finally, a man came to say the thief had been caught. The word had spread. Everyone had gathered to see who it was.

A single gasp raced through the crowd as the thief emerged between two guards. The tribal leader's face fell in shock and grief. The thief was his very own mother, old and frail.

"What will he do?" the people wondered aloud. Would he uphold the law or would his love for his mother win over it? The people waited, talking quietly, collectively holding their breath.

Finally, the leader spoke. "My beloved people." His voice broke. In little more than a whisper he continued, "It is for our safety and our peace. There must be 40 lashes; the pain this crime has caused is too great." With his nod, the guards led his mother forward. One gently removed her robe to expose a bony and crooked back. The appointed man stepped forward and began to unwind the whip.

At the same moment, the leader stepped forward and removed his robe as well, exposing his broad shoulders, seasoned and solid. Tenderly, he wrapped his arms around his mother, shielding her with his own body. He whispered gently against her cheek as his tears blended with hers. He nodded once more, and the whip came down again and again.

A single moment, yet in it love and justice found an eternal harmony.[6]

Father Dan pauses for a moment and then quotes the lines from the letter to the Romans:

Christ, while we were still helpless, died at the appointed time for the ungodly. Indeed, only with difficulty does one person die for a just person, though perhaps for a good person one might even find courage to die. But God proves his love for us in that while we were still sinners Christ died for us.[7]

He concludes by saying the following:

Tonight we celebrate the truth that the death and resurrection of Jesus have brought us into that eternal harmony of love and justice. Teresa will be baptized into that eternal harmony in a few minutes and the rest of us will be invited both to remember the price Christ paid to bring about that eternal harmony and to recommit ourselves to living as people of love and justice. May the eternal harmony we touch in these waters this evening truly make a difference in our lives and in the lives of those we meet.

After the homily, Father Dan invites Teresa to come to the baptismal pool with her sponsor. It is a portable water trough used for livestock. To look at it, though, one would think it was an indoor pool. It is decorated with flowers and discreetly covered in white cloth. The Litany of the Saints is sung, and then Father Dan blesses the water in the pool with the paschal candle. Once the water is blessed, he asks Teresa to make a renunciation of sin and a profession of faith. She is invited to face west (just as candidates for baptism did in ancient times) to reject sin. After doing so, she is invited to face east, the place from which the first light of dawn comes and from where Christ will appear at the end of time, to profess her faith. After these professions, Father Dan invites her to step into the pool. With Phyllis to help her, she steps into the pool, kneels down, and is gently but firmly pushed completely into the water three times while Father Dan baptizes her in the name of the Father, and of the Son and of the Holy Spirit. When she arises after the third immersion, the people sing an "Alleluia" while Phyllis wraps a large white towel around her. A white baptismal gown and a candle lighted from the paschal candle are presented to Teresa and Phyllis takes her away to dry off and change clothes.

As Teresa leaves with Phyllis, Father Dan invites the Burnetts and Joe Preston to come to the font with their sponsors. He then invites the community to stand. Together they renounce sin and profess their faith facing east and west as Teresa did. Then the pastor invites everyone to come to the baptismal pool to bless themselves with the holy water.[8] The organist and cantor lead the people in a song while they bless themselves. When everyone has been blessed, Joan and Joseph are invited to the front of the sanctuary with their sponsors.[9] Father Dan explains to the community that these two are about to come into full communion with the Catholic church. In a gesture of ecumenical sensitivity, he acknowledges their churches of baptism and expresses his gratitude to those who have shaped their Christian faith in these denominations. After explaining to the candidates what they are about to do and inviting their sponsors to place their hands on their candidate's shoulder, he asks them to make a profession of faith in the Catholic church. The two have memorized the two-line profession and individually proclaim it in a loud voice. After receiving their profession, Father Dan officially receives them into the full communion of the Catholic church.[10] Immediately after this, Teresa, who has changed into her white baptismal robe and is standing with her lit candle in hand, is invited to join Joan and Joseph in the front of the sanctuary. She and her sponsor come forward. Then Keith and Sue with their sponsors are invited forward so that all five may be confirmed.[11]

Father Dan addresses the community briefly, explaining why Keith and Sue are being confirmed at this time. After this explanation, he addresses the confirmation candidates and then lays hands on their heads in silence. After this laying on of hands, he stretches out his hands over the candidates and prays the prayer of confirmation (RCIA, 590). Then he invites the sponsors to place their hand on the shoulder of the candidate they are sponsoring, and he anoints them with chrism. He pours some on their heads, smears some of it on their faces, and then makes the sign of the cross on their foreheads as he says, "N., be sealed with the gift of the Holy Spirit." He then embraces them and says, "Peace be with you." After they are confirmed, they are invited to return to their places.

The liturgy of the eucharist follows. The five bring the bread, wine, collection and gifts for the poor to the altar. When the time comes for them to receive holy communion, each comes forward with his or her sponsor to receive communion under both kinds. Again, the sponsors place their hand on the shoulder of their candidate as they receive the body and blood of Christ. The community waits until all five have received and then comes forward. After the prayer after communion, Father Dan makes a few announcements. He invites everyone to a reception in honor of the newly initiated and asks the community to offer their congratulations. The people stand and offer an enthusiastic round of applause. The newly initiated smile broadly, and the sponsors spontaneously embrace their candidates. The liturgy concludes with a traditional Easter hymn, and a lavish reception follows in the parish hall.

Analysis of the Easter Vigil Celebration

Father Dan has used the combined rite of initiation (RCIA, 566–594) that incorporates into one celebration those to be baptized (Teresa), those coming into full communion (Joan and Joseph), and those baptized but formerly uncatechized Catholics who are completing their reception of the sacraments of initiation (Keith and Sue). Had there been no one to baptize, he would have used the rite of reception of baptized Christians into the full communion of the Catholic church (RCIA, 473–498), and he would have invited Keith and Sue to come forward after Joan and Joseph had been received into full communion. It should be noted that when there is no one to baptize at the Easter Vigil, it is preferable that the reception of candidates into full communion take place at another time, although it appears to be commonplace in rural communities to initiate them into full communion at this time if candidates are ready.[12]

A review of this celebration will show several ritual moments in which a choice was made that was sensitive to both a community and a group of initiates who view and live life as oral people. It has already been noted that stories, symbols and traditions are especially important to rural people. This liturgy is rich in all these dimensions. Father Dan used a story as the basis of his homily. The readings, especially from Genesis and Exodus, have a story-like character to them and should be proclaimed in this manner to the extent that the lector(s) can do so. The symbols are powerful in this liturgy.

Light and darkness, water, white garments, oil, bread and wine, gesture, and music are major symbols in this celebration. This is why a large bonfire, a large paschal candle, baptism by immersion, a full-length white alb, oil placed on more than just the forehead, real bread (using approved recipes) and wine for everyone, laying on of hands (rather than simply their extension over the candidates) for confirmation, and simple refrains that are easily repeated by an assembly at prayer are recommended for this liturgy. People who live close to nature will appreciate the natural symbols used in this celebration. The Easter Vigil is very ancient in its structure. In a rural setting, it will be particularly important that this celebration be experienced in a similar manner from year to year so that a sense of tradition becomes attached to it.

In selecting his homily, Father Dan's choice was motivated by the fact that compassion motivates rural people more than knowledge. So, rather than preaching about the paschal mystery, he illustrates it with a story filled with compassion. Because of the importance of relationship and family, Father Dan and the parishioners made sure that all were welcomed before the liturgy began and that ecumenical sensitivity was considered during the celebration in light of the fact that several people were present for the celebration from other denominations. The ministry of hospitality and the reception are important bridges for rural people, who connect the relationships that exist before and after worship with the relationship they experience during worship. Not to welcome guests before the liturgy—or worse, to have no reception after the Easter Vigil for the newly initiated—would be a serious oversight in the eyes of rural people.

Rural people prefer a liturgy that is more oral and less "printy." While it might be more common for candidates from urban and suburban settings to read their profession of faith from a card during the liturgy of reception, indigenous rural people generally prefer to profess their faith by memorizing the two-line text or by responding "I do" to the profession presented in the form of a question by the priest. Refrains and responses made by the community using simple, call/response or repeat-after-me styles encourage fuller participation and stronger responses by rural people.

The pool was a plastic water trough used by farm livestock. It is relatively inexpensive and portable. It can be nicely decorated and is deep enough for someone to be baptized by immersion in it. It will also be an object with which people in a rural farming setting can relate. It should be used exclusively for baptisms and located in a place where the weight of the water can be sustained. Placing very hot water into the pool just before the liturgy begins usually ensures that it is at a tolerable temperature when it is time to baptize. This requires some organization, but the benefits are worthwhile.

Mystagogical Catechesis on the Celebration of the Sacraments of Initiation at St. Al's

Easter Sunday is a very important day in rural communities. Many people go to church and enjoy a special meal together, frequently in the afternoon. It was agreed several weeks earlier that the newly initiated and their sponsors would gather at the Smiths' home on Sunday evening for some food and conversation. There is no school on Monday so the children have no homework. As always, Alice has food galore for everyone to eat, and Joan has brought an Easter basket filled with goodies as a gift from her family to the Smiths.

When they finally sit down in the living room after the meal, Alice passes out a sheet of paper with an Easter hymn to the well-known melody of "Ode to Joy" by Beethoven. The group sings the song and at its conclusion Alice invites everyone to sit quietly as she recalls the previous evening's liturgy. She notes the bonfire and the people gathered around it, the lighting of the paschal candle and of the tapers. She sings, "Christ our Light," and everyone responds, "Thanks be to God." She notes the Exsultet, the readings and the Gloria with bells clanging and lights going on. They sing the Alleluia and Alice recalls the story of the tribal chief embracing his mother. She sings a few of the saints' names, to which they respond, "Pray for us." She recalls everyone facing west to denounce sin and facing east to profess faith. She describes Teresa's baptism, everyone coming to the pool to bless themselves, Joan and Joe being received into full communion and the lavish anointing with chrism. She recalls the reception of holy communion, the applause of the community and the wonderful reception.

When she is finished she pauses and then asks them, "As you remember the Easter Vigil, what memories stand out for you?" Teresa is the first to speak and describes her experience of being baptized. She tells them she felt totally cleansed, that when she emerged from the waters she felt as though all her sins were washed away. Keith jokingly says that she looked like a drowned animal. They all laugh, and Teresa says that she did feel as though she was drowning once when Father Dan held her down under the water a little longer than she expected. Alice asks Teresa if she felt as though she had died to sin as Bishop Reese has exhorted her to do at the rite of election. Teresa agreed. Alice then looked to the others and asked if anyone wanted to comment on their renewal of baptismal promises with the rejection of sin, profession of faith and blessing with the holy water at the baptismal pool.

Pauline spoke first and said that she liked facing east and west because it seemed to give more emphasis to her "I do." Alice reminded them of Bishop Reese's comments to the baptized at the rite of election about making a deeper commitment to Christ. She exhorted them to remember that their response of "I do" means they are serious about deepening this commitment. Alice speaks a few words about covenant and tells them that what they celebrated last night was a liturgy of promise making, and that Teresa and God entered into a covenant that will never end. Alice then tells the others that they recommitted themselves to living the covenant they entered at their baptism in a deeper way.

Alice asks for other memories. Phyllis comments on the image of the tribal leader with his mother that Father Dan described in his homily. She says she could see her elderly mother shielded by her brother Frank, who is quite large and strong. She goes on to say that the image really struck her as an image of Christ embracing all the sinners for whom he died. She says it reminded her how much she is loved by Christ.

Sue wants to talk about confirmation. She mentions that the oil smelled wonderful and that she can still smell it in her hair. Keith remembers the laying on of hands and how it felt as though he was receiving power as Father Dan placed his hands on top of his head. Teresa comments on the anointing as well and says she knows what King David must have felt like when he was anointed by Samuel.

Alice speaks to them of the Holy Spirit and how the Spirit, as the third person of the Holy Trinity, is the perpetual presence of God among us. She tells them that in confirmation they have been marked by God and are God's anointed children. She tells them that the word *Christ* means "anointed" and that through confirmation they are now to be like Christ in the way they live. She concludes by telling them that to help them be Christlike they have received the gift of the Holy Spirit, who will be with them the rest of their lives to help them in their efforts to be like Christ.

Alice then asks them about holy communion. They all make comments about it. Teresa comments that she fasted on Saturday and was hungry when she arrived for the Easter Vigil. She says this hunger reminded her of Alice's comments about the soul being hungry for the eucharist and that she was amazed how good the bread and wine tasted. Joan says that the reception of holy communion was the highlight for her. She tells the group she has watched with a little envy those who have gone forward to receive holy communion week after week at St. Al's and says she was especially happy that she can finally receive the body and blood of Christ. She tells the group that she went to the 10:00 Mass earlier that morning because she wanted to receive the eucharist again.

Alice comments briefly on the eucharist. She reiterates that it is another gift from God to help them remain faithful to the covenant they established with God in baptism. She tells them that God understands how easily people can lose their enthusiasm for living the often-difficult Christian lifestyle. To help them, God gives them the very gift of his Son, present in the consecrated bread and wine, to strengthen them. She mentions how important food and drink are to the human body. Without them, people become steadily weaker and eventually die. She tells them that in the same way their souls become weaker without spiritual nourishment and then encourages them to receive the eucharist regularly, at least once a week.

She then asks them if they remember the foot washing ceremony at St. Elizabeth's on Thursday evening. They all remember it. She takes a few minutes to explain the connection between the Last Supper and the foot washing ceremony in John's gospel and the reception of holy communion and service for today's Christians. She tells them that receiving holy communion commits them to serving others, just as Jesus served his followers by washing their feet after the Last Supper. She tells them that over the next few weeks they will be reflecting more deeply on how they see themselves serving others in light of the fact that they can now receive holy communion.

As they continue their conversation, Keith comments on the bonfire and the candles. Sue remembers the bells and all the lights going on in the church when the people began to sing the Gloria. Joan expresses gratitude for the kind way her parents were welcomed to the church, the kind words made about her Methodist baptism, and the presence of her husband John at the liturgy. Teresa says she really felt like she belonged when she heard the applause at the end of the Mass. The others agreed. Alice confirmed that they indeed belong to the Catholic faith, especially after all they have been through to reach Easter Sunday.

Alice then tells Teresa and Joan that they will meet with Father Dan in his home for the next seven Sundays after the fellowship hour to reflect on their lives as Catholic Christians. Their discussion will last about an hour. She then tells Pauline and her children that they will meet with Keith and Sue at the same time in the living room of Father Dan's house, so that they too may continue to learn about their new life as fully initiated Catholic Christians.

Alice asks everyone to stand up and together they sing the "Alleluia" they sang during Easter Vigil. They exchange a few more words with each other and then return home.

Analysis of the Mystagogical Session

As she had done in earlier mystagogical sessions, Alice took a few moments to recall the main elements of the Easter Vigil liturgy. Doing this helped to jar their memories and bring back into focus a very complex rite. The participants remembered a great deal about the liturgy, and Alice used some of their comments as a springboard to offer some deeper insights about various parts of the liturgy, especially the key elements of baptism, confirmation and holy eucharist. The conversation was informal, used memory and incorporated some music from the liturgy.

Alice gave a brief explanation, which was called a "mystagogical catechesis" in the early church, on the important meaning of the sacraments of initiation as part of the session. She kept the explanation simple, basically restricting herself to one or two key ideas per sacrament.

Alice confirms their relationship with the community. Because relationship is so important for rural people, she also emphasizes that through their initiation they are now fully members of the Catholic Christian faith and the community of St. Al's.

She had a mental checklist of points to cover but found that the group remembered most of them. Her list follows below:

- darkness and light: paschal candle, tapers, church in darkness

- stories of faith/homily: scripture stories of salvation, paschal faith

- the saints: communion of saints present for baptism

- renunciation of sin, profession of faith: facing east and west to symbolize commitment

- baptism by immersion: dying in the waters of sin and death and rising to eternal life

- renewing baptismal promises at the baptismal pool for baptized: rededication to Christ and baptismal covenant

- profession of faith in the Catholic tradition for candidates for full communion

- confirmation: chrism, laying on of hands conferring gift of the Holy Spirit

- holy eucharist: receiving the body and blood of Christ for spiritual nourishment

- holy eucharist: spiritual nourishment for Christian service to others

- community: initiation makes one a member of the church, both universal and local.

Notes

[1]It would appear as though the Paschal Triduum lasts four days as one normally counts the days of the week (Thursday to Sunday). However, as is the case with marking time for Sunday (sunset of Saturday until sunset of Sunday, as the Sabbath is counted in Judaism), the Triduum is only three days since it begins with sunset on Thursday and concludes with sunset of Sunday (Day One: Thursday sunset to Friday sunset; Day Two: Friday sunset to Saturday sunset; and Day Three: Saturday sunset to Sunday sunset). *Triduum* means "the three days."

[2]RCIA, 26, allows for this adaptation while clearly stating that the Easter Vigil is the preferred and normal time to celebrate sacramental initiation with unbaptized adults and children of catechetical age.

[3]RCIA, 185, recommends that the elect (and by extension the candidates) observe a fast on Holy Saturday. This is a fast of anticipation and not of penitence.

[4]RCIA, 16, explains that catechists may be deputed by a bishop to preside over some of the minor rites of initiation. Among the rituals designated in RCIA, 193–205, only the Ephphetha rite (RCIA, 197–199) appears restricted to priests or deacons. If the presentation of the Lord's Prayer occurs on this occasion, the presider for this rite is a priest or deacon (see RCIA, 178–184) because the Lord's Prayer is presented in the proclamation of the gospel.

[5]A model for a service is found in RCIA, 187–192.

[6]John MacArthur, heard on his radio program, "Grace to You," June 10, 1990.

[7]Romans 5:6–8.

[8]RCIA, 583, indicates that the celebrant sprinkles all the people at this time. However, to allow more time for Teresa to dry off and change her clothes, Father Dan has invited the people to come out of the pews and bless themselves at the baptismal pool.

[9]RCIA, 584, indicates that the newly baptized join those who are to come into full communion in the sanctuary at this time. Experience shows that the newly baptized are often not finished dressing by this time. Consequently, Father Dan moves to the celebration of reception for Joan and Joseph so that the people in the body of the church are not made to wait for Teresa. If she is ready by the time the reception into full communion is to occur, she should be invited to join the candidates in the sanctuary for this portion of the liturgy.

[10]RCIA, 585, indicates that the candidates for full communion say the words of the profession of faith in the Catholic church. In a rural community, there may be some wisdom in having the presider present the profession of faith in the form of a question to which the candidates respond, "I do."

[11]The only time confirmation is omitted is when a candidate has already been confirmed in the Orthodox church, in an Eastern rite of the Catholic church (for example, Maronite rite, Ukrainian rite), or in a church with legitimate apostolic succession (for example, Polish National Church, Old Catholic Church). Those belonging to an Eastern rite of the Catholic church do not make a profession of faith because they are already members of the Catholic faith. Orthodox Christians become members of an equivalent Eastern rite (for example, Greek Orthodox become Greek Catholic) when they make a profession of faith.

[12]National Statute 33 legislates this preference. If candidates are ready for reception into full communion when the Easter Vigil is celebrated and there is no one to baptize, it is permissible to welcome then at the Easter Vigil. In light of the solemnity of the Easter Vigil, the reception should not appear to be triumphalist.

Chapter 8

The Period of Mystagogy

This chapter will explore:

- maintaining attendance for catechetical sessions between the Easter Vigil and Pentecost

- what to do during this 50 day period of time in a rural or small-town setting

- bringing the new Catholic Christians together on a monthly basis between Pentecost and their first anniversary of baptism or reception into full communion.

Now comes the end of the formal initiation process but what is for the newly initiated the beginning of their life as Catholic Christians. To continue with the marriage analogy, this phase may be likened to both the honeymoon period of newlyweds and the experiences of their first year of marriage. Joe and Maria are on an emotional high from their wedding. They have returned from the wedding reception to Joe's house where they will live as husband and wife. With bags packed, they drove to St. Louis, where they would spend their honeymoon. In the car, Maria sat next to Joe and kissed him on the cheek from time to time, saying, "We're married!"

When they arrived in St. Louis, they checked into a riverfront hotel. A little later, they went out to dinner and took a stroll on the River Walk along the Mississippi River. During dinner and their walk, they talked about the wedding and the reception, recounting the highlights. Both spoke about how they felt as they were saying their vows to each other and laughed as they recalled the frustrated best man who couldn't get the rings off the ring bearer's pillow. Joe commented how beautiful Maria looked as she came down the aisle with her mother and brother escorting her. They laughed as they remembered feeding each other cake and how Maria ended up with

Boy meets girl/ First dates	Commitment to go steady	Building the relationship Meeting the family Learning the traditions	Engagement	Pre-Cana/ Marriage prep	Wedding	**Honeymoon/ First year of marriage**
Precatechumenate	Rite of Acceptance into Order of Catechumens	Catechumenate	Rite of Election	Purification and enlightenment	Sacraments of initiation	**Mystagogy**

a frosting mustache. Maria got teary-eyed as she remembered the touching toast offered by her brother. They returned to their room and spent their first night together as husband and wife.

The next day they continued to reminisce. After breakfast, they went to the old cathedral near the Arch for Mass. They loved the architecture of the building and noted that the priest wasn't quite as good a homilist as Father Dan. The music, however, was much better! Later, back in their room, they remembered their first dance. Maria teased Joe about having two left feet. Joe remembered how nervous his mother was at the rehearsal and how Father Dan was able to calm her down. Joe turned on the radio in the room and asked Maria to dance with "Left-foot Louie." As they danced, it was as if they were back to the local Ruritan Club Hall where they had their reception.

After their honeymoon, they returned to Oakville to begin their life as a married couple. Now they would begin to explore the real implications of married life. Their conjugal life was rich and fulfilling, and Joe was learning how important it was to Maria that they spend some time cuddling and holding each other as an expression of their love. Living life together under one roof with only one bathroom was more of a challenge! Joe was a bit of a slob in the bathroom, and Maria was on him about cleaning up after himself before long. Maria was pleasantly surprised to learn that Joe could and liked to cook. Maria hogged the blankets, and Joe liked to wear his socks a day longer than he should. Compromises loomed on the horizon! They had their first sharp words with each other when Joe came home very late from work one evening and dinner was ruined.

They had much to figure out: who would buy the groceries, who would pay the bills, and who would clean up the house! They had to set up a joint bank account and adjust to the fact that Joe was a morning person while Maria was a night person. They enjoyed looking at their wedding pictures, recalling the wonderful people and events associated with their important day. Maria made sure they celebrated their first week anniversary, first month anniversary, six-month anniversary and so forth. Bob and Martha Henderson invited them over to their home regularly and enjoyed watching this newly married couple grow and adjust to each other, and they occasionally passed on some of the wisdom they had learned from their thirty years of marriage. About 10 months into their marriage, Maria discovered she was pregnant. They rejoiced that God would bless them with a child, and they spent a lot of time pondering what adjustments they would have to make once their baby was born.

THE FIFTY DAYS

The period of mystagogy is to the celebration of the sacraments of initiation what the honeymoon period (the first weeks and months of married life) is to the wedding. It is an opportunity to experience over a brief but extended period of time (50 days) the incredible love of God (grace) continually poured out in the liturgical/sacramental life and to begin exploring life as Catholic Christians.

Threefold Objective of Mystagogy

At the time of their initiation, Teresa, Joan and her children experienced the love of God at a very profound level. Now they are invited to experience that perpetually available grace in the liturgical/sacramental life, to ponder the purpose of the gift of grace given to them in the sacraments, and to consider how they can share that grace with others in the life of discipleship. To facilitate these three objectives during this 50-day period between Easter and Pentecost, the ritual text of Christian initiation offers some guidelines (RCIA, 244–251).

The diagram below may help visualize the objectives of the period of mystagogy.

God's grace is experienced in the course of the liturgy itself, during the catechetical session that follows, and in the day-to-day life of the newly initiated disciple. An explanation of these objectives and how they are used during the mystagogy period to manifest God's grace, using the Third Sunday of Easter, Year A, follows.

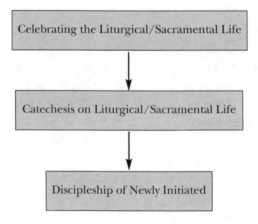

The Eucharistic Liturgies of the Easter Season

On the Third Sunday of Easter, the gospels for all three years have a eucharistic focus. In Year A, the Emmaus story is featured. Father Dan has decided to preach on the connection between the eucharist and discipleship in light of the response by the Emmaus disciples after recognizing Jesus in the breaking of the bread. He looks at the music list provided by the organist and sees that the recessional hymn emphasizes the same connection between eucharist and discipleship. He reviews the general intercessions provided through a subscription the parish has with a publisher of liturgical aids. He sees two petitions that explicitly connect eucharist to discipleship. This will also be First Communion Sunday for the three grade school children in the parish. He notes that his homily will need some examples of discipleship appropriate to young children. He writes a story about a young Catholic girl who befriends a new immigrant Hispanic girl in her class and helps her with her homework. He will use this story in his homily.

The parish gathers at 10:00 on Sunday morning for the liturgy. The celebration unfolds fairly smoothly. The people know the hymns, the lectors are prepared, the families of the three first communicants are in their places before the Mass begins, and the three children are ready to walk in the entrance procession. Father Dan tells the story of the young Anglo girl who helps the new immigrant girl in her class. He speaks about the importance of being a disciple of Jesus and then explains, using St. Augustine's famous saying ("Become what you eat"), how the reception of holy communion obligates us to be disciples. He connects these points to the gospel story in which the Emmaus disciples go tell the others about Jesus' resurrection after they recognized him in the breaking of the bread. The rest of the Mass unfolds nicely, with the three first communicants bringing up the gifts and receiving holy communion at the front of the sanctuary with their families gathered around them. They sing the closing song and proceed to the parish hall for a reception in honor of the three grade school children and their families.

Mystagogy Session Using the Liturgy-Catechesis-Discipleship Dynamic

Thirty minutes after the fellowship hour began, Teresa, Joan and Phyllis met with Father Dan in the kitchen of his home for their catechetical session. This conversation lasted about 45 minutes. While they were speaking with Father Dan, Joan's children were spending time with Pauline and her children talking about the eucharist in the pastor's living room.

Father Dan had placed an open lectionary on the kitchen table with a candle and a copy of the recessional hymn before Teresa, Joan and Phyllis arrived. They began with some informal conversation, catching up on the latest family news and events. When everyone seemed ready to begin, Father Dan lit the candle and invited the three women to be still for a few moments and to remember the Mass they had just celebrated in the church. After an appropriate period of silence he asked them to describe something they remembered and what it expressed to them.

Teresa mentioned the joy she experienced watching the three children receive holy communion for the first time and how that triggered the memory of her first reception of the eucharist only two weeks earlier. It reminded her how wonderful she felt knowing that Jesus was so close to her. Joan also spoke about the first communicants and how they reminded her of her children who recently received the eucharist for the first time. Phyllis said she was struck by the saying of St. Augustine about being the body of Christ for others because we have received the body of Christ. This connection between receiving holy communion and discipleship was a new insight for her. Father Dan said he was struck by the way the musical selections supported the connections he was trying to make between the eucharist and discipleship in his homily and invited the two women to pick up the music sheet on the table and join him in singing one verse of the recessional hymn they had just sung at Mass.

Father Dan then led them in a further conversation about eucharist and discipleship, explaining that the eucharist always calls those who receive it to a life of service. Father Dan then spent a few moments describing anonymously some of the ways parishioners serve. He mentioned the three women who bring holy communion to the sick and elderly of the parish who cannot come to Mass, a man who teaches reading to an illiterate neighbor, and a family who has been helping an elderly neighbor who can no longer take care of her yard. Teresa asked how the women bring the eucharist to the sick and elderly, and Father Dan told her about the reservation of the eucharist in the tabernacle and how this is one of the purposes of reserving the eucharist.

Next, Father Dan reviewed the dismissal rite of the Mass with the women and explained how the final words (in this case, "Go in peace to love and serve the Lord") are an explicit call to live as a disciple. He then asked them to sit quietly for a few minutes to think specifically how God might be calling them to be disciples in the coming week. At the conclusion of this period of silence, he invited them to share their insight if they care to. Joan mentioned that she had thought about helping her husband with a home project she had been avoiding. Teresa said she needed more time to think about it but that bringing holy communion to the sick sounded interesting. Phyllis thought she might give some of her time in the coming week to the food pantry the parish sponsored with three other local churches. Teresa thought that sounded interesting also. Father Dan led them in a prayer of thanksgiving for the gift of the eucharist followed with a petition for the Holy Spirit to help them be better disciples. At the end of the prayer they said their good-byes and returned to their homes.

Preparing for the Catechetical Session

As has been the case with the other liturgical rites of initiation (for example, the rite of scrutiny), the catechetical session that follows and is a direct reflection upon the rites is called a mystagogical catechesis. This is what is being done for the weekly reflections on the liturgies of the Easter season. Father Dan sat down between the Second and Third Sundays of Easter and determined how the mystagogical session would unfold. Using the Mystagogical Catechesis Preparation Form (found in the back of the book as Appendix 13 for further reproduction and use), which he acquired at a mystagogy workshop,[1] he prepared in the following manner.

He reviewed the scriptures and prayers of the Mass of the Third Sunday of Easter and determined that he wanted to focus on the connection between the eucharist and discipleship. There were many ideas connected with the eucharist to choose from, but this was the one he felt inspired to pursue. After determining the focus, he filled in the box marked "A: General Focus" on the planning form. Next he wrote down the relevant scriptures that might be proclaimed during the session and placed the citation in "Box B: Scriptures." Then he noted in Box D that he would want to have a lectionary and candles for the session. Afterward, he tried to figure out what other elements of the Mass would support the focus he had chosen for his session. Fortunately, he had the music list and the general intercessions to check. He thought it might be good to review the dismissal rite so he marked these down in "Box C: Other Supportive Liturgical Elements."

Now he was ready to structure the format of the session itself. He knew that the responses to the first two steps follow a standardized format and noted them in Boxes E1 and E2. In "Box E3: Exploring One Belief of the Church Proclaimed in the Sunday Liturgy," he wrote a few comments about the relationship between eucharist and discipleship. Then he looked at the ritual elements of the Mass that support this belief and noted them in Box E4. Rounding out his preparation, Father Dan noted the perennial call to discipleship in Box E5 and then jotted down a general idea for a spontaneous prayer to conclude their session.

Father Dan's completed form appears on page 146.

Four Fountains of Grace During Mystagogy

The RCIA provides a formational guideline for this period. Paragraphs 244–246 suggest that the newly initiated ponder the implications of their Catholic Christian life by meditating on the gospel, sharing in the eucharist and doing the works of charity.[2] These three elements are explored in light of an additional element: the community of faith (see the diagram that follows). These four elements reveal God's grace, first in the actual liturgical celebration of the Mass, second in the reflection about the eucharistic liturgy that follows, and third in the day-to-day life of discipleship that the newly initiated are invited to embrace.

These four components become the primary source of grace to help the newly initiated experience and explore the meaning of their lives as Catholic Christians. Catechetically speaking, this is not a time devoted to those topics there wasn't time to address before their initiation at the Easter Vigil. Paragraphs 244–246 are clear that this is a time to do liturgical and mystagogical catechesis, a continuation of the same kind of catechesis Teresa and Joan experienced during the periods of the catechumenate and purification and enlightenment.

MYSTAGOGICAL CATECHESIS PREPARATION FORM

Sunday in Easter/Liturgical Year: *Third Sunday of Easter, year A*

A. General focus:

   Connection between the holy eucharist and discipleship

B. Scriptures:

   Luke 24:13–35: Disciples on the road to Emmaus

C. Other supportive liturgical elements (for example, music texts, propers of Mass):

   General intercessions, dismissal rite of Mass, recessional hymn

D. Environment for session (for example, lectionary, candles):

   Lectionary and candles

E. Format of session:

   1. Remembering the experience of the liturgy:

   Invite all to silence. Pause until all are settled. Invite them to remember the Mass just celebrated. Review in mind for a minute in silence. Tell what you remembered.

   2. Exploring the meaning of the liturgy as experienced by participants:

   What was your reaction to what you remembered? What did it say to you? What connections did you make? What stories, sayings, did it remind you of?

   3. Exploring one belief the church proclaims on this particular Sunday liturgy:

   Eucharist–Discipleship. The eucharist always invites us to/strenghthens us for service. We are to become like the One whose Body and Blood we share.

   4. How this belief is ritualized at Sunday liturgy:

   See "C" above

   5. Implications for discipleship (invitation for my life/message to others/cost):

   Participants reflect on this in silence for three minutes. Those who want to, share with group.

   6. Closing prayer:

   Catechist initiates: Prayer of thanksgiving for gift of Eucharist; followed by petition to help us be disciples.

This period is devoted to learning the Christian life by first doing the liturgy.[3] This has profound implications for the liturgy, and those who are charged with the responsibility to celebrate it well. If this is true, it will be especially important that the Sunday celebration of the eucharist be the best the rural and small-town parish can offer the neophytes and newly received, so that the best opportunity for catechesis may occur. This means, among

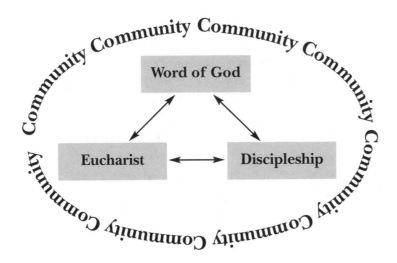

other things, that lectors are prepared and proclaim the word of God well, that presiders pray the liturgy and avoid merely reciting the words found in the sacramentary, and that the music be accessible to the community, relevant to the focus and season of the liturgy and accompanied by a competent musician (or sung unaccompanied when necessary). This means that preachers are making explicit, rural-sensitive connections (for example, stories, practical wisdom, relationally based) between the scriptures of the day, the eucharistic liturgy being celebrated, and the real world to which the community will return after the celebration.

This does not mean that additional kinds of catechesis are no longer important or helpful. Like Joe and Maria, those who are experiencing the sacramental life for the first time have much to talk about. Therefore, it will be beneficial to connect the neophytes and newly received to someone for some conversations about their experience of the sacraments of initiation as well as their first experiences of celebrating with a community of faith gathered to hear the word of God, to celebrate the eucharist and to renew their commitment to be Christ's disciples. For Teresa and Joan, this will be Father Dan; for Joan's children, it will be Pauline and her children, but in other situations it may be with a catechist and/or godparent.

But that does not mean a formal meeting is necessary. For example, such conversations might take place between a newly initiated person and his or her godparent or sponsor. Recall that Pauline and her children had such a conversation with Joan's children while Joan and Teresa met with Father Dan. It might take place in someone's home at a convenient time. It might take place with other members of the parish who gather during the week to discuss how the eucharistic liturgy invites them to live their lives as Catholic Christians. It might take place in a car ride, on someone's porch or at the local diner. Where and with whom these mystagogical conversations take place seems secondary to the fact that they actually do take place. If the newly initiated are interacting with some member(s) of the community about the word of God, the eucharist, charity and their interconnectedness during the 50 days of the Easter season, they are being faithful to the vision of this period. It need not be a formal session in the way it might have been during the previous two periods of formation. Be sensitive about setting something up that makes the newly initiated think and feel that they are still in some ways outsiders. Now they are insiders. Be careful about inadvertently setting up a dynamic that communicates "outsider" once they have become insiders. People from rural and small-towns are very sensitive to this.

How this conversation occurs is left to the wisdom of the local community. In the rural world, where informality is a way of life and where stories and relationships are very important, a relaxed, informal setting and conversation may be the best way of doing mystagogical catechesis during mystagogy. What is important is that a conversation is occurring on a weekly basis during this period.

Meditating on the Gospel

The newly initiated have meditated on the word of God throughout their formation, so it might seem strange that the church invites them to continue meditating on the gospel. Why is this? The church says that meditation on the word of God is a lifelong task because Christians never become masters of the word of God, only better servants of it. Building on the good beginnings from their days as catechumens and candidates, they now ponder the word of God in relation to the eucharist they may now participate in with a faith community. In the same way, Joe and Maria regularly pondered the events and advice of others during their courtship. As newlyweds, they now ponder the events of married life and the ongoing advice of friends and relatives in light of their new life as a married couple and will spend the rest of their lives becoming better at marriage through the experiences they will share over many years.

Doing the Works of Charity

In addition, the newly initiated are called to an explicit doing of the works of charity, this too done in the context of the eucharist. They have slowly grown in their understanding and commitment to discipleship over the course of their preparation for the sacraments of initiation. Here they are charged with the responsibility of "doing discipleship" on a regular basis because this is what those who share in the eucharist, the perpetual presence of Christ's death and resurrection, do. In a parallel way, Joe and Maria have shared life together as an unmarried couple on dates, on the telephone, and in church, and they have practiced this life by the way they have accommodated themselves to each other's needs before marriage. Building on those premarital experiences and the grace of their covenantal bond with God and each other in marriage, they now commit themselves to learning how to live together as husband and wife.

Sharing in the Eucharist

What is new for the recently initiated in this three-fold focus of word-sacrament-discipleship is sharing in the eucharist. Both newly baptized and received share in the eucharist for the first time with Catholic Christians. Sharing in the eucharist configures the newly initiated to both Christ and the community and acts as a perpetual presence of the paschal mystery in the here and now so they won't forget its significance for themselves and the world. The newly initiated now share in the sacramental life of the Catholic church. And this sharing has implications. Sharing in sacramental marriage has implications for Joe and Maria. They have been configured to God in a bond that is dissolved only by death. Just as the grace they receive from God in the sacrament of matrimony is a well-spring offering strength and encouragement to them throughout their married life, so too is the grace the recently initiated receive in the sacrament of the eucharist.

Community

Sharing in the sacraments also binds the newly initiated to the community and the community to them.[4] They now share the experience of being an insider with this community of faith and the community rejoices over the arrival of a new family member. This bond exists for support, consolation, encouragement and, at times, challenge. In the same way, Joe and Maria receive the support of the church, their families and other married couples who will offer them support, counsel and encouragement as they discover the joys and complexities of married life.

The Scriptures of Mystagogy

Part of the liturgical catechesis of the Easter season consists of the scripture texts chosen for this period of time. Year A readings are recommended during the period of mystagogy.[5] Rural and small-town initiation ministers ask how sacrosanct are the A readings for Years B and C when the parish has only one Mass on the weekend and/or their pastor is reluctant to restrict the parishioners to Year A readings when newly initiated members are present in years B and C, or is unwilling to prepare two homilies for one weekend when neophytes are present during the Easter seasons of Years B and C (one homily on Year A readings and the other on Year B or C readings).

First, don't make a mountain out of a molehill. Year A readings are recommended but not required. A review of the gospels of Easter in Years B and C reveals a harmony between them and the gospels of Year A. The scriptures of Years B and C also provide an opportunity for the newly initiated to bask in the joy of the sacraments celebrated at the Easter Vigil and to explore the implications of their new life.

The following table is offered to illustrate the connections between the three cycles of readings and the themes of Mystagogy when the Year A readings cannot be proclaimed in Years B and C.

All the gospels connect the dots between word, sacrament and discipleship. Year A has historical significance because these are the gospels used since antiquity but there is no requirement to use these readings exclusively.

BETWEEN PENTECOST AND THE FIRST ANNIVERSARY OF INITIATION

Joe and Maria look forward to a long life together. At some point in time, however, the honeymoon phase of their marriage ended as it does for almost every couple. The euphoria of the wedding became an increasingly distant memory and the routine of day-to-day life as a couple began to settle in. Joe and Maria continued to discover new things and deeper truths about each other. They learned that in order to stay in love they must continue to foster their relationship with each other and that they must devote time and energy to their relationship. Joe knows that remembering their anniversary, her birthday, and other important days is very important to Maria. Maria knows that during hunting season she will become a "hunting widow." They learned the reality of living with a spouse who is not perfect, and that they themselves are not perfect. Sometimes Joe forgets a special day in Maria's life and sometimes Maria complains about being alone on Saturdays during hunting season. Over time they discover how to live out the ebb and flow of their vocation as husband and wife. They also learn that their vocation called them forth from the comfort of their lives as a couple in service to others. For example, after a few months of marriage, Joe and Maria's pastor ask if they would be willing to help with the annual Harvest Festival. They also learned shortly before their first anniversary that they were expecting their first child. While things went fairly well during their first year of marriage, Joe and Maria had the normal trying moments every married couple experiences. Fortunately, the Hendersons were nearby and they had a deep enough friendship that they could talk to this couple, Maria speaking with Louise, Joe speaking with Ralph.

The period of time from Pentecost Sunday up to the next celebration of the Easter Vigil is like the period during the first year of marriage that occurs after the honeymoon phase ends. The newly baptized and the newly received have begun their journey as Catholic Christians, not completed it. Like a newly married couple, they too will continue to discover deeper truths about God, their church, themselves and their world. They too will discover that in order to grow in the relationship established in the sacraments of initiation, work and effort are involved. They will discover that discipleship is not always easy and that sometimes they are lazy in this area. They will discover

Sundays of Easter	Gospel Focus Year A	Gospel Focus Year B	Gospel Focus Year C
2nd Sunday	Faith in the resurrected Christ (Thomas/ New Disciple)	Faith in the resurrected Christ (Thomas/ New Disciple)	Faith in the resurrected Christ (Thomas/ New Disciple)
3rd Sunday	Emmaus story (Word/Eucharist/ Discipleship)	Resurrected Christ eats a fish (Word/Eucharist/ Discipleship	Christ serves breakfast on seashore/Peter's reconciliation-commission (Eucharist/ Discipleship)
4th Sunday	Good Shepherd/Sheep (Christ cares for/ protects his disciples)	Good Shepherd/Sheep (Christ cares for/ protects his disciples)	Good Shepherd/Sheep (Christ cares for/ protects his disciples)
5th Sunday	Those who believe God and Christ are one/Will do great things (Discipleship)	God is vinedresser/ Christ is vine/Disciple is branch (Disciples faithful to the word remain on vine)	Love one another (Disciples who love like Christ attract others to Christ)
6th Sunday	Those who love Christ keep his commandments (Discipleship)	Love one another/ I chose you to go out as witnesses (Discipleship)	Those who love Christ keep his word/Promise of advocate (Discipleship/ promise of helper)
Ascension	Christ ascends and commissions to baptize/teach (Discipleship)	Christ ascends and commissions to baptize/teach (Discipleship)	Christ ascends and commissions to baptize/teach (Discipleship)
Pentecost	Christ gives the Holy Spirit and commissions the disciples (Discipleship)	Christ gives the Holy Spirit and commissions the disciples (Discipleship)	Christ gives the Holy Spirit and commissions the disciples (Discipleship)

a church filled with sinful people and that they too continue to sin. Likewise they will be invited to explore how God is calling them to live out their baptismal vocation as disciples. Their bond with God, Christ and the church must bear fruit if the bond is authentic. This will require the help of a community at prayer, the word of God and the sacramental life, as well as a tradition rich in spirituality, knowledge and history. All of this is to be discovered and explored in the first year (and beyond) of life and service as a Catholic Christian. There is plenty going on that might merit occasional conversations between the newly initiated and the more seasoned Catholics in the parish.

In the United States, the Catholic bishops have legislated[6] that the newly baptized (and it may be inferred to include those baptized candidates who had received relatively little Christian upbringing before entering the parish's catechumenate process,[7] like Joan) gather at least monthly until the anniversary of their initiation for ongoing formation and incorporation into the life of the faith community. (It would appear that this requirement is entirely optional for those baptized Christians coming into full communion with the Catholic church, like Richard, who have lived the Christian life and who needed only instruction in the particulars of Catholicism and a degree of probation within the Catholic community.[8] An invitation might be extended to him, but the choice to participate should be entirely his.)

Why have the bishops imposed this requirement on the newly baptized and those newly received candidates who had little Christian upbringing prior to entering the catechumenate process? Experience has shown that pastoral care and concern for the newly initiated described above is still important as they become grounded in the day-to-day life of the Catholic Christian faith, even beyond Pentecost. There is evidence that more than a few newly initiated struggle in their new life as Catholic Christians in the months that follow their initiation. There also is evidence that ongoing support is helpful as a sign that the community cares for the newly initiated, something very important in rural society where relationship is a primary lens through which life is viewed and lived.

In their wisdom, the U.S. bishops have asked parishes to bring the newly initiated together at least monthly in what might be described as a kind of support group experience. Similar to what occurs in married life in rural and small-town communities, informal conversations occur from time to time to provide ongoing help for the recently married.

For example, Louise Henderson invites Maria to join the parish Quilting Club, an organization to which she and some other women of the parish belong. At their weekly gatherings, the members make quilts to be sold at the annual parish Harvest Festival and discuss the events of their lives. Problems are shared and wisdom is offered for the benefit of everyone, including Maria. Ralph Henderson invites Joe to join him and another friend for an occasional fishing trip. During their outings, they discuss work, politics, religion and family life. Joe finds helpful counsel from these older men.

The monthly gatherings between Pentecost and the first anniversary of initiation function in a similar way. These are times to check in with the newly initiated to see how they are doing, to support and encourage them, and to provide wisdom as they seek to live the life of a Catholic Christian.

Issues they had not considered before initiation are bound to arise. The initial enthusiasm of initiation may be wearing off and the newly initiated may be backsliding a bit. The gathering may provide an opportunity to discuss these and other issues arising from the ebb and flow of life and faith.

These gatherings, like those during the period of mystagogy, need not be formal. Anything with a classroom atmosphere should be avoided. Conversations over a meal or in someone's living room may be more fruitful for rural initiates. Conversations with people they respect (a godparent or sponsor, a catechist, or perhaps a wisdom figure like the parish matriarch) may be more beneficial than bringing the newly initiated together to discuss in a group setting how their life is going. This is not to say that a group gathering should never occur. It might be nice to bring folks together a couple of times during the first year of initiation for prayer, a meal and a conversation about some questions they may have about their life in the Catholic faith, about the Mass, the sacrament of reconciliation, or other matters.

Be flexible and look for various ways to give the newly initiated the care and support they will need in their first year in the church. Keep the conversations focused on practical experiences and concerns. Keep the settings informal and be sure that relationships are being nourished. Be particularly sensitive to avoid experiences that give the new initiates a feeling that they are still, in some way, outsiders. With these dynamics present, a rural and small town initiate should flourish during the period of mystagogy and the months leading up to his or her first anniversary as a Catholic Christian.

SOME FACTORS CONTRIBUTING TO POST-INITIATION ABSENCES

One of the most important suppositions about the period of mystagogy and the months afterward leading to the first anniversary of initiation is that they build upon what has preceded throughout the entire process of formation. It has been the general observation of initiation experts that frustrations associated with this period in rural and small-town parishes are frequently connected in some way to misunderstandings associated with one, two or three of the components associated with Christian initiation in these communities: catechesis, liturgy and/or a process that is not rural-friendly.

The Catechetical Method

The ritual text provides many clues about the way formation should occur over the course of the initiation process. It describes a formation model that incorporates spiritual formation, conversion, life lived in the midst of a praying community, discipleship and intellectual formation in a balanced manner.[9] This model is called initiation catechesis and is much more evangelical than educational, both in structure and content. In other words, it asks those who facilitate the initiation process to ensure that inquirers, catechumens and candidates are being spiritually awakened to a living relationship with

God and Christ, appropriately catechized in the faith, developing a committed relationship to the church (especially to a weekly praying community) and practicing discipleship. It is also important for them to understand that conversion is a lifelong task.

This model is different from an educational one that concentrates fairly exclusively on learning the content of the Catholic Christian tradition as described in, for example, the *Catechism of the Catholic Church* or other sources of Catholic teaching. The former model is holistic, involving mind, heart, spirit, body and behavior. The latter model frequently focuses almost exclusively on the acquisition of information about the Catholic Christian tradition. While learning the content of the faith is important, the rite clearly says that it is only one part of the formation process.[10] The former model asks that all components of formation be explicitly incorporated into the process, whereas the latter model tends to emphasize the intellectual dimension of formation in an explicit manner, frequently leaving the other components to be incorporated sporadically. A process that concentrates on intellectual formation without balancing it with spiritual, affective, ecclesial and moral formation may unwittingly contribute to a mindset in the initiates that the initiation process is like a course one takes in school. This is because it looks like the education model experienced in most schools, a model that concentrates on the acquisition of information. If this mindset predominates, it might come as no surprise that rural initiates perceive the process as a classroom course whose goal is graduation rather than initiation. If those going through the process see the celebration of the sacraments of initiation as a point of termination (accompanied by a diploma called a baptismal certificate or a certificate of reception into full communion), then initiation ministers should not be surprised if the newly initiated stop coming to formation after the Easter Vigil.

Some reflection questions might help to determine the dominant model used in your parish. Look at the way your process is structured. Does it look more like a 30-week catechism class in which the catechist is offering instructions about the faith with little interaction with the initiates? Does it begin in September and end in May like a school year is structured? Is everyone required to begin in September, even if they express interest in starting the initiation process in January? If you answered "yes" to any of these questions, you may be contributing to a mindset that sees the Easter Vigil as the moment of completion rather than as the moment of beginning. Don't forget that initiation is about beginning, not ending.

An initiation model consistent with the vision of the church looks different.[11] In addition to the teaching component of a catechetical session, does your session include prayer every time? Are other members of the parish invited to participate in the sessions and in the lives of the initiates as sponsors or simply as parishioners who want to become acquainted with them through conversation and hospitality? Is the "teaching" component of every session after the rite of becoming a catechumen or the rite of welcome connected explicitly to the word of God? Are the participants asked to consider how the central idea discussed at the session invites them to a concrete decision to follow Christ? The rite presumes an affirmative answer to these questions and that these components are incorporated into the three periods leading up to sacramental initiation.

Anecdotal evidence suggests that many rural or small-town parishes using an education model based on a school-year timeline (September to May) complete with predetermined topics for each session are struggling with participation during the mystagogy period. This model may contribute to a mindset within the inquirers that they are taking a course that has as its goal graduation rather than initiation.

A Formation Process That Underutilizes the Power of Liturgy

The initiation process of the church is called the Rite of Christian Initiation of Adults. From the celebration of the rite of acceptance into the order of catechumens to Pentecost, when the formal process concludes, nearly every catechetical session is rooted to a liturgical celebration, be it the Sunday liturgy of the word, a major initiation rite like the rite of election, or a minor rite incorporated into a catechetical session during the period of the catechumenate. There is an intrinsic relationship between the liturgy of the church and initiation catechesis. They are two sides of one coin.

It is the belief of the church that rites have a power to change people. The U.S. bishops teach us that "good [liturgical] celebrations foster and nourish faith; poor ones weaken and destroy it."[12] In other words, a person does not leave a liturgical celebration the same person who entered it. He or she is either better or worse for the experience.

The rites of Christian initiation also form those who participate in them. If the initiation rites are done poorly (or worse, not at all), or if liturgical formation with a parish community around the Sunday scriptures is not included or well celebrated, then it might not be surprising that the initiates see liturgical prayer as an optional or auxiliary part of their lives. To the extent that it is seen in this light, it may contribute to an attitude among the newly baptized or received that Sunday worship and other celebrations of liturgical prayer are not that important to the people who belong to that church because they do not celebrate liturgical prayer in a manner that clearly says it is important. The end result may be a new Catholic Christian who does not worship on Sunday (sometimes within the period of mystagogy itself) or who may begin visiting churches of other denominations where the worship is of a higher quality!

But if Sunday worship and the initiation rites are celebrated well the participants have a much better chance of encountering the very presence of divinity, a presence that makes a difference, fosters a relationship between God and the initiate, gives hope, and deepens faith. If the liturgical rites of initiation are well celebrated and the Sunday gathering around the table of God's word with a believing community is a normative experience for catechumens and candidates, it will not be surprising that Sunday worship becomes an indispensable part of their lives. In other words, it matters that the rites of initiation are given a priority by those who preside over them as well as by the community that celebrates them with the catechumen and/or candidate. It matters that the parish puts time and energy every week into the best celebration of the Sunday worship it is capable of and that preachers, readers, musicians and community do their best to foster the presence of divinity as well as possible each week through their respective ministries. In a rural, small-town context, this does not mean that parishes must duplicate what exists in suburban ones. This is impossible. What is important is that the liturgical celebrations are the best the parish can celebrate despite the limitations that are often the reality of these communities.

Here's another checklist. Do you celebrate the major and minor rites of Christian initiation? If you do, are they well celebrated or simply read out of a book? Once they are catechumens and declared candidates for full communion, are the Sunday lectionary readings the springboard for their weekly formation? Do your liturgical ministers—especially lectors and preachers— give evidence that they have spent time preparing for the exercise of their ministry? Does your preacher give a rural-friendly homily? Is your liturgy reverent? If you answered in the negative to any of these questions, it will be important to learn what can be done to improve your parish's experience of liturgy.

A Formation Process That Isn't Rural-Friendly

As we have seen, people from rural and small-town communities tend to live life in what has earlier been described as the oral tradition.[13] As such, their approach to life and the church is different from those who live in the other dominant culture in our society, the literate culture. (Again, remember this does not mean that rural people are illiterate, for most can read and write. Rather, it means their preferred form of communication or way of engaging their world and the people who inhabit it is tied to relationships and stories rather than theories and discourse.) The meaning of life is found in relationship with others, stories, plain talk and concrete applications to life. Their thinking process tends to be experiential rather than introspective. They tend to live out their faith in more practical ways, preferring traditions and practices to theoretical knowledge about their faith.

People living in this culture who seek initiation into the Catholic Christian tradition are intuitively looking for a church community that initiates in a way that is reflective of their culture, in a place where they feel at home. Sometimes well-meaning ministers (usually college educated and/or operating out of a literate culture) provide an initiation process that is more reflective of a literate culture than the one in which they are serving. To the extent that it does, initiates may view the celebration of the sacraments of initiation as a good time to conclude their participation in a well-intentioned but uninspiring formation process.

A comparison between your present formation process and oral culture may provide some insights about the exodus after initiation. Here are some questions to explore. Do the rural participants see your catechist as someone who is more comfortable in a literate culture, where abstract thinking, big words and theological ideas abound, or is the catechist seen as "one of us"? Would you say your process gives more time to learning about the content of Catholic Christian faith from a book or from the experiences and relationships found daily in a rural or small-town world? Is your catechist's methodology more like lecture (tell me) than apprenticeship (show me)? Does your catechist use more language of the head than of the heart during formation sessions? Is the catechist more concerned about starting and ending on time and getting through the topic than about developing a relationship with the participants? Would it be rare for a catechist to use stories, proverbs, witticisms and other folksy sayings to help rural initiates learn about the faith and how it should be lived? Would your catechist be more inclined to tell participants what some theologian or author says about Jesus than to tell about what Jesus means to him or her?

If your answers to these questions tend to be more "yes" than "no," then you may be contributing to the misfire between the formation process and those who live their life in an oral tradition, and unconsciously motivating your rural participants to excuse themselves from the process once they have been initiated.

There may be other culturally motivated issues contributing to diminished attendance after the Easter Vigil. Many rural and small-town people are connected to the land in some way. In North America, the Easter season coincides with spring and the months after Pentecost coincide with summer and fall. In an agricultural area, planting season may coincide with the Easter season, creating significant conflict for those whose survival is rooted to the land and who therefore must choose how to use their time very wisely. In other rural areas, tourism may increase during the spring and seasons that follow. Those who earn their annual income during the tourism season, especially in family-owned businesses, may be hard pressed to attend sessions that require them to leave work, jeopardizing their business or their job.

One other rural dynamic is worth noting. Relationship is very important in rural society, and being an "insider" is highly prized. Once initiated, the newly baptized or received are insiders. They belong. It will be important that their experiences during the period of mystagogy and the monthly gatherings leading up to their first anniversary do not create the impression that they are still outsiders. Some parishes reserve special seats for the newly baptized during the period of mystagogy as is recommended in paragraph 248 of the RCIA. This practice may actually contribute to a feeling of separateness, creating a sense that they have not yet become true insiders since all the other insiders sit wherever they want in the church. Rural people do not like to draw attention to themselves. They prefer to blend in. Special seating draws attention to those sitting in the special section, which is usually in the front of the church. If special seating has not been a feature through the initiation process (and it doesn't appear to be recommended in the ritual text, even for the rites), it might appear strange for them to be asked to sit, after becoming insiders through initiation, in a place where they have never previously sat.

For those who struggle with attendance during the period of mystagogy, a review of your process in light of these three issues might help you identify ways to keep the newly baptized and/or received involved in the initiation opportunities provided by your parish during this period and the months leading up to their first anniversary of initiation.

Notes

[1]The format of this model is an adaptation of one developed by Sister Gael Gensler. I am grateful to her for the inspiration her original model gave me and for her permission to adapt it.

[2]See RCIA, 244.

[3]The late Mark Searle said there "is hardly any serious theological issue which does not surface, in one way or another, in the liturgy: theological epistemology, God-language, theological anthropology, ecclesiology, salvation history, even the issues of critical theology." See "Renewing the Liturgy Again," in *Commonweal*, 115 (November 18, 1988), p. 622.

[4]See RCIA, 246.

[5]See RCIA, 247.

[6]See National Statute 24 (Appendix III) in the ritual text.

[7]See National Statute 31 (Appendix III) in the ritual text.

[8]Ibid.

[9]See RCIA, 4–8, 36–38, 75–76 and 138–139, which describe this holistic formation over the course of the entire process.

[10]RCIA, 75, describes the formation as consisting of: appropriate acquaintance with dogmas, precepts and the mystery of salvation accommodated to the liturgical year and solidly supported by celebrations of the word of God; life in a faith community that inspires catechumens and candidates in the development of their spiritual life and witness to the faith; formation through liturgical rites and celebrations of the word of God; and discipleship.

[11]See the *General Directory for Catechesis* from the Congregation for the Clergy, especially paragraphs 60– 72 and 85– 86.

[12]See *Music in Catholic Worship*, 6.

[13]See Tex Sample, *Ministry in an Oral Culture: Living with Will Rodgers, Uncle Remus, and Minnie Pearl* (Louisville: Westminster/John Knox Press, 1994). I am grateful for Sample's numerous insights about oral culture. His book may be considered a primer on rural life and ministry.

INQUIRY SESSION PREPARATION FORM

Date of Session:_____

1. Building relationships/community/hospitality

2. Appropriate prayer/music/symbols, etc.

3. Question(s) from the inquirers

4. Responses to the question(s)

    A. Key stories or issues linked to human experience

    B. Key stories from scripture

    C. Key stories from tradition

    D. Summary of church teaching

5. So what? The challenge to living faith daily

6. Prayer from the treasury of the church

Appendix 2 — RESOURCES FOR THE PRECATECHUMENATE

1. *The Rite of Christian Initiation of Adults* (Ritual Text). Various publishers. (This is the official text of the RCIA, which everyone working in this ministry should own and read.)

2. *Catechism of the Catholic Church.* Various publishers. (This is a resource for catechists in planning catechetical sessions.)

3. *Catholic Update.* St. Anthony Messenger Press, Cincinnati, Ohio. (This series of four-page pamphlets on various aspects of the Catholic church is an excellent resource for catechists. Many back issues are available in three-hole punched binders.)

4. *Handbook for Today's Catholic.* Ligouri Publications, Ligouri, Missouri. (This is a quick-reference booklet for major beliefs, practices and prayers of the Roman Catholic Church.)

5. *The Harper Collins Encyclopedia of Catholicism,* General Edition. Richard McBrien. Harper-Collins Publishers, New York. (This is a one-volume collection on the Catholic faith.)

6. *The Serendipity Bible Study Book,* Catholic Edition. Zondervan Publishing House, Grand Rapids, Michigan. (This is an excellent resource for finding discussion questions for scripture-sharing sessions.)

7. *Come Follow Me: Resources for the Period of Inquiry in the RCIA.* Edited by Joseph Sinwell. Paulist Press, New York, 1990. (This is an excellent resource for ideas on discussion starters for inquiry session.)

8. *The Catholic Sourcebook,* Third Edition. Peter Klein. Harcourt Brace & Company, Orlando, Florida, 2000. (This is a comprehensive collection of information about the Catholic church.)

POPULAR BIBLE STORIES

Creation:	Genesis 1:1—2:4a or 2:4b–25
The Fall:	Genesis 3
Cain and Abel:	Genesis 4:1–16
Noah and the Ark:	Genesis 6:5—9:28
Tower of Babel:	Genesis 11:1–9
Call of Abram:	Genesis 11:31—12:6
Covenant with Abraham:	Genesis 15
Jacob Deceives Isaac:	Genesis 27—28
Joseph:	Genesis 37—45
Burning Bush:	Exodus 3
Passover:	Exodus 11:1—12:36
Crossing the Red Sea:	Exodus 13:17—15:21
The Ten Commandments:	Exodus 20:1–17; Deuteronomy 5:6–21
Golden Calf:	Exodus 32
Great Commandment:	Deuteronomy 6:4–9
Arrival in Canaan, the Promised Land:	Joshua 3—4
Samson:	Judges 13—16
Goliath and Saul's Reaction:	1 Samuel 17—19
David and Bathsheba:	2 Samuel 11:1—12:25
Elijah Meets God:	1 Kings 19:1–13
Job and Suffering:	Job 1:13–22
	Psalm 23
Call of Jeremiah:	Jeremiah 1:1–10
Infancy Narratives:	Matthew 1:1—2:23; Luke 1:1—3:52
Temptation of Jesus:	Matthew 4:1 - 11; Mark 1:12 - 13; Luke 4:1–13
Beatitudes:	Matthew 5:1–11; Luke 6:20–23
Lord's Prayer:	Matthew 6:5–14; Luke 11:2–4
Sower and the Seed:	Matthew 13:1–9, 18–23; Mark 4:1–9; Luke 8:4–8
Feeding of the Multitudes:	Matthew 14:13–21; Mark 6:30–44; Luke 9:10–17; John 6:1–14
Prediction of Jesus' Death:	Matthew 16:21–28; Mark 8:31—9:1; Luke 9:22–27
Lost Sheep:	Matthew 18:10–14; Luke 15:3–7
Great Commandment:	Matthew 22:34–40; Mark 12:28–34; Luke 10:25–28
Final Judgment:	Matthew 25:31–46
Passion and Death of Jesus:	Matthew 26—27; Mark 14—15; Luke 22—23; John 13—19
Lord's Supper:	Matthew 26:26–30; Mark 14:22–26; Luke 22:14–23; 1 Corinthians 11:23–25
Resurrection:	Matthew 28:1–15; Mark 16:1–8; Luke 24:1–12; John 20:1–10
Ascension:	Matthew 28:16–20; Mark 16:14–18; Luke 24:36–49; John 20:19–23; Acts 1:6–8
Good Samaritan:	Luke 10:25–37
Martha and Mary:	Luke 10:38–42
Prodigal Son:	Luke 15:11–32
Lazarus the Beggar and the Rich Man:	Luke 16:19–31
Zacchaeus:	Luke 19:1–10
Disciples on the Road to Emmaus:	Luke 24:13–35
Wedding at Cana:	John 2:1–12
Samaritan Woman:	John 4:3–42
Bread of Life Discourse:	John 6
Woman Caught in Adultery:	John 7:53—8:11
Man Born Blind:	John 9:1–41
Raising of Lazarus:	John 11:1–44
Doubting Thomas:	John 20:19–29
Pentecost:	Acts 2:1–13
Stoning of Stephen:	Acts 6:8—8:2a
Conversion of Paul:	Acts 9:1–30

CHURCH TEACHINGS THAT EMERGE FROM THE LITURGICAL YEAR

Solemnities and Feasts

Day/Feast	Doctrine/Precept/Teaching/Tradition
Mary, Mother of God	Mary is human mother of divine son
Epiphany	Universal salvation; mission of the church
Baptism of the Lord	Baptism; social justice
Passion Sunday	Passion and death of Jesus; obedience
Easter Sunday	Resurrection
Ascension	Enthronement of Christ in heaven; new body of Christ on earth
Pentecost	Holy Spirit; mission: renewing the earth; birth of the church
Holy Trinity	Mystery of the Holy Trinity
Body/Blood of Christ	Eucharist
Assumption of Mary	Assumption of Mary, body and soul, to heaven
All Saints/All Souls	Communion of saints; intercession for the dead; purgatory
Christ the King	Final judgment; end of time
Immaculate Conception	Conception of Mary without original sin
Christmas	Incarnation
Holy Family	Fourth commandment; Christian marriage; family values

Sundays

Year A

Advent 1	Second coming of Christ; peace
Advent 2	Universal salvation; reconciliation/forgiveness of sins
Advent 3	Hope; patience
Advent 4	Virgin birth
Lent 1	Sin; redemption
Lent 2	Universal call to holiness; transfiguration-resurrection
Lent 3	Sin/forgiveness; justification
Lent 4	Social sin
Lent 5	Death/resurrection of the body
Easter 2	Faith; resurrection; reconciliation
Easter 3	Eucharist; the Mass; discipleship as witness
Easter 4	Church vocations; service as discipleship
Easter 5	Diaconate; royal priesthood of the baptized; Christ as way to God
Easter 6	Love as commandment of disciples; suffering as discipleship
Easter 7	Disciples continue the mission; suffering as discipleship
Ordinary Time 2	Fifth commandment; pro-life issues; Christian unity
Ordinary Time 3	Baptismal vocation; religious vocation
Ordinary Time 4	Beatitudes
Ordinary Time 5	Option for the poor; works of mercy; eighth commandment

Ordinary Time 6	Choosing life; spiritual wisdom in following the law of Christ
Ordinary Time 7	Love of neighbor and of enemies; body as temple of Holy Spirit
Ordinary Time 8	Fidelity of God; trust in God; final judgment
Ordinary Time 9	Obey commandments (for example, first); justification; discipleship as action
Ordinary Time 10	Discipleship as love; Jesus calls sinners; faith and righteousness
Ordinary Time 11	Covenantal bond; justification; discipleship as mission
Ordinary Time 12	Discipleship as hardship; salvific grace
Ordinary Time 13	Christian hospitality; discipleship as prophetic
Ordinary Time 14	Sovereignty of God; humility and praise before God
Ordinary Time 15	Word of God; eschatology
Ordinary Time 16	God as mighty/merciful; Holy Spirit; sinners/saints coexisting
Ordinary Time 17	Spiritual wisdom; justification/glorification; value of reign of God
Ordinary Time 18	Generosity of God; Jesus eliminates separation between God/humans
Ordinary Time 19	Divine revelation
Ordinary Time 20	Universal salvation; mercy of God
Ordinary Time 21	Responsibility of spiritual leaders; Jesus as messiah; role of Peter
Ordinary Time 22	Suffering messiah; disciples suffer
Ordinary Time 23	Admonishing the sinner; love as fulfillment of law; reconciliation
Ordinary Time 24	Golden rule; sacrament of reconciliation
Ordinary Time 25	Conversion; final judgment; God's generosity
Ordinary Time 26	Conversion; obedience; christology: Jesus is human/divine
Ordinary Time 27	Divine justice; intercessory prayer
Ordinary Time 28	Eschatological banquet; dependence on God
Ordinary Time 29	First commandment; church/state relationships
Ordinary Time 30	Love of God/neighbor
Ordinary Time 31	Christian leadership
Ordinary Time 32	End of time; final judgment; resurrection of the dead
Ordinary Time 33	Discipleship as exercise of one's talents; preparation for the end

Year B

Advent 1	Second coming of Christ; end of time
Advent 2	Second coming; repentance and the sacrament of reconciliation

Advent 3	Gifts of the spirit; baptism
Advent 4	Annunciation; Mary's virginity
Lent 1	Sin; redemption; covenant
Lent 2	Fifth commandment; Christ removes separation between God/humans; transfiguration-resurrection
Lent 3	Ten Commandments; suffering messiah; disposition for worship
Lent 4	Consequences of sin; God so loved the world; role of good works and merit
Lent 5	Jesus as new covenant; obedience; suffering-sacrifice
Easter 2	Faith; resurrection; reconciliation
Easter 3	Eucharist; bodily resurrection; Jewish culpability for paschal mystery
Easter 4	Priesthood; discipleship causes hardship; disciples as healers
Easter 5	Universal call to holiness; love as theological virtue
Easter 6	Love as theological virtue; ecumenism; impartiality of God
Easter 7	Episcopacy; ecumenism; discipleship
Ordinary Time 2	Theology of the body; vocation as call from God
Ordinary Time 3	Repentance/conversion; universality of God's love; responding to call
Ordinary Time 4	Authority/magisterium; value of virginity
Ordinary Time 5	Prayer; theology of suffering; healing and anointing of the sick
Ordinary Time 6	Freedom; theology of suffering; healing and anointing of the sick
Ordinary Time 7	Forgiveness of sins; Holy Trinity
Ordinary Time 8	Reconciliation; fasting/abstinence
Ordinary Time 9	Third commandment
Ordinary Time 10	Original sin; theology of the body; forgiveness of sins; inclusivity of God's reign
Ordinary Time 11	Kingdom of God; final judgment
Ordinary Time 12	Faith; Christians are a new creation
Ordinary Time 13	Death/eternal life; healing of the sick/anointing
Ordinary Time 14	Prophecy; suffering
Ordinary Time 15	Disciples as missionaries; paschal mystery
Ordinary Time 16	Christian leadership; sacraments of order; unity
Ordinary Time 17	Eucharist; unity
Ordinary Time 18	Eucharist; conversion
Ordinary Time 19	Eucharist; examples of discipleship
Ordinary Time 20	Eucharist; real presence; behavior of disciples
Ordinary Time 21	Eucharist and service; marriage
Ordinary Time 22	Dogma/doctrine/precepts/laws/customs; discipleship with the poor

Ordinary Time 23	Spiritual/physical healing; disciple is impartial
Ordinary Time 24	Jesus' suffering/death; love for the poor
Ordinary Time 25	Servant-leadership; behavior of a disciple
Ordinary Time 26	Wealth; hell; prophets in the church
Ordinary Time 27	Marriage/divorce; christology
Ordinary Time 28	Ten commandments; wealth/greed; scripture
Ordinary Time 29	Jesus as high priest; sinlessness of Jesus; authority; honor/service
Ordinary Time 30	God hears the poor; healing of the sick
Ordinary Time 31	Love of God/neighbor; eternal priesthood of Jesus
Ordinary Time 32	Support of the church; sacrifice of the Mass
Ordinary Time 33	Judgment (heaven/hell); sacrifice of the Mass

Year C

Advent 1	Second coming; social justice; disciples love others
Advent 2	Second coming; repentance; hope
Advent 3	Hope; joy; moral conversion
Advent 4	Visitation; new covenant
Lent 1	Sin/grace; justification
Lent 2	Covenant between Abraham/God; transfiguration-resurrection
Lent 3	Name of God; repentance; moral life
Lent 4	Sacrament of reconciliation; forgiveness of sins
Lent 5	Discipleship as gratitude to Jesus; forgiveness of sins; sixth commandment
Easter 2	Faith; resurrection; reconciliation
Easter 3	Eucharist and the cost of discipleship; conscience; apostolic church
Easter 4	Christian leadership; salvation and Judaism; martyrdom
Easter 5	Virtue of Christian love; heaven; apostolic church
Easter 6	Magisterium of church; peace; Holy Trinity
Easter 7	Unity; martyrdom; end of the world
Ordinary Time 2	Marriage; gifts of the spirit
Ordinary Time 3	Word of God; church as body of Christ; Christian unity
Ordinary Time 4	Christian love; prophets
Ordinary Time 5	Call to holiness; call to ministry
Ordinary Time 6	Beatitudes; resurrection
Ordinary Time 7	Mercy/compassion of God; love of enemies; resurrection
Ordinary Time 8	Judging others; resurrection
Ordinary Time 9	Universal salvation; magisterial teaching
Ordinary Time 10	Resurrection; call of Paul to discipleship
Ordinary Time 11	Forgiveness of God; justification

Ordinary Time 12	Self-renunciation as discipleship; suffering messiah; children of God
Ordinary Time 13	Commitment in discipleship; prophets; freedom
Ordinary Time 14	Disciples as evangelists; images of God; cross of Christ
Ordinary Time 15	Love of God/neighbor; Christ as image of God
Ordinary Time 16	Christian hospitality; word of God; disciples suffer for Christ
Ordinary Time 17	Lord's Prayer; intercessory prayer; baptism
Ordinary Time 18	Greed; behavior of disciples; impartiality of God
Ordinary Time 19	Hope; faith
Ordinary Time 20	Cost of discipleship
Ordinary Time 21	Universal salvation; suffering disciples
Ordinary Time 22	Pride as capital sin
Ordinary Time 23	Slavery; price of discipleship
Ordinary Time 24	Ministry of reconciliation; forgiveness/mercy of God
Ordinary Time 25	Social justice; prayer
Ordinary Time 26	Social justice; fidelity as disciple
Ordinary Time 27	Faith; belief in God; intercessory prayer
Ordinary Time 28	Anointing of the sick; salvation with baptism; gratitude to God
Ordinary Time 29	Intercessory prayer; cost of discipleship
Ordinary Time 30	Justice of God; self-righteousness
Ordinary Time 31	Second coming; mercy of God
Ordinary Time 32	Resurrection; intercessory prayer
Ordinary Time 33	Last judgment; suffering/persecution

CATECHUMENATE SESSION PREPARATION FORM Appendix 5

Sunday/Feast _____ Cycle ___ Date _____

1. Scriptural passages for the Sunday/feast

2. RCIA, 75.3: Prayer/music/symbols connected to the liturgy of the word

3. Setting up the catechesis/doctrine: experiences from daily life

4. RCIA, 75.1: Suitable catechesis/doctrine connected to the liturgy of the word

5. RCIA, 75.2: Christian way of life in community connected to liturgy of the word

6. RCIA, 75.4: Works of mercy/outreach/witness that emerge from liturgy of the word

7. Prayer from the treasury of the church (including minor rites from RCIA text)

RESOURCES FOR CATECHESIS
DURING THE CATECHUMENATE PERIOD

1. *Catechism of the Catholic Church.* Various Publishers. (This is a resource for catechists in planning catechetical sessions.)

2. *Catholic Update.* St. Anthony Messenger Press, Cincinnati, Ohio. (This series of four-page pamphlets on various aspects of the Catholic church is an excellent resource for catechists. Many back issues are available in three-hole punched binder.)

3. *Cultural World of Jesus.* John Pilch. Paulist Press, Mahwah, New Jersey. (This is a three-volume exegesis of the Sunday gospels based on the Mediterranean culture of Jesus' day, with striking similarities to contemporary oral culture.)

4. *Footprints on the Mountain.* Roland Faley. Paulist Press, Mahwah, New Jersey. (This is an excellent resource for background on the Sunday readings.)

5. *Handbook for Today's Catholic.* Ligouri Publications, Ligouri, Missouri. (This is a quick-reference booklet for major beliefs, practices and prayers of the Roman Catholic Church.)

6. *Harper Collins Encyclopedia of Catholicism.* Harper-Collins Publishers, New York. (This is a one-volume compendium on Roman Catholicism.)

7. *Preaching the New Lectionary.* Dianne Bergant. Liturgical Press, College-ville, Minnesota. (This is a three-volume commentary on the Sunday scriptures with topical suggestions for preachers and catechists.)

8. *Serendipity Bible Study Book.* Zondervan Publishing House, Grand Rapids, Michigan. (This is an excellent resource for finding discussion questions for scripture-sharing sessions.)

9. *The Catholic Sourcebook,* Third Edition. Peter Klein. Harcourt Brace & Company, Orlando, Florida, 2000. (This is a comprehensive collection of information about the Catholic church.)

10. *Living the Good News,* Catholic Version, Adult Edition. (Harrisburg, Pennsylvania: Morehouse). (This is a resource for preparing the content of a catechetical session. Published three times a year.)

UNIFIED CATECHUMENATE SESSION MODEL
(NO DISMISSAL AFTER HOMILY)

1. Mass concludes; catechumen(s) and/or uncatechized candidate(s) dismissed with assembly

2. Hospitality and fellowship (with parishioners when available and with initiation group)

3. Read featured scripture(s) (first reading, psalm, second reading and/or gospel).

4. First impressions of/reaction to the reading(s) without critique by catechist

   a. Exercise in imagination. What did they see, hear, smell, taste, feel?
   b. What did the passage(s) say to the catechumen/candidate?

5. Offer brief commentary on each passage.

6. Bridge to catechetical focus of session: experiences from daily life that will connect to catechesis of step eight.

   a. Practical examples from daily life
   b. Conversation by participants recommended

7. Reread relevant scripture passage(s) used as connection to catechesis of step eight.

8. Catechesis on church teaching incorporating principles of paragraph 75 of the RCIA (doctrine, liturgy, community, discipleship)

9. Invitation to participants to identify affirmation, information, inspiration, challenge encountered in teaching discussed in step eight

   a. Silent reflection
   b. Conversation among participants

10. Invitation for deeper integration of topic with daily life
    a. Silent reflection
    b. Journaling (concrete, practical application of catechetical focus to daily life)
    c. No discussion

11. Questions, announcements and other miscellaneous issues

12. Closing prayer (for example, minor rites [RCIA, 90–103], prayers from the tradition) and conclusion

Part One: Dismissal Catechesis

1. Homily concludes; catechumen(s) and/or unbaptized candidate(s) dismissed with catechist

2. Immediate reassembling of group with catechist

3. First impressions of the readings/liturgy (for example, homily, music) without critique by catechist

    a. Exercise in imagination. What did they see, hear, smell, taste, feel?

    b. What did the readings/liturgy say to the catechumen/candidate?

4. Offer brief commentary on each reading.

5. Conclude with opening prayer of the Mass.

6. Hospitality and fellowship (with parishioners now dismissed from Mass and/or initiation group)

Part Two: Post-Liturgy Catechesis

1. Bridge to catechetical focus of session: experiences from daily life that will connect to catechesis of step three below.

    a. Practical examples from daily life

    b. Conversation by participants recommended

2. Reread relevant lectionary reading(s) used as connection to catechesis of step three.

3. Catechesis on church teaching incorporating principles of paragraph 75 of the RCIA (doctrine, liturgy, community, discipleship)

4. Invitation to participants to identify affirmation, information, inspiration and challenge encountered in catechesis of step three

    a. Silent reflection

    b. Conversation among participants

5. Invitation for deeper integration of topic with daily life
   a. Silent reflection
   b. Journaling (concrete, practical application of catechetical focus to daily life)
   c. No discussion

6. Questions, announcements and other miscellaneous issues

7. Closing prayer (for example, minor rites [RCIA, 90–103], prayers from the tradition) and conclusion

DISCERNMENT OF READINESS FOR INITIATION IN PREPARATION FOR THE RITE OF ELECTION

Discernment for Baptism or Full Communion

You have traveled many miles on your faith journey with us. We are excited by the growth you have experienced. You have indicated your readiness for baptism or reception into full communion. To help you in this final discernment for readiness, you will find some reflection questions below. Please think about these in preparation for your conversation with your sponsor, catechist and me in the near future. We look forward to meeting with you.

A. Tell us about an experience or experiences you have had that have helped you grow in your awareness of God's love for you. Some suggestions to trigger your memory follow.

   1. An experience of God through prayer and/or worship

   2. An awareness of Christ's death on the cross as an expression of his love for you

   3. A spiritual healing from God

   4. A gift of inner peace from God

   5. An experience of God's love through a parishioner or group of parishioners

   6. Some other experience?

B. Once we experience one of these divine encounters, we want to deepen our relationship with God. So we look for opportunities to meet and spend time with God. Frequently, we want to express our gratitude to God for loving us so much. So we find ways to say thank you by serving God and others. Sometimes we want to share what we have received from God with others. So we tell others about God and Jesus. Tell us about some of these experiences since you started coming to our church. Some suggestions to trigger your memory follow.

   1. Prayer/Worship:

     a. What is it like coming to our parish on Sunday to worship God with us?

     b. What is speaking/listening to God in private prayer like for you?

2. Community:

   a. What has it been like becoming part of our church family?

   b. Tell us about some of the parishioners you have met or gotten to know better.

3. Tradition:

   a. Please tell us some important things you have learned about God, Christ, the Catholic church, and Christian life while with us.

   b. Please tell us a scripture story you have heard here that has been helpful for you?

4. Service:

   a. Has your commitment to discipleship grown since you began to spend time with us? If so, could you tell us about it?

   b. Have you told anyone about the good things happening in your life since you began to spend time with us? If so, could you tell us about it?

Instructions: After reading the gospel of the Samaritan Woman at the Well (John 4:5–42), repeat the following sequence for each intercession that appears below.

1. Invite someone to read an intercession aloud (from RCIA, 153b). After a few moments of silence, read the intercession again.
2. Invite the participants to reflect in silence on the intercession for 30 seconds.
3. Read aloud the reflection question that follows the intercession, allowing for timed pauses where indicated.
4. At the end of eaach reflection read the intercession a final time.

- That, like the woman of Samaria, our elect may review their lives before Christ and acknowledge their sins.

    Part of the process of entering into a relationship with Christ for the Samaritan woman included an acknowledgment of sin. The same is true for us, whether we are beginning or deepening our relationship with Christ. Lent is a time to acknowledge and repent of personal sins. Take two minutes in silence and remember some sins for which you have not repented.

- That the elect may be freed from the spirit of mistrust that deters people from following Christ.

    The Samaritan woman did not trust Christ at first because of some stereotypes she had about Jews and some bad experiences she had had with other people in the past. She eventually came to trust Christ when she learned he was not like the people she had heard about or knew. Take two minutes in silence to think of a situation in the past that caused you to mistrust someone. (Pause for two minutes.) Unlike sinful people, Christ is always trustworthy. Do you believe this? (Pause for five seconds.) Do you *really* believe that Christ is *always* trustworthy? In silence, ponder about this for a minute. (Pause for one minute.) If you believe this, are you willing to place greater trust in Christ? Take one minute to ask for an increase of trust in Christ. (Pause for one minute.)

- That while awaiting the gift of God, the elect may long with all their hearts for the living water that brings eternal life.

    Although she did not know it until she met Christ, in the depths of her heart the Samaritan woman longed for God. She substituted her longing for God with five husbands and a live-in boyfriend. Our hearts also long for God but sometimes we seek fulfillment from other people or things instead of God. Take two minutes to think about a person and/or thing that you substitute for God. (Pause for two minutes.) Since God alone can fill the deepest longings in our heart, take a minute to ask God to help you in your desire to put/keep God in the center of your life. (Pause for one minute.)

- That by accepting the Son of God as their teacher, they may become true worshipers of the Father in spirit and in truth.

  The Samaritan woman accepted Jesus as the Messiah and became a true worshiper of God. We believe Jesus is the Son of God and worship both him and his Father. Have you worshipped and prayed to God and Jesus regularly? Take two minutes to review your weekly presence at Mass and your daily prayer life. (Pause in silence for two minutes.)

- That they may share with their friends and neighbors the wonder of their own meeting with Christ.

  Having established a relationship with Christ, the Samaritan woman went back to her village and told everyone about him. We frequently tell our friends about the people in and the events of our lives. Do you tell others about Christ, your friend, or are you silent about your friendship with Christ? What makes you able to tell others about Christ? If you are silent about Christ, what do you need from him to help you speak about him to others? Take two minutes to reflect on these questions. (Repeat the three questions and pause for two minutes.)

- That those whose lives are empty for want of the word of God may come to the gospel of Christ.

  The Samaritan woman's life was empty until she met Jesus, the Word-made-flesh. Life is empty without the word of God and without Jesus, the Word-made-flesh. Do you know someone whose life is without the word of God or without Jesus, the Word-made-flesh? Take a minute to lift them up in prayer. (Pause for one minute.) Is it possible for you to bring them Jesus and his good news, either through serving them by good example, or by telling them about the bible or Jesus? If so, take two minutes to think of one way you could help them. (Pause for two minutes.)

- That all of us may learn from Christ to do the Father's will in love.

  Jesus faced many challenges to bring the Samaritan woman the gift of eternal life. He even had to say some difficult things to her about her faith and morals. Christ is inviting you to do the will of God more faithfully. Doing God's will requires growth and change in all of us. Take two minutes and think of one area in your own life where you need to learn from the example and word of Christ how to do God's will in love. (Pause for two minutes.)

After reading the gospel of the Man Born Blind (John 9:1–41), repeat the following sequence for the each intercession that appears below.

1. Invite someone to read an intercession aloud (from RCIA, 167a and b).
2. Invite the participants to reflect in silence on the intercession for 30 seconds.
3. Read aloud the reflection question that follows the intercession, allowing for timed pauses where indicated.
4. At the end of each reflection read the intercession a final time.

- That God may dispel darkness and be the light that shines in the hearts of our elect.

    God prefers light to darkness and looks for opportunities to bring people who are in darkness into the light. One such opportunity is described in today's gospel. Through Christ, God brought the man born blind out of darkness. There is darkness in our lives. We call it sin. God is looking for an opportunity to bring the light of grace to the darkness of our sin. What sins do you keep in darkness? In silence, take two minutes to remember them. (Pause for two minutes.) Now, let us ask God to shine the light of his grace upon our darkness. Let us take a minute to ask this favor from the Lord. (Pause for one minute.)

- That God may heal the elect.

    Through Christ, God healed the man born blind. For what do you seek God's healing during this Lenten season of forgiveness, healing and reconciliation? Let us take two minutes to place our infirmity before the Lord and to ask for the healing we need, whether spiritual, physical, emotional or mental. (Pause for two minutes.)

- That, freed by the power of the Holy Spirit, the elect may put all fear behind them and press forward with confidence.

    Freed from his blindness, the religious leaders of that time asked three times how he was cured. His parents were afraid to answer these leaders because they had the power to expel them permanently from the synagogue. However, the healed man overcame his fear and answered them, even though it resulted in his expulsion. Of what are you afraid? Take two minutes to identify something of which you are afraid. (Pause for two minutes.) Now, take a minute in silence and ask God to free you in some way from your fear. (Pause for one minute.)

- That, enlightened by the Holy Spirit, the elect may never fail to profess the good news of salvation and share it with others.

  As the healed man is asked by the Pharisees a second time to explain how Jesus could heal on a day on which he was forbidden to heal, the man proclaims the good news of salvation by saying that the man who healed him must be from God. You too are asked to profess your beliefs and to share them with others. Take two minutes to think of someone who might need to hear good news from you and what that might be. (Pause for two minutes.) Now pray that you may be given the strength you need from the Holy Spirit to bring that news to him or her.

- That those who suffer persecution for Christ's name may find their strength in him.

  The healed man was persecuted by the religious leaders for speaking the truth about Christ to them. Sometimes Christians face difficulties for following or speaking the truth about Christ. If you are aware of an individual or a group of people who are being persecuted for their Christian faith, take a minute and intercede to God on their behalf. If you have suffered for your Christian beliefs, take a minute and thank God that you were found worthy to suffer for Christ. If you have not suffered for your Christian beliefs yet, take a minute and ask God for strength when the day comes for you to suffer for your beliefs. (Pause for one minute.)

- That all of us, by the example of our lives, may become in Christ the light of the world.

  Christ says in today's gospel that while he is in the world he is the light of the world. Christ is no longer in the world and calls us to bring his light into the world through the example of our lives. Take two minutes and think of some ways that you have been light for someone else. (Pause for two minutes.)

Preparation for the Third Scrutiny

After reading the gospel of the Raising of Lazarus (John 11:1–45), repeat the following sequence for the each intercession that appears below.

1. Invite someone to read an intercession aloud (from RCIA, 174a and b).
2. Invite the participants to reflect in silence on the intercession for 30 seconds.
3. Read aloud the reflection question that follows the intercession, allowing for timed pauses where indicated.
4. At the end of each reflection read the intercession a final time.

- That the elect may be given faith to acknowledge Christ as the resurrection and the life.

    In faith, Martha proclaims that Jesus is the resurrection and the life and that those who believe this will live forever, including dead Lazarus. Do you believe Jesus is the resurrection and the life? Do you believe you will live forever due to your faith in Jesus? Think about this for two minutes. (Pause for two minutes.)

- That the elect may be freed from the sin that binds them.

    Lazarus is wrapped in burial linen. It symbolizes the death that binds him. Sin binds us. Take two minutes and think of those sins from which you seek liberation. (Pause for two minutes.) This liberating gift from God will be experienced by the elect in baptism and by the baptized in the sacrament of reconciliation. For the elect, offer thanks to God for the liberation you will receive shortly. For the baptized, ask God for the grace needed to celebrate the sacrament of reconciliation. (Pause for 30 seconds.)

- That we, the baptized, may again be confirmed at Easter in our hope of living forever with Christ.

    Lent is a time when the baptized prepare to renew their baptismal commitment to Christ, victor over death and Lord of life. Sometimes sin, death, and evil dim our hope of Christ's victory over death and his lordship over all. Place before the Lord anything that has caused your hope to weaken and ask him to renew your hope in him. Take a couple of minutes to do this. (Pause for two minutes.)

- That all of us may walk in newness of life and show to the world the power of the risen Christ.

    When Lazarus came forth from the tomb he showed the world the power of Christ. You too are called to show others the difference the risen Christ has made in your life. What difference has Christ made in your life? How would others describe this difference in you? Name one way you might ask Christ to help you walk in a new

and different way. Take two minutes to consider this.
(Pause for two minutes.)

- That the eucharistic food, which the elect are soon to receive, may
  make them one with Christ, the source of life and of resurrection.
    Catholics believe that they received the body and blood of the
    resurrected Christ every time they receive holy communion.
     In sharing in this holy food, Catholics believe they become one
    with Christ. They also believe that by sharing in this holy food they
    are called to be Christ for the world, to bring life and resurrection
    to others. If you are preparing for holy communion, reflect on the
    oneness you will have with the resurrected Christ when you receive
    the eucharist for the first time. If you already receive holy commun-
    ion, think of one person to whom Christ is calling you to bring life
    and resurrection. Take a few minutes to think about this. (Pause
    for two minutes.)

- That the compassion shown by Christ for his friend Lazarus may
  be shown toward all who are bound by sin, evil and death.
    Despite the price Jesus would pay for setting Lazarus free, he called
    his friend forth from the tomb. You know people who are bound
    by sin, evil and death. They too need Christ's compassion. Think
    of someone in need of Christ's compassion. Lift him or her up
    in prayer to Christ and ask Christ to unbind him or her. Take
    a few moments to do this. (Pause for two minutes.)

MYSTAGOGICAL CATECHESIS PREPARATION FORM

Sunday in Easter/Liturgical Year: _____

A. General focus:

B. Scriptures:

C. Other supportive liturgical elements (for example, music texts, propers of Mass):

D. Environment for session (for example, lectionary, candles):

E. Format of session:

1. Remembering the experience of the liturgy

2. Exploring the meaning of the liturgy as experienced by participants

3. Exploring one belief the church proclaims in this particular Sunday liturgy

4. How this belief is ritualized at Sunday liturgy

5. Implications for discipleship (challenge for my life/message to others/cost)

6. Closing prayer

Baptism by immersion, pouring or sprinkling of water together with the Trinitarian formula (I baptize you in the name of the Father, and of the Son and of the Holy Spirit) is of itself valid.

What is necessary and sufficient is evidence that the minister of baptism was faithful to these norms. For this purpose, one should generally obtain a written baptismal certificate with the name of the minister. When a certificate cannot be produced, an affidavit from a witness of the baptism may be used. When neither can be produced, conditional baptism becomes necessary unless the individual remembers the event of his/her baptism and testifies to its validity as described above.

—

Information in this appendix is from John Huels, *The Pastoral Companion* (Chicago: Franciscan Herald Press, 1986, pp. 50– 51).

Adventists
African Methodist Episcopal (AME)
Amish
Anglican
Assembly of God
Baptists
Church of the Brethren
Church of God
Church of the Nazarene
Congregational Church
Disciples of Christ
Episcopalians
Evangelical Churches
Evangelical United Brethren
Liberal Catholic Church
Lutherans
Old Catholics
Old Roman Catholics
Orthodox Churches (all of them)
Polish National Church
Presbyterian Church
Reformed Churches
United Church of Christ

—

Information in this appendix is from John Huels, *The Pastoral Companion* (Chicago: Franciscan Herald Press, 1986, pp. 50– 51).

CHURCHES WHERE
CONDITIONAL BAPTISM APPLIES

Apostolic Church
Bohemian Free Thinkers
Christadelphians
Christian and Missionary Alliance
Christian Scientists
Church of Divine Science
Church of Jesus Christ of Latter Day Saints (Mormons)
Jehovah's Witnesses
Masons
Pentecostal Churches
People's Church of Chicago
Quakers
Salvation Army
Unitarians

—

Information in this appendix is from John Huels, *The Pastoral Companion* (Chicago: Franciscan Herald Press, 1986, pp. 50– 51).